By Any Means

Also by Charley Boorman

Race to Dakar

By Any Means

from Wicklow to Sydney

CHARLEY BOORMAN

with JEFF GULVIN

sphere

SPHERE

First published in Great Britain in 2008 by Sphere

A CIP catalogue record for this book
is available from the British Library.

ISBN 978-1-84744-246-8

Typeset in Times by M Rules
Printed and bound in Great Britain by
Clays Ltd, St Ives plc

Papers used by Sphere are natural, renewable and recyclable products made from wood grown in sustainable forests and certified in accordance with the rules of the Forest Stewardship Council.

Mixed Sources
Product group from well-managed
forests and other controlled sources
www.fsc.org Cert no. SGS-COC-004081
© 1996 Forest Stewardship Council

FSC

Sphere
An imprint of
Little, Brown Book Group
100 Victoria Embankment
London EC4Y 0DY

An Hachette Livre UK Company
www.hachettelivre.co.uk

www.littlebrown.co.uk

For my darling family: Olivia, Doone and Kinvara.

And for Françoise and her dear family she leaves behind.

Picture credits

1 (both pictures), 2, 3 (all three pictures), 4 (all three pictures), 27 (bottom), 28 (all three pictures), 29 (all three pictures), 30 (all three pictures), 31 (top) · Ollie Blackwell

22 (bottom), 23, 24 (top) · Julian Broad

12 (middle) · Jo Ford

17 (both pictures), 24 (bottom), 25 (all three pictures), 26 (bottom) · Anne Holst

31 (bottom), 32 (both pictures) · Nick Long

5 (bottom), 6 (middle and bottom), 7 (middle), 9 (all three pictures), 10 (top and middle), 11 (both pictures), 12 (top and bottom), 13 (both pictures), 14 (all three pictures), 15 (middle), 16 (top), 18 (both pictures), 19 (top), 20 (top), 21 (all three pictures) · Russ Malkin

5 (both top pictures), 8 (top), 10 (bottom), 26 (top), 27 (top) · Mungo

22 (top) · Nick Ray

15 (top and bottom), 16 (bottom), 19 (bottom), 20 (bottom) · Robin Shek

7 (top and bottom) · Lucy Trujillo

Contents

1
Permission to Board

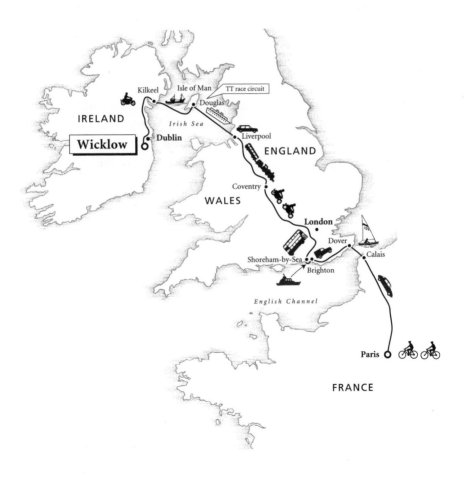

The weather in Ireland is like nowhere else in the world.

Take the morning of 12 April 2008. I'm standing outside my dad's house on the edge of the Wicklow Mountains and I can see blue sky and sunshine. I can also see a dull, wispy cloud, and – on the other side of the house – some ominous-looking thunderheads.

Russ comes out. Gazing up he raises one eyebrow. 'Which way are we going?'

I point to where the sky is bluest. 'That way: where you can feel the love.'

I'm wearing an open-faced helmet and goggles, and my Belstaff jacket. Russ is wearing old-fashioned motorbike boots, an aged leather jacket and a silk scarf. I throw my leg over my hand-built T110 'Bobber'. In just a few moments we'll be on our way. To Sydney. Australia.

It had been Russ's idea.

In August 2007 Ewan and I had completed our 'Long Way Down' trip from John O'Groats to Cape Town. Russ Malkin was our expedition leader – he's also a great friend and along with Ewan had been instrumental in getting not only Long Way Down off the ground but also our first trip, Long Way Round. It was now the back end of 2007, and Russ and I were kicking around a few suggestions about what we should do next.

In November we flew to Valencia for the last Moto GP of the season. I've got a lot of friends in the paddock: Chris Vermeulen, Randy Mamola, Kenny Roberts – it's a race we always try to get to. I was really excited because I had been invited to do a couple of laps on the back of Randy's two-seater Ducati on the race day itself. I think Russ was jealous. He said nothing, but he had to be, didn't he? I'd be green with envy: a couple of laps on a GP bike that weighs 165 kg and produces in excess of 250 bhp. Michael Schumacher himself had ridden it just a few weeks before.

On Saturday night we ate dinner in the hotel. Qualifying for the race was over and Dani Pedrosa was on pole. It was going to be a cracking finale to the season and I was looking forward to it. At the same time, I couldn't stop thinking about what I would do once the season was over. I was eager to start on a new adventure. As we finished eating I brought up the subject of the Australian Safari: a southern hemisphere 'Dakar' with bikes, cars and trucks. It started in Kununurra, Western Australia, and finished in Perth six days later.

'I wouldn't mind doing it,' I told Russ, 'but I don't know if it's feasible.'

'We could do it,' Russ said. 'You know we could. We did the Dakar, we could do this.'

'What about the logistics?'

He shrugged. 'We could set most of it up down there. It wouldn't be hard, but then it wouldn't be that challenging either. All you would have to do is jump on a plane.'

Jump on a plane, right. Somehow that didn't inspire me. Jump on a plane and get where we're going just as fast as we can. I can't help feeling sometimes that we're all rushing through our lives, living so quickly that we're burning out in the process. It reminded me of what Ewan had said about our trip through Africa: we hadn't always allowed ourselves enough time. I wanted to be sure with my next trip that we always factored in enough time to experience everything properly.

Russ opened his wallet to pay the bill and his boarding pass fell out. I picked it up. 'It's all so easy,' I said, turning the pass round in my hand. 'You go to an airport, get one of these, jump on a plane and fly off to wherever you're going. Anywhere you like. Anywhere in the world.'

Russ looked at me thoughtfully. 'You know what?' he said. 'We don't have to do the Safari, but we can still go to Australia.'

'What do you mean?'

Taking the boarding pass he scribbled the word 'London' in the top left-hand corner. Then he wrote 'Sydney' in the bottom right-hand corner. 'You remember back in Cape Town, Charley: you said how lucky we were to travel all those old roads while they were still there.'

I nodded. I remembered only too well: it had been all I could think about as Ewan and I rode the last bit of dirt to Cape Agulhas.

'You remember how we talked about doing an expedition just

for the hell of it, packing up and taking off: no back-up trucks, no medic, no security? So why don't we?' Russ traced a line on the boarding pass between London and Sydney. 'We could do that,' he said. 'London to Sydney. Only we don't take a plane. The roads in Africa were made by donkeys and camels; they were made by thousands of people walking. They were made by tuk-tuks and old taxis, those ancient buses with a million people packed on them.' He paused for a moment, thinking. 'How about this: we go to Australia by any means we can other than taking a plane from Heathrow. We pick a route and cross each country, each piece of water, using a different form of transport. We jump on trains and old buses: we hitch a ride with some long-distance lorry driver somewhere; someone who's been making the trip for years.'

Now I could see where he was coming from. 'I get you,' I said, starting to catch his excitement. 'We'd have to do some of it on motorbikes, though; Christ, I'd get withdrawal symptoms. Maybe we could ride some old British bikes: Ewan and I were going to Bantam around Britain one day. Bloody hell, I like this, Russ! It sounds like a lot of fun. It's the kind of thing I used to do as a kid. Dad would be off to the Amazon or God knows where, and we'd all just clear off with him.'

'How is your dad by the way?'

'He's really well.' I started telling Russ how my dad was working on a project about Hadrian. It was the usual nightmare – trying to find an 'A' list lead in order to green-light the film.

I soon realised Russ wasn't really listening to my thoughts on the perils of working in the film industry. I could see his mind was whirring again. 'Wouldn't it be great to start the trip from County Wicklow?'

'You mean from Dad's place?'

'Why not? It's where you grew up, it's where you rode your first motorbike.'

I felt a smile spread across my face. 'County Wicklow to Sydney, by any means possible. You know, it does have a ring to it, Russ . . .'

Since then everything had happened so quickly. After just a couple of months' preparation, here we were in Ireland, ready to leave my dad's house at the start of another major expedition. My only regret was that I would be away from my wife and daughters again so soon after the last one.

Along with our new cameraman, Mungo, Russ and I had stayed the night with my dad in the house I'd grown up in – an old rectory with the River Avonmore running through the grounds. I remember Dad always said that although the house might belong to him, and the land perhaps, the river was only passing through.

The whole expedition was going to be filmed as a fly-on-the-wall documentary and we'd considered a few different camera operators: what we needed was someone who could do the job day in day out for three and a half months, carry the gear we'd need and put up with Russ and me at the same time. Not much to ask, was it? When we met Paul Mungeam (or Mungo as he's known to his mates) we knew we had the right guy. Emerging from the kitchen now, he took a lingering look at my saddle; very small and very thin. 'You're going to have a numb bum,' he said.

Dad came out with his hands in his pockets. 'I wish you'd fuck off,' he said. 'You're churning up my lawn.' He looked at me with a glint in his eyes. 'Motorbikes,' he muttered. 'I have no feeling for them, nothing at all. I suppose they're a nice way of prolonging adolescence, but when I was a boy I wanted to be a man.' Then he grinned and gave me a hug. 'Good luck, Charley. I'm proud of you.'

I hugged him back – and I'll admit we were both a little tearful. I'm not sure if my dad realised this, but in a way it was because of him that I was doing this trip. He and my mum instilled in me the sense of wanderlust, the desire to see new places and get to know people I'd never ordinarily meet.

I climbed onto my 1953 Triumph and looked up the hill to where a group of my friends were standing, looking on. My old childhood friend Tommy Rochford was grinning at me, cropped hair gelled stiff and sticking straight up from his head. Him and Mick Bolger, Caz and Ziggy Balinski: the five of us used to hang out all the time. In the summer we'd float miles down the river on inner tubes. Mostly, though, we rode motorbikes. It was Tommy and his Maico 400 Enduro that got me hooked: I remember listening to him racing through the woods above our house.

'Good seeing you, Charley,' he called out now. 'I'll see youse when you get back.'

Russ started his Norton 850 Commando, and Mungo his Triumph Trident T160. I fished out the crude map I'd drawn on a scrap of paper.

'I thought we had GPS,' Russ said.

'We do. This is for back-up. Annamoe to Dublin, Dublin to Kilkeel. Then over here,' I tapped the bottom right-hand corner, 'that's Australia.'

'Right. See you there, then.'

Our first stop was Kilkeel in County Down, where we planned to stay the night. The next morning we were due to join a scallop boat that would take us to the Isle of Man. In all the years of the TT I'd never made it there; now I would be arriving on a dredger.

It was suddenly a little surreal, trundling down the drive while Tommy and the others waved from the hill where I used to jump my old Yamaha DT100. Glancing back at Dad I felt a mixture of excitement and sadness to be leaving him. I thought of Olly, Doone and Kinvara – at least I would see them briefly on Tuesday in London. But after that I wouldn't be back until August. I hadn't intended to do another expedition so soon and I had a lump in my throat and a bit of a wobble in the old chin. Yet in the same moment I could not have been more excited.

The countryside we were riding through now was so familiar; the roads wet, pine trees covering the lower slopes that dominate this part of Wicklow. I might live in London but this was home away from home and it was a thrill to be back. As we climbed the hills we passed a spot where Dad and I had filmed an autobiographical film in 1991 called *I Dreamt I Woke Up* with John Hurt and Janet McTeer. There had been a scene involving a mummified body in a peat bog. When lunchtime came we took off to the Roundwood Inn as we always did. We didn't bother to tape the area, just took the equipment down to the village and left the dummy half-buried in the marsh. While we were having lunch a couple of Australian backpackers came across what they thought was a bronze-age body. Convinced that they'd made the discovery of the century, they phoned the police in Dublin. The local guard,

Sergeant Cronen, knew all about the filming, but as no one bothered to involve him, he didn't tell them anything. By the time we got back up the hill the place was alive with *gardai* and reporters. It was hysterical, particularly when Dad asked them what the fuck they thought they were doing trampling all over his film set.

Remember what I said about the weather in Ireland being like nowhere else in the world? We were hit by every kind of weather imaginable on this first leg through the mountains to Dublin. Wind, rain, sunshine, hail and even snow.

I was a bit worried about my saddle, which was a tad uncomfortable – the bike was designed for blatting about town, not really for long runs like this. Ewan had ordered a similar bike after seeing a feature on 'The Baron Speed Shop' in *Classic Bike* magazine. The Speed Shop is all about 'Bobbers': cut-down stock bikes; a style that grew up in America in the 1950s. When I saw what they'd produced I'd wanted one myself.

At the beginning of the year I phoned the owner, Dick Smith, and arranged to meet him at his workshop. Dick works with his partner Del Russell, burning the midnight oil to build these really incredible hand-crafted bikes. He's real south London – he was like the kind of guys who hung out at the Ace Cafe back in the sixties.

Dick met me in a quiet residential street in Catford and led me down a grassy alley to his workshop. Well, I say workshop – it was actually a garden shed. The end wall was draped with the skull and crossbones, a rigid frame hung from the ceiling and boxes of parts were stacked right up to the roof. It was barely big enough to swing a cat, never mind build a bespoke motorbike.

Leaning on the work bench, Dick lit a cigarette. 'So what kind of thing were you thinking of?'

Good question. I'd always known what I wanted in my mind's eye, but to describe it . . .

Ten minutes later he was nodding. 'So we're talking about something in black, something with big bore TT pipes coming up under the crank case . . .'

'Yes,' I said. 'That sounds about right.'

'Rigid frame with a two-inch stretch,' he was making notes

mentally. 'Like a sort of 1930s broad-track racer. OK, mate; leave it with me and I'll scribble something down.'

The rigid frame had been stretched all right but as for 'something in black' . . . We all wanted black, apparently. Dick delivered something in cherry red instead. I suppose that's designers for you – you tell them what you want and they build what they've always wanted to build. You pay for it and they're happy. But then so are you because the bike is absolutely gorgeous.

Although we had no back-up vehicles this time, we had planned as much as we could. That was only sensible: you can't just travel across the world without proper planning. We'd created an operations centre at our old workshop on Avonmore Road, with computers and maps, and books covering some forty different countries scattered all over the place. This time we needed not only a route, but also a rough idea of some of the transport we would use. We'd had lots of ideas: North Sea trawlers, the Danish Coastguard, the ICE-T train in Germany. There were a bunch of people working on it, most of whom had worked on our three previous trips – Lucy, Jo, Ollie and Lisa. We worked out there were some thirty-eight countries to get through between Ireland and Australia – including China, which had closed the border from Nepal into Tibet. We had to find a way around that problem and we had to consider the politics of other places. So much of Asia was in a state of flux: Afghanistan, Pakistan . . . Burma was closed to any kind of film-maker. We also wanted to do something with UNICEF along the way, as we had with Long Way Round and Long Way Down.

It was a movable feast and things changed all the time: much of what we thought we could do we found out was impossible, and some of what we thought might be impossible turned out to be OK. After a lot of hard graft we came up with a route and a list of different forms of transport. The first handover, if you like, was from motorbike to the fishing boat at Kilkeel and it would be monumentous.

That's not a word, is it? My mum's always telling me that being dragged around the world without proper schooling has given me what she calls a sort of 'unsophisticatedness'. (Which isn't really a word either.)

It felt *monumentous* to me, though, standing at Kilkeel harbour later that afternoon. I wondered how big our boat would be: some looked pretty small. My sense of adventure began to wane as I had visions of massive waves and throwing up all the way to the Isle of Man. Oh well, I'd find out before the sun came up.

We were due to sail with the morning tide and had booked a hotel in town for the night. What we hadn't counted on was the Orangemen's marching season. I'd always thought the bands marched in July yet here we were in April and they were out in numbers. We were told they'd be parading up and down outside the hotel until at least midnight. After that there was a disco, and my room was right above it. I had a feeling it was going to be a long night.

Upstairs I went through my gear. When Russ first talked about the trip he was thinking about the spirit of the old days, a sort of 'round the world in eighty days' feel. His forte is getting things done, working with production teams and logistics, but this would give him a chance to pursue some of his passions too. I just knew that somewhere along the line we'd be on a steam train. A friend of mine called Richard Gauntlet runs an antique shop in Pimlico, and he found this old case and had my initials printed on it. It was great, and I loved it, but it was also, I have to say, really heavy. Now I was handing my bike over, it was mine to carry pretty much till we got to Australia.

The alarm woke me at four-forty-five a.m. At least I think it did. I don't know if I actually got any sleep; the night was full of drums and flutes; disco music pounding into my room. Bleary-eyed but excited I met Russ and Mungo downstairs and the three of us made our way to the harbour.

I needn't have worried about the size of the boat. We would be sailing on the *Q-Varl* of Ramsey, Isle of Man, one of the largest scallop vessels out there. The skipper was a white-haired, bearded guy called Raymond Hatton, who spoke with a broad Lancastrian accent. He'd been in the merchant navy before becoming a scallop diver and buying his own boat. In fact it actually belonged to the whole Hatton family, which meant that if he wanted some time off either his son or his grandson Danny could run the crew. This seemed a great idea to me. He introduced us to the five crewmen. One of them – a tall, lanky guy – seemed familiar. I soon realised why: this was Conor Cummins, a road racer who also rides short circuit in the British Superstock series. He's lapped the Isle of Man at an average speed of 126.4 mph, only six miles an hour slower than John McGuinness's lap record. I had thought Conor was part of the regular crew, but it turned out that his cousin worked the boat. Conor told me that when he found out we'd be aboard he decided to come along for the craic.

After requesting permission to board we took a look around. The boat was blue-hulled with a white wheelhouse; a dredging arm on each side with ten enormous chain-link scallop nets. It was tall, I mean high in the water, three decks: one for the gear, another where they sorted the catch and the fish deck where the bagged scallops were stored.

The channel was narrow and we sailed with the tide because Raymond wanted plenty of water under the keel. It still looked very difficult to me; we had to zigzag to make it beyond the tight harbour walls before negotiating a sandbank. It was a masterful piece of captaincy, all performed against a dramatic backdrop – street lights reflected in the still water, the town dominated by low cloud draping the Mountains of Mourne. I stood on deck thinking: 'This is it.' We were leaving our first block of land, heading out on a brand-new journey.

Russ came over. 'They say there's a bit of weather out there: that'll be a laugh.'

I looked sideways at him. 'Will they give us breakfast, d'you reckon?'

Would they ever – we were soon presented with kippers, bacon, eggs, toast and beans, the first of many fabulous meals on our trip. As we ate we discussed our schedule for the day. The plan was to steam across the Irish Sea to the twelve-mile fishing zone round the Isle of Man. The zone was known as Area 7, and was closed from June to the end of October to allow scallop stocks to recover. From the beginning of November the boats could fish from six p.m. until nine p.m. If they wanted to fish after nine p.m. they had to go outside the twelve-mile limit where the catch was a lot more scarce.

As we headed into the open sea I was soon caught up in the adventure of it all. David Jackson, who'd cooked breakfast, showed us the engine room where 500 hp of diesel was hammering away so loudly you couldn't think without ear defenders. The crew had bunks with alarms fitted above them so that when the dredges were down and they grabbed an hour's sleep, they could be woken in time to bring the gear in. They'd spend a week at sea, sleeping little and working hard: fishing until the fish room was stocked with three to four hundred large bags of scallops. Each bag was worth between £65 and £100 and they needed to fill at least four every time they pulled up the dredges.

It was a four-hour steam to the fishing grounds, 46 nautical miles. We were travelling at 8.4 knots per hour; a knot being 1.16 nautical miles. (The difference between a nautical mile and a land or statute mile is that the nautical mile takes account of the curvature of the earth.) When we got to the fishing grounds we gave the crew a hand with the dredges, which are hoisted by crane, hooked on to two massive booms and then run out on a cable and dragged along the sea bed. Raymond's grandson Danny told me that one time he was working the cable and chatting away to another member of the crew when the wire ran out: it just rolled off the winch and disappeared over the side leaving thousands of pounds of dredge lying on the bottom.

An hour and a half after we'd dropped them the dredges were hauled in again and the catch was shaken into a trough that runs along the sides of the boat. The scallops and much of the debris that came with them were shunted to the conveyor on the deck below – a great clattering, vibrating machine that sorted everything in about fifteen minutes. Along with scallops we had lumps of rock, squid, starfish, as well as scallops that were less than 110 mm in size. These had to be thrown back. Raymond told me that if the boat was found to have even two or three undersize scallops among the catch they'd be fined at least £500. The penalties for fishing a 'closed box' – a no-go area where you were not allowed to fish – were far more severe: a £7,000 fine and your gear confiscated.

The crew shared the work between them; when the alarms went off they'd pile out of their bunks and on to the deck, music blasting through speakers made from a couple of old tool boxes. As soon as the catch had been shaken out the nets were back in the water.

Meanwhile, David fried up some of the catch for lunch, fresh scallops with a bit of garlic and a green salad. God, this was the life.

After a couple of hours at the fishing grounds we headed for Douglas, the capital of the Isle of Man. Russ and I leant on the rail with the wind in our faces, watching the rocky coastline, the surf crashing against the base of the cliffs. A lighthouse dominated the headland and we chugged into the harbour with whitewashed buildings scattered across the hillside.

So many great racers lived here: Neil Hodgson, who was riding for Honda in the AMA Superbike series, James Toseland, the only Brit in MotoGP. Though I'd never been before, the place evoked bittersweet emotions. Ewan and I used to run David Jefferies in British Superstock. He was one of the great characters of bike racing and was killed practising for the TT in 2003. I couldn't help but think about him now: he'd been undisputed king of the mountain and I still missed him – but he died doing what he loved.

2
King of the Mountain

The following morning I was outside the hotel with a classic MV Agusta burbling away in front of me. Older bikes need to be warmed up properly to avoid placing unnecessary stress on the engine: it's when a bike is cold that things can break suddenly.

I was really excited about today. A little later I'd be hooking up with John McGuinness, the current 'king of the mountain', and together we'd do a lap of the 37.75-mile circuit. There was somebody I needed to speak to first, though, and he was waiting for me on the start–finish straight.

The Isle of Man TT is the most famous and the most dangerous motorbike race in the world. Someone who can testify to the latter is Richard 'Milky' Quayle. Milky – a tall, slightly built guy with glasses – got his nickname from his resemblance to the Milky Bar Kid. He's Manx, a local who won four TT races in his time. His final race was last year and with his wife expecting a baby, he decided enough was enough. Not before he'd spent two weeks in a coma, though. I met him by the pit board where the lap times and rider placings are still recorded manually by local scout troops. He pointed out a few racing landmarks and we talked about the speeds riders get up to. Then he took me to the spot where his 160 mph crash had been captured on home video.

It had been an horrendous crash – and standing with Milky on the exact spot where it happened really brought it home. Milky knows the circuit like the back of his hand but he'd had set-up problems and the bike wasn't working quite how he wanted it to. He was blatting through a narrow, wooded section when he came to a jagged rock wall at a really fast left-hander. Tipping in a fraction too early, he brushed the wall with his shoulder. There was barely any contact but at 160 mph it was enough to rip his hands off the bars and send him and the bike careering across the road and into the far wall. The wall exploded, the bike disintegrated and Milky was thrown twenty feet into the air and a hundred and fifty feet down the road before he landed under some trees. His left shoulder was smashed, his ankle was shattered, his lungs collapsed, one kidney packed up and he lost his spleen. He doesn't remember much about it because he was knocked unconscious and stayed that way until he woke up in hospital two weeks later. Having watched the footage on the web then listened to him talk me through it, I was staggered he was standing there at all. It just shows that no matter how many races you've won or how intimately you know the circuit, all you have to be is a fraction off line and it can be curtains.

The video footage Milky showed me was still raw in my mind as I waited for John to arrive: I was about to do the lap myself and would ride through that cutting. Before long I saw a white sports bike gunning up the road towards me, the rider wearing race leathers. Pulling up, he lifted the visor on his helmet. 'Hello, Charley,' he said. 'John McGuinness.'

Since 2004 John's won every superbike race on the island. He is a superstar of road racing, one of the gods, yet he's the most down-to-earth guy you could wish to meet. Milky told me that – professional or amateur – there are no prima donnas at the TT; everyone is there because they love racing bikes and John is no different. His favourite part of the track is a left/right kink where he's doing just shy of two hundred miles an hour. No matter how many times he does it he gets the same rush. He's a lovely guy, a great laugh, and he was really up for showing me round.

I was on the classic MV which threatened to tank slap when I let go of the handlebars: John was on a stock Fireblade and he popped the front wheel beautifully as we set off. It was an incredible couple of hours, riding right behind the world record holder. The lap was so varied it was soon clear to me that it would take years to learn it well enough to be both safe and competitive. There are long, blisteringly fast straights, hairpins in the middle of villages, flying sections through built-up areas that scare the shit out of you, wooded glens like the one where Milky overcooked it, not to mention the mountain and the wind-blown roads bisecting farmers' fields.

Riding at my side, John talked me through the technical parts and the really fast stretches. There are a couple where you flash by the houses at more than 190 mph and one in particular sent my stomach into a flip. You're tearing along when suddenly this wall appears as if it's right in front of you. It's actually marking a bend, but as you race up it looks like it is dead ahead and you're going to crash into it. Your eyes are telling you there's nowhere to go while your memory is telling you it's a corner and to keep going. Steve Hislop was a few centimetres off line there once and banged his head on the wall.

There's no speed limit on the open road and I tried to follow as John wound the Blade up to more than 170. I had the MV off the ground at Ballaugh Bridge, landing with a bit of wobble, but this was the TT circuit and Ballaugh is one of those magical landmarks. Out of the village, John cranked the throttle again. The road was incredibly bumpy now and I was thinking: 'Oh my God, imagine taking this at one sixty with the wheels off the deck one minute, and suspension and the forks on full compression the next.' I suddenly remembered something that Milky had told me. He said that it's a long lap and riding it in race conditions your mind can begin to wander. The thought of taking my mind off what I was doing even for one second made me laugh out loud.

We were approaching the mountain now. It was very windy here, with the fields rolling down to the sea. We were climbing, John leading me into a hard and fast right-hander: past the waterworks where a low wall marks the edge of the road and beyond . . . a hell of a long fall. It's only when you ride the roads, even at relatively slow speeds, that you have any idea of just how on the edge the racers really are, not to mention the hundreds of amateurs who come here from all over the world.

John led me to the goose neck and the start of the mountain. From fourth gear you're on the brakes and down to second, then accelerating hard to the mountain mile itself. By the time you get to Guthrie's memorial you've taken three consecutive left-handers and are all but flat out. (Jimmy Guthrie raced for the first time in 1923: he rode a Matchless in that race before winning in 1930 on an AJS. He was killed in 1937 at the German Grand Prix. The memorial marks the cutting where he was forced to retire from the TT.)

The whole island is steeped in history – not just the course and the competitors, but the crowd, the pit crews, the volunteers. Every year hundreds of people help out, including marshals like Gwen Crellin, who has been outside her house in Ballaugh at five a.m. every TT day for the last thirty-eight years. Like all the riders, John would give her a wave as he passed during practice. In the races he'd try and lift a finger; Gwen understood: he was a little busier then.

We stopped at the Creg Ny Baa, a pub that marks a right-hand bend on the hill and honours Geoff Duke, the six-time TT winner and six-time world champion. He's eighty-five now, but meeting him there and seeing him face to face, you would never know it.

It was an amazing experience to sit with a former king of the mountain along with the current one, talking about a racing history that's spanned one hundred years. I asked Geoff if the course had changed much since his time.

'The basic shape hasn't changed,' he said. 'But the way you ride it has. Windy Corner, McQuarrie's, they used to be taken in second gear and now they're just about flat out.'

He told me that during his first race, the Manx TT of 1950, he pulled into the pits for fuel. His mechanic topped him up with both petrol and oil and as he rode away Geoff could feel the back end slithering. He realised that oil was spilling onto the back tyre. Cursing his mechanic for overfilling the tank he had to scrub the speed off until the heat in the tyres burned up the oil. But in fact the mechanic hadn't overfilled the tank. Unbeknown to either of them it had actually split. Just as Geoff approached the mountain the engine seized. Managing to keep control he got the bike stopped and leant it against the wall. Helmet off, he wandered over to a mechanic at the mountain mile checkpoint.

'What number are you?' the mechanic asked him.

'Twelve.'

'Really.' The man nodded calmly at the stricken bike. 'Shame about that, you were leading.'

It was the end of his race that day but Geoff went on to win six times. He told me he loved every minute of racing. In 1950 the prize money for winning the senior TT was £200 but he couldn't have cared less; he did it for the sheer enjoyment. It's much more commercial today but even so, John races for the love of it just as Geoff did. In Geoff's time the roads weren't so smooth, the bikes were less powerful and the tyres less sticky. They had to use the same tyres for both wet and dry conditions. The roads were heavily cambered back then, which meant the riders had less road surface to play with, all of which made a huge difference. Different eras mean different standards of bike and therefore different hazards: Geoff rode his machinery every bit as hard as John rides his now.

Sitting there with the two of them, the spirit of the race was really brought home to me. John told me that every year before the race began he would visit Fairy Bridge to say hello and keep the fairies on his side – he'll do anything that he thinks might help him when it comes to race day. He even wears the same socks and underpants throughout the entire festival for luck. He does wash them daily, though, he assures me.

As Russ and I boarded the ferry to Liverpool I vowed I'd be back. I stood at the rail and watched as the island with its banks of three-storey terraces slipped away, still not quite believing that I'd just ridden a lap with the fastest man ever around the circuit. What an incredible experience.

However, it was time to turn our attention to the next stage of our journey. Russ and I headed to the bridge, and asked the captain of the ferry if we could join him. His name was Joe and his assistant was a mad-keen biker chick called Laurie. She lived on the Isle of Man and rode a Honda 350. Every year during the racing she made sure she was on the car deck to tie down the three hundred bikes that crossed every time the ferry sailed.

Joe showed us the bridge and its mind-boggling array of screens and dials, sonar, radar and GPS systems. It looked very hi-tech, though in fact the vessel was ten years old. I was looking for the wheel, but Joe just pointed to a tiny little joystick, like something from a games console. The skipper steered the ferry with it using just his left hand. Meanwhile four massive engines powered jets which chucked water out of the stern at a rate that could fill an Olympic-sized swimming pool in thirty-six seconds.

We raced across the Irish Sea at 34 knots with Joe calm and composed at the 'wheel'. When we docked in Liverpool – after cruising up the Mersey past the Liver Building – he eased the massive boat into the berth just by feathering a couple of levers. He was as much in his element as Geoff Duke had been; as John McGuinness when he was catching air at Ballaugh Bridge. It struck me that this was what this trip was all about; a chance to step into other people's lives for a little while.

From the docks it was a mad dash to the station and Platform 7 for the train to Coventry. Russ had jumped in a cab but Mungo and I had been messing around and had to wait for the next one. Sitting hunched in the back with my suitcase on my knees, I realised we were ten minutes away from the station with the train leaving in five.

No worries, our cabbie knew a short cut and beetled through the traffic, pulling up as close to Platform 7 as he could get. We piled out, bags in hand, and legged it towards the train. I could hear the whistle blowing. I could see the guard on the platform. I could also see Russ trying to keep the doors open. Stumbling past the guard I threw my bag in and followed it just as the doors closed.

Russ tapped the face of his watch. 'If we're going to cut the whole trip this fine, we ain't going any further. You know what I mean?'

We were planning to camp for the night at the Coventry Transport Museum. My bike from Long Way Round was on display there and it made sense (or so I thought) to call in. That was before I learned that the museum was haunted.

We met Steve, one of the curators, outside the museum. It's a wonderful place, well worth the visit. The timelines of the world are lit up in blue across the concourse and arriving in darkness we had the full effect. Inside there's a fantastic scene of London during the Blitz, with rubble everywhere and an old Austin lying on its side.

Russ marched in, stripped off his clothes, dumped them in a pile in front of a classic Bentley, and headed for a shower. I shook my head, suddenly remembering why I always refused to share a room with him.

'Is the place really haunted?' I asked Steve. 'Russ will be up for that; he's into ghosts. One night he slept in a haunted hotel room with a couple of cameras set up.' I didn't mention that I'd had my own encounter with a ghost just last year, while staying in a haunted sixteenth-century Scottish castle at the start of Long Way Down. I'd woken up with a mysterious black bruise around my eye, and really didn't want a repeat of that experience.

'Did he see anything?' Steve asked.

'No.'

'He might here.'

'Oh great.' I could feel a shiver up my spine.

'We've got a collection of old bicycles upstairs,' Steve explained. 'They were donated by an old chap who died while he was riding one of them.'

I could feel the shiver extending to my buttocks.

'One of our assistants was in there the other day,' Steve continued, 'and she saw this old gentleman in tweeds, bald head and a beard, sitting on one of the bikes. I had an old cycling magazine in the office and . . .'

'Don't tell me.'

He nodded. 'I found his obituary from years ago. It was the same man the assistant had just seen up in the bike room.'

'Cool, eh, Charley?' Russ had returned from the shower. 'I don't know where you're sleeping, mate, but I'm going to camp in the bike room.'

No chance. Instead I camped alongside the motorbike I'd ridden round the world. It was exhibited next to a pristine E-type Jag convertible. My old rally suit was there, too. I still miss that suit. There was a glass case with some of the stuff Ewan and I had left in our pockets: a compass, some coins, a couple of cassette tapes.

It brought back lots of great memories. Leaving Russ to the ghost of Sammy Bartley, I blew up my mattress and unrolled my sleeping bag.

I glanced at my bike, my old suit and helmet. I looked up at the ceiling. Not quite out in the cuds, but it was near enough.

3
Let There Be Bikes

The floor was hard, and my sleeping bag was a bit too hot, but I slept pretty well, all things considered. I woke up a few times but there were no ghosties; at least none that I saw. No black eye either, which was a relief.

Russ came down at six looking bleary-eyed but rested. I asked him if he'd seen any ghosts.

He shook his head. 'I was knackered. That old man could have ridden his bike right past me and I wouldn't have heard him.'

This morning we were back on the bikes, heading for the Ace Cafe in London. We'd ride to junction 10 of the M40 where, please God, there would be some bikers waiting for us. We'd advertised the ride on our website and I was hoping a few people would come out to support us. *Motorcycle News* had also done a piece about the expedition the previous week and we'd invited anyone who wanted to join us as far as the Ace Cafe to show up at eight-thirty at the services. Twenty would do. If there were twenty I'd be really happy. It would be a real downer if there were only one or two.

My bobber looked gorgeous this morning. Turning the petrol on I tickled the carb, kicked her over and the little beauty thundered into life with a snarling crackle. We were escorted from the museum by a Vintage Daimler limo – I followed it off the slip road but Russ and Mungo, giving it large, missed the turning completely.

Lost already and we'd not even left Coventry.

At last Russ appeared from the roundabout in front of me and not long after him Mungo showed up looking a little sheepish.

I could only manage 55 mph without being blown off: being a bobber the bike is naked; the consideration being style rather than aerodynamics. I started thinking about sailing across the Channel the next day. I was nervous: Russ and I had spent a few days in Southampton getting 'boat and wind aware', as the instructor called it. We'd capsized our dinghy in no wind at all and tomorrow we'd be sailing one of the busiest shipping lanes in the world. I knew I should have practised more, but instead of learning to sail properly I'd been taking flying lessons.

The exit for the services came up, and all thoughts of sailing left my mind. Leaving the motorway I climbed the hill and swung left into the services. Please God, let there be bikes . . . Bloody hell! Forget twenty – there were more like three hundred. I was gobsmacked; the whole car park was solid with chrome and leather. A sea of bikes and riders surrounded us. It was incredible, and I could feel a lump in my throat as they crowded around, patting us on the back and offering to buy tea and coffee. This was Tuesday, a work day, and here we were at eight-thirty in the morning with hundreds of bikers who had taken the time and trouble to see us off. We were all speechless.

We set off again and I'm afraid to say that with so many motorbikes we ended up blocking all three lanes of the M40. We had just never expected such a turnout. I rode at the head of the convoy, feeling euphoric and humbled by the support. Every now and then we'd manage to squeeze into two lanes to let the traffic by.

Riding into London we joined the North Circular, heading for Willesden and the Ace Cafe. A large, flat-roofed, white building, it is the caff of all caffs. Built in 1938, it was destroyed by the Luftwaffe in World War Two, but rebuilt in 1949. Rockers started hanging out there in the fifties, making the most of the twenty-four-hour service. Ever since then it has been a bikers' haven, and is rightly famous around the world.

As we pulled in we brought the North Circular to a standstill, three hundred bikes trying to turn into the cafe. I saw my wife Olivia standing with my daughters, Doone and Kinvara, along with Russ's parents Jill and Tony. My mum Christel was also there with my twin sister Daisy. (My mum says the first time she saw me on a motorbike was when she asked me to go to the garden and fetch some potatoes. I was with my mate Caz and we rode through the patch on his bike as fast as we could, using the back wheel to churn the spuds from the ground. Bucket after bucket we brought in, broken – or, as we saw it, 'ready mashed'. My mother thought it was very ingenious . . .)

With my family around me it was hard to accept that it would be months before I saw them again. Olly copes but it's not easy. Doone and Kinvara go to different schools which are in opposite directions. Normally I take one of them but for the next few months I wouldn't be there. Olly passed her motorbike test recently and planned to buy a moped so she could drop Kinvara, then come back for Doone.

But at least they were joining me on the next short leg of my trip. I was leaving my bike at the Ace Cafe in exchange for a bright red London Routemaster, which I would drive down to Shoreham-by-Sea. I'd never driven a bus before and was dying to get going. It would be the perfect way to say goodbye. In Shoreham we'd hook up with the RNLI and take a lifeboat to Brighton.

We said goodbye to all the friends who'd come to see us off and then, climbing into the cab, I slid open the window. My instructor, a man called Peter Barrington, was hunched behind me. My first lesson would be driving the North Circular. My family were in the back along with Jill and Tony, Russ's daughter Emily and his girlfriend Sarah. They wouldn't be seeing him for a long time either. I started the engine and pulled out with hundreds of people waving us off. It was the most brilliant send-off, and I couldn't have asked for a more positive start to the expedition.

Ever since I was a kid I'd wanted to drive a Routemaster. First built in 1954, it's a design classic. I couldn't think of a better way to leave the capital. It wasn't hard to drive – a bit like an automatic car (only bigger, of course). Steering is the only tricky part; the wheel is huge and flat and you have to make constant adjustments to keep the thing straight.

It was wild, like something from *Summer Holiday*. Once we got to Shoreham I drove through the narrow streets to the harbour, squeezing past parked cars. Somehow, miraculously, I managed not to take one of them out along the way. I found a space, parked and jumped down.

I gave Emily a squeeze and told her I'd look after her dad, and said goodbye to the rest of Russ's family. Then I kissed Olly and the kids. Olly patted me on the bum. 'You'll be fine,' she told me. 'And don't worry, so will we.'

Russ, Mungo and I crossed the beach to the square brown building where the lifeboat was housed. Talk about 'by any means'; I was going to pilot a 47-foot All Weather Lifeboat. We met up with coxswain Peter Huxtable, who explained that the boat could capsize and right itself whilst remaining watertight, which was reassuring. He was going to launch it down the slipway just as they would for a rescue and then take us on to Brighton. From there we'd pick up a Land Rover and drive to Dover.

The RNLI is funded solely by donations. The charity costs £100 million a year to run – there are 230 stations covering the UK and the Republic of Ireland – and they have to raise that money entirely themselves. As an island, Britain is particularly vulnerable to accidents at sea, and when people get into difficulty their lives depend on these brave volunteers. We were a couple of novice sailors ourselves, and it was good to know that when we crossed the Channel tomorrow the RNLI would be there if, God forbid, we needed them.

When the RNLI was founded in 1865 the boats were rowed out to rescue in all weathers. Now – thankfully – they are powered by diesel, but Peter said the RNLI was finding it harder and harder to get crews together. In my eyes, the people who volunteered were true heroes, risking their lives 24/7. If you're going to volunteer for something and you live by the sea, I can't think of anything more fulfilling or worthwhile.

Keen to get going as always I asked Charlie Hubbard, the

second coxswain, to explain how the boat was launched. We were standing in the boathouse under the massive blue hull.

'We lower her forwards,' he said, 'then take off the safety chains and she falls over on the cradle.'

I gazed the length of the concrete slipway. It had what looked like a tramline – known as a keelway – running down the middle, not much wider than the boat itself. It was V-shaped with concrete sides topped with wooden pilings. There were metal walkways above our head, and beyond the keelway I could see the harbour walls and the open sea.

'The cradle is hydraulically controlled,' Charlie explained. 'It comes down level with the slipway and away she goes.' He showed me how the keel fitted into the greased keelway before the boat slid into the sea under its own weight.

A few minutes later Russ and I were kitted out in drysuits, standing on the bows as the crew prepared to launch. I couldn't get the smile off my face. First the convoy, then a London bus and now a lifeboat for God's sake – all in one day. We gripped the rail and moments later we were moving, sliding towards the water at a thirty-degree angle. It was low tide, and as we hit the water it erupted, spray exploding high over the bows, soaking us and foaming about our feet. It was brilliant – like a rollercoaster ride – and yet much smoother than I'd thought it would be.

Outside the harbour Peter let me take control and I piloted from the open cockpit. It was a great boat, very powerful and very manoeuvrable. I guided us the five miles to Brighton where we were met by a RIB from that station. They had one of their crew fall overboard and we performed a rescue, coming around him upwind then drifting in gently. A couple of the crew climbed over the side and hung off the rope netting to haul him on board.

I steered the ALB into harbour at five knots then handed over to Peter to take us alongside. Shaking hands, we grabbed our bags and ran up the weed-encrusted steps to the harbour wall where the Land Rover was waiting for us.

I got behind the wheel with Russ in the passenger seat and Mungo perched among the gear we'd tossed in the back.

'It's a double declutch,' I said. 'I bet I do nothing but grind the gears all the way.'

As we headed gingerly out of town, I pointed out the house where my grandmother used to live.

'Right on the seafront,' Mungo said. 'Nice.'

'She used to swim in the sea every day. Well almost every day – right up until she was eighty.'

'Really?' Russ looked back: the house was part of a Georgian terrace and whitewashed like those on the Isle of Man.

'Yeah. Don't forget – my dad's seventy-five and he still swims in the river at Annamoe.'

We plodded up the hill. Russ sat back with his arm across the seats. 'You know how these old Mark I's came about, don't you? Mr Wilks, the man who owned the Rover car company, had an old World War Two jeep. He and his brother put a Rover engine in it then realised they could build something better. They made the first one of these in 1948 as a sort of stop gap to boost sales at the car company.'

I looked round at him. 'You getting those voices in your teeth again, Russ? Like in Long Way Down?'

'Nope.' Russ grinned. 'Roger, the guy we got it from, told me.'

We held up the traffic all the way along the white cliffs to Dover. Bit of a theme for the day, that. The Land Rover broke down twice, well once actually: the first time I accidentally switched the engine off when I was trying to find the lights to flash someone. The second time we were spluttering a bit and coughing smoke and finally it conked out. An electrical lead had come off. Between us we got it going again and finally made it to the seafront hotel in Dover. Unloading my case I looked at the water, half excited and half terrified. I was only too aware that tomorrow we were leaving the country in a twelve-foot dinghy.

That night I prayed for good weather, I prayed for the right tides and I prayed that I'd know what to do after spending too much time in a small aeroplane instead of a boat. We would be sailing a Laser Bahia dinghy made of plastic: the kind we'd trained in and capsized. I didn't sleep well.

*

'It'll be fine,' Russ assured me on the beach the next morning, gazing across the sea towards France. It was a bright day, the Channel grey but calm. 'Just think of the sense of achievement. And who gets to do this, Charley? How many people sail the English Channel in a twelve-foot plastic boat?'

'How many would want to?' I muttered miserably.

We headed for the marina where lots of small boats were berthed; it wasn't cold but it was cloudy. I was glad that Russ was so calm and on the case – he was enjoying himself, I could see that. Mungo too seemed to be unfazed, but then he'd be filming from the support boat. However, I was still feeling very unsure about the whole thing.

'It's exactly the right thing to do,' Russ was saying. 'Twenty-two miles to France, Charley. It's perfect.'

The support boat was called the *Gallivant*, which seemed pretty apt: the three of us gallivanting across the world without the kind of back-up we'd had on previous trips. The skipper, a guy called Lance from Margate, sounded more like a cabbie than a boat skipper. Nelson, his right-hand man, was as laid-back as they come. Glen and Rob, two sailors from Laser, would also be joining us. They would take turns in the dinghy with us if we needed them.

The boat was on the beach and ready to launch as Russ and I got into our black and grey drysuits. They were made of neoprene and very awkward. It was like pulling on some kind of giant body condom.

Mungo wandered over. 'So anyway,' he said. 'Just to cover our arses: what's plan A and what's plan B?'

'You think we've got a plan, Mungo?' I laughed. 'Of course – you've never been with us before, have you? It's simple: plan A is to get in the boat, get in the water and sort of follow the support boat so we know roughly the direction we're going.'

'And plan B is to capsize,' Russ added.

'Seriously,' I said. 'I'm more concerned about this part of the trip than any other.'

Russ looked supremely confident. 'I'm excited. It'll be a doddle; we'll sit there on one tack and get there in time for tea.'

I wasn't convinced. I spoke to Lance. 'So what's your salty sea-dog opinion?' I asked him.

He just smiled knowingly. 'Simple, Charley: as the wind gets up the faster you go.'

Glen, the younger of the two guys from Laser, was rigging the mainsail. 'Don't worry,' he said. 'A light breeze scheduled to build, perfect sunshine. It'll be great.'

'See,' Russ said. 'Perfect conditions. Your dad said you lead a charmed life. Remember?'

'What he *actually* said was, he's spent his entire life swimming against the current, while I just floated downstream.'

'There you go then. No worries.'

With that we dragged the boat into the water.

If we crossed in good time, Russ was right – we would have perfect conditions. But later that afternoon the wind was due to get up. With that thought in mind I took the rudder; Russ, Glen and Rob sitting next to me on the port gunwale to keep the weight spread. It felt all right, but we hadn't even left the harbour yet and already a fucking great catamaran ferry was pulling in and lifting waves to rock us from a couple of hundred yards away.

'Over there is France,' I said, trying to lift my spirits. 'Good food, good wine, good cheese and sexy women.'

Once we left the harbour it was just me and Russ and our threadbare experience. It was only now that I wondered why I had spent all my time training in a small plane instead of at sea. I'm fine with motorbikes, I can ride well enough on a track, I can ride the dirt, I'd leap one off a cliff if I was asked. I don't know what it is about boats, but when you're steering you have to work the mainsail as well as the steering and that sort of freaks me out. In the Channel on our own with massive ferries steaming by, I felt incredibly vulnerable. We seemed to be all over the place, tacking when we should be gybing, gybing when we should be tacking; upwind; downwind, the sail dipping viciously towards the water. And all the time Rob, the serious sailor, was yelling at us from the support boat: 'Main off! Main off! Straighten up. Straighten up. Let it out, Charley, let it out; that red rope is your accelerator.'

We almost capsized; the boat coming round too quickly, the mainsail filling just as it had when we were training. Only this wasn't training. The waves were slapping the hull and we were spinning around. Russ grabbed the tiller and we hauled the sail in hard. With the boat heeling all but right over, somehow we managed to save it.

'Close one,' Russ said as we got on course again.

'Close? Close? Fucking hell, mate!' I was really freaked out now. 'Ten hours of this, and with the wind getting up this afternoon.'

'We'll be all right.'

'No, we won't, we'll drown.'

It was more than daunting – it was absolutely miserable. I kept thinking of ten or more hours at sea in a boat that in my view shouldn't be on anything bigger than a lake. Something could go very wrong. There were ships ahead and ships behind; there seemed to be ships all round us. We both knew we couldn't get across on our own whilst avoiding the heavy shipping. The guys in the support boat knew it too. We did our best for a while then Glen and Rob took turns sitting in the bows, directing us.

With that little bit of guidance our confidence grew immeasurably, and with the sky clear above us, we were cutting through the waves. We had wind in the mainsail; the spinnaker fully powered and I couldn't believe it when Lance yelled across to tell us we were halfway. Halfway! We'd only been going a couple of hours. 'Shit, Russ,' I said. 'We might be able to make this.'

We'd left the English zone and were now in the 'separation zone': pretty soon we'd be into French waters. It was actually very enjoyable, though our hands were like prunes and freezing cold because we hadn't thought to wear gloves. The time flew by, the wind was perfect and I forgot about everything and just concentrated on the sailing.

In the distance I could see sandy beaches, little towns hugging green hillsides. I saw a smile of satisfaction spread over Russ's face.

'How many people get to do this?' he said again. 'Sail the Channel in a twelve-foot boat?'

'Not many,' Rob piped up from the bows. 'Between you and me it's the first time I've done it, too.'

We could have sailed directly into Calais harbour but that would have taken another three hours so we headed due north for the beach. Terra firma, wow: I was elated. We'd done it; despite all my fears, my nerves, the way small boats had always freaked me out. We'd crossed the Channel in five hours. I danced on the sand. We all shook hands and I hugged Russ: he was jumping about, with elation but also because he needed a pee. With nowhere to go on the beach, he trotted up to the nearest house. A woman answered the door and peered suspiciously at him. It was our first encounter in a new country.

Russ, standing there in his rubber suit, gave her his best smile. '*Toilette s'il vous plaît, madame?*'

'*Non,*' she said, and shut the door in his face.

4
Black Tie and Bullet Holes

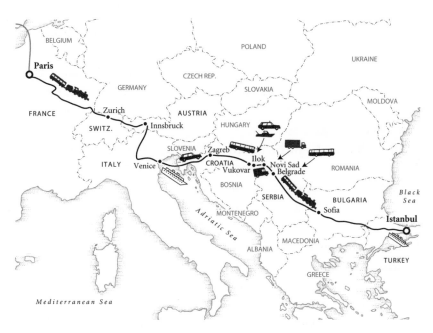

After the last few hectic days, we were looking forward to a leisurely drive to Paris. We'd arranged to borrow a classic Citroën DS from a wiry-looking guy called David, which he delivered on a curtain-sided trailer. It was a real gentleman's car, way ahead of its time and very much in keeping with the next stage of the expedition. The plan was to drive it as far as Paris where we'd swap it for bicycles. We needed to reach the Gare de l'Est by nine o'clock that evening to catch the *Orient Express* to Venice.

Checking over the silver Citroën, I was confident we would make Paris in good time. Manufactured in 1969, it was in pristine condition, with smart leather upholstery, power steering, lights that turned with the steering and hydropneumatic self-levelling suspension. The bodywork had been designed by an Italian sculptor called Flaminio Bertoni. After the exertions of our Channel crossing yesterday, the car was right on the money.

From here on it would be just Russ, Mungo and me. I jumped in, Mungo piling into the back with his camera. Russ sat next to me, the map on his knees, ready to navigate. We said goodbye to Lucy, who was standing on the pavement waiting to see us off. Lucy Trujillo is our producer; she has worked on every one of my trips and is absolutely fantastic – completely unflappable in a crisis. She had been working on our visas with Jo and Lisa – always a complicated process on a trip like this. Apart from Iran, the only country we still needed visas for was Laos. A former French colony, it didn't have an embassy in London but there was one in Paris, so Lucy was using this opportunity to go and get them. But for some strange reason she thought she would get there faster without us.

I got the car going, working out the semi-automatic gearbox and the little plastic button the Citroën had for the brakes. For the first mile or so it was a nightmare, the brakes so sensitive I almost had Russ through the windscreen. But this wasn't a dinghy, it had an engine and I could work it out. Thinking back on yesterday's boat trip, I realised it had been a mad idea. We were complete novices and the Channel had been so busy: a container ship would pass miles away and twenty minutes later we'd be rocked by massive waves from the wake. Thank God for the two guys from Laser – if they hadn't been there I'm not sure we would have made it in ten hours, never mind the five we managed.

Halfway to Paris the Citroën conked out. We were cruising along discussing the expedition and looking forward to a night on the *Orient Express*, when the car started to splutter. Moments later the engine stopped and we rolled to a halt on the side of the busy dual carriageway.

'It feels like fuel,' I said, lifting the bonnet. 'But the gauge says the tank's half full.'

Russ got on the radio to David, the car's owner, who was following in his van. 'David,' he said, '*la voiture est morte.*'

David pulled up and took a quick look. He fiddled about for a moment then twisted the key and the car fired into life.

I glanced a little sheepishly at Russ. 'Didn't you just know that would happen?'

Back behind the wheel I studied the fuel gauge. It was still reading half full. No problem there then.

I was soon back in my element. On this trip the journey itself was the real destination, and I couldn't think of anything better than bimbling through France in this wonderful gentleman's car. 'This car was so advanced when they built it,' I said. 'The faster you go the stiffer the steering gets.'

There was a pregnant pause, then Russ said slowly, 'The faster you go the stiffer it gets.'

'The *steering*, Russ.' I shook my head sadly. 'You know, I drove an old Le Mans Jag from Italy to London once; one of those massive soft-tops with a fin on the back. All the way through France people were honking and waving and whenever I stopped they'd crowd around the car.'

Russ was nodding. 'There's something personal about old cars; they've got a soul, haven't they?'

'Especially when they break down,' Mungo muttered.

'Anyway,' I said, 'people were all over it all the way to Dover.'

'What happened at Dover?'

'A lorry driver spat on me.'

Russ took a call from Lucy, then turned to me with a smile. 'Lucy arrived in Paris about forty minutes before the embassy closed. There was a massive queue for taxis outside the station.'

'What did she do?'

'Rented a limo.'

'She did what?'

'She didn't have a choice. It was either queue for ever or take the only form of transport available. She made it to the embassy with five minutes to spare then begged them to process the application. She told them she'd come from London by boat, train and car and they took pity on her. She's got to hang around for three hours but she'll get the visas.'

Good old Luce. We were sorted. Now we just had to work out how to get in. We'd originally planned to enter Laos from the north, after crossing from Nepal to Tibet and then into China. But back in March the Chinese closed the Tibetan border and it looked as though it would stay that way until after the Olympics.

'We'll have to think about it nearer the time,' Russ said. 'There doesn't seem to be an option right now though; except maybe trying to go through Burma as tourists.'

Mungo didn't look convinced. 'With all this camera gear?' he said. 'Somehow I don't think they'll go for it.'

Twenty minutes later the Citroën lost power and the engine died again: we were on the motorway now and the closer we got to Paris the busier it was becoming.

David drove past and pulled over. It was too dangerous for him to back up so Russ jumped out and pushed the car to the van. We had the bonnet up again and David cleaned the fuel filter: the car started and off we went again.

The third time it stopped we were in sight of the city: the Eiffel Tower in the distance with blocks of ugly flats defining the sprawl of the suburbs. We were still on the motorway and I managed to glide the car to a slip road and drift down to the exit on the brakes. 'Fuck, this is wild,' I said. 'It's the last place you want to break down.'

We pulled over and got out. Russ looked at his watch. 'It's getting late,' he said. 'We've got to be at the station by nine o'clock and still we have to cycle from your niece's place. I think we'll have to load the Citroën onto the trailer.'

David took another look. He thought it had to be petrol. The gauge still said half-full but we couldn't think of anything else so between the four of us we loaded it onto the trailer. The van only had three seats and the back was separated off by a panel: with David driving one of us would be back there with no windows, hunched on the chipboard floor.

'Rock, paper, scissors,' Russ said. 'Mungo, are you ready? One, two, three, go.'

Mungo lost.

'You're in the back, mate,' Russ told him.

'No, he's not,' I interrupted. 'He can't sit in the back, Russ: he's the cameraman.'

With Russ squatting on the bags we headed into Paris. David pulled into the first petrol station we came to and filled the Citroën as it sat on the trailer. I got behind the wheel and it started first time. Basically, we had run out of petrol, which was a bit embarrassing.

I sat there revving the engine and thinking that it was a pity we'd not figured it out earlier because the car was beautiful to drive. The suspension was so good that production companies used to strip these Citroëns to the chassis and use them for filming platforms.

Still, all was not lost. We had petrol now and we still had some time. I was really keen to drive into the city and brave the Arc de Triomphe as originally planned, so after backing the car off the trailer we set off again.

Paris was manic, worse than I'd ever known it. I remembered the first time I drove in the city, almost crapping myself with fright. At least this time I knew my way around. We were heading for my mum's flat in the Rue Saint Honoré where we'd meet Daphne, my sister Telsche's daughter. Telsche died from cancer when Daphne was only six and I always think of her when I'm travelling. She was on the bike with me on Long Way Round and again when we rode through Africa.

Daphne, who works as a translator, lives in my mum's flat: it's a great spot, very central, just behind the Louvre. My favourite museum, the spectacular Musée d'Orsay, isn't far away. It used to be a station and amongst many other amazing works it houses sculptures by Rodin and Camille Claudel. Camille was Rodin's model and then his lover. There was something about their tempestuous relationship – and the fact that she was a brilliant sculptress herself – that has always inspired me.

We made it to the apartment, met up with Daphne and grabbed a crêpe from the patisserie across the road. It was exciting to be in Paris again, soaking up the atmosphere. Time was getting on, though, so Russ and I grabbed a couple of bicycles from one of the many stands dotted around the city. It's a great idea; you put your credit card in the slot and take a bike, and you can then cycle to any of the other stands around the city and park it up again. It's quick and easy and of course there's no pollution. Weaving in and out of the traffic we made our way to the Gare de l'Est.

It's a beautiful station with its fine cobbled concourse and pillared façade. The fabulous domed entrance hall is the perfect, decadent setting for the *Orient Express*. After the motorbikes, the challenges of the Channel crossing and the car breaking down all the way to Paris, I was looking forward to a bit of rest and luxury.

The only problem was – I'd forgotten to bring any shoes. You have to dress for dinner on the *Orient Express* and I'd carefully packed my suit and black tie, but had nothing to wear on my feet except my chunky old bike boots. I couldn't believe it. I was so unprepared for this section of the trip it was ridiculous. I'd just have to hope I wouldn't get kicked out of the dining car.

The cars themselves are blue with white roofs, and polished till they gleam. The wood panelling in the corridors and cabins is varnished to the point where you can see your reflection. Our cabins were in car 3309, one of the two oldest and most beautifully decorated, with beautiful murals lining the walls. Built in 1926, the other of the two oldest cars had been used by King Carol of Romania. More alarmingly, some other parts of the train had been used as a brothel for occupying German officers in World War Two.

The stewards wore blue uniforms and kepi-style hats – round, flat-topped caps with a visor. The bartenders and waiters, a cosmopolitan mix of French, Italian, Serb and even Australian, worked quietly and unobtrusively, seemingly oblivious to the roll of the carriages.

My cabin was small but beautifully formed, the bed folding out ingeniously from the seat. My case was stored on a luggage rack above a panel of polished wooden cupboards, and there was a small table fitted up against the window. I felt a tingle of excitement – I couldn't believe I was about to set off on one of the most famous and historic trips in the world. I pulled down on the window's ancient lever and poked my head out, sucking up the sights, smells and sounds as we left Paris. Tomorrow morning I would be able to lie back and gaze at the Alps as we rolled through the countryside on our way to Venice.

Wandering along the corridor I discovered a bucket of wood and coal under a shelf just along from my cabin. A little bit of investigation revealed a cupboard housing a pot-bellied stove. I realised that the water must be heated now as it always was, by a solid fuel boiler in each sleeping car.

I dressed for dinner. I reckoned I looked all right – apart from my boots of course, which were battered and clumpy and completely at odds with the image of sartorial elegance I was hoping for. Oh well, it couldn't be helped and I wasn't going to let it spoil the evening. Ready to go at last, I looked for the key and couldn't find it anywhere. I began rummaging through my clothes, the cushions, my suitcase, getting increasingly annoyed with myself. Just when I thought I'd never find the bloody thing I saw it hanging where I'd left it on a hook designed for a gentleman's pocket watch. I sighed to myself and grabbed it. Sometimes I'm more organised than I think.

I found Russ and Mungo in the bar, already well into a bottle of champagne. I relaxed and soaked up the atmosphere, enjoying a few drinks before a fabulous dinner. That said, we didn't actually sit down to eat until almost midnight – passengers from Paris have to wait until those who started in London have finished their meal.

When I finally got back to my cabin at two-thirty I was delighted to see that the stewards had prepared the bed while I'd been eating dinner – all I had to do was fall into it. I fell asleep to the train's gentle swaying motion, thinking I could definitely get used to this . . .

I woke the next morning to find we were in Switzerland, snow settled on the ground about us. The steward brought breakfast: croissants, jams and cheese, fruit cocktail and a thermos of hot coffee. I ate leisurely, watching the world go by and thinking how lucky I was.

We stopped in Innsbruck to change engines: each train has an engine front and back and they're changed at the border crossings. The engine is the only bit of the train that looks modern. I watched as it was uncoupled; the platform overlooked by the ski jump from the Winter Olympics. Once the new engine was in place we had a new driver: a local man from Innsbruck who'd been driving for sixteen years. He invited me onto the footplate to have a look.

I'd driven a steam train once – a sister engine to the *Mallard* – at the Watercress Line in Hampshire. It had been built in the 1930s and was powered by steam. The only resemblance here was the button the driver had to push every time he saw an orange light ahead. It was a track security system: if he didn't hit the button within a few seconds the train would automatically shut down. He had to drive with his feet on two pedals and there was another pedal by the window. If his feet came off the pedals the train would stop. It was all to avoid disaster if he blacked out, had a heart attack or fell asleep. The train is a quarter of a mile long and driving it carries huge responsibility.

Not far out of Innsbruck we stopped and he jumped down and walked up the track. I took the opportunity to steal his seat, the fascia a mass of dials and switches, nothing like the old steam engine with its gauges and levers, its blazing hot fire-box. Moments later the driver was back. He explained that this track system had different electronics from the one we'd just been on – he had to throw a relay switch before we could continue.

He took us through lush green meadows that drifted into the snow-clad mountains, over bridges and through tunnels, past pretty little ski-towns. We rode on through the Brenner Pass to the Italian border; the same pass used by German tribes when they invaded Italy in the fifth century. At the station in Brenner our driver said goodbye, jumped down and made his way to the back of the train where he would drive the other engine back to Innsbruck.

I took some time out in my cabin to think about Venice. I'd only been there once – Olly and I had taken the kids – but it had been one of the most moving and emotional experiences of my life. One night we'd eaten dinner at a restaurant by the canal. The kids were messing about on the terrace. Looking over at my wife I saw she had a tear in her eye.

'What is it?' I asked her.

'Nothing,' she said. 'It's just this place. You know, Charley, today has been one of the most perfect days of my life.'

I decided to call her from the train. I told her where I was and how I wished she was with me. But Olly had other things on her mind. She'd just had some awful news – Françoise, one of our friends, had been ill for some time. The doctors had thought it was pneumonia but in fact she was suffering from a form of skin cancer. She'd just been told it was terminal. And there I was rolling into the city of canals and bridges aboard the *Orient Express*. God, it put things into perspective. Life is such a leveller; no matter what you're doing, it never quite allows you to get carried away with yourself. Arriving at the station I was still thinking about Françoise, her husband Steve and their two children. There was nothing I could do and a sense of helplessness flooded through me.

At the Stazione Santa Lucia we said goodbye to the stewards and headed for a water taxi to transport us through this magical city, where there are no cars and everything is delivered by boat. Venice covers a hundred or so little islands dotted around a salt lagoon at the northern end of the Adriatic. We passed under bridges, gliding by some truly spectacular buildings. One house in particular stood out: an orange and white building with a tiled roof and sun terrace, twin porticos on either side built right over the water. It was a chilly day, the sky overcast and the water grey and murky; but that couldn't dampen the spirit of old world adventure.

'Look, there's the Rialto,' Russ pointed out as we came out of a smaller channel. The Ponte di Rialto, one of the most famous landmarks in Venice, is one of three bridges that span the Grand Canal. Originally a pontoon, it was replaced by a wooden bridge in 1250. The Rialto itself was completed in 1591. It's very wide, with covered arches on each side and an open cobbled walkway in the middle.

We stayed the night in the Hotel Gritti Palace on the Grand Canal, a last bit of luxury before we headed for Eastern Europe. In the morning we were up early and into another taxi that took us through the smaller channels. Some of them were really narrow with very low bridges, most no more than two metres. Standing on deck we had to duck our heads each time we passed underneath. We were on our way to meet a woman called Chiara, whose brothers run a fruit and vegetable company, supplying restaurants all over the city.

The buildings seemed to crowd the boat; they're erected on closely spaced wood piles that originally came from Russia. If there's no oxygen wood doesn't decay and underwater there's no oxygen. The piles were driven into layers of sand and clay and because of that the buildings look as though they grow right out of the water. It's an incredibly dramatic, gothic effect.

Everything is moved via the water; we saw laundry boats, yellow ambulances and the postman; we even saw an undertaker complete with coffin and flowers. Heading down one tight canal we passed a grey-haired fishmonger. He stood up when he saw us and yelled across the water.

'Hey, Charles Boorman!'

I waved to him, not quite believing I'd been recognised by a man selling fish from his boat in the middle of Venice.

'I read your book,' he called out with a grin. 'I love it. You're number one, you and Ewan McGregor.'

The taxi dropped us at a small piazza where Chiara was waiting. She led us into a narrow side street where the buildings blocked the sun, and boxes of exotic fruit were stacked against the stone walls. I could smell lemons and strawberries, pomegranates, the finest quality oranges. Chiara introduced us to her brother Alessandro who took us into a hectic-looking shop where a dozen or so men were weighing fruit and shifting boxes. Alessandro told us they start work about three in the morning and finish around noon. They buy the produce from the main market by the station and ship it back to the shop in a big boat. There it's sorted before being delivered to various parts of the city in smaller boats.

I went out with a driver, criss-crossing the canals; some narrow, some wide. We called at restaurants and shops, dropping off box after box of the kind of fruit that caters to the expensive palates you find here in Venice. I loved it – it was so laid-back, so beautiful: another job I wouldn't mind doing. We'd motor down tiny canals and unload the boxes. Then we'd be back on the Grand

Canal with the sun on our faces and the smell of the city in the air. It was all very different from delivering fruit and veg somewhere like London: no white-van man and no road rage either.

It was still early in the morning and none of the gondolas were out; we were part of the Venice of everyday Venetians. You don't see many gondolas before ten a.m. Alessandro told us there is an unspoken agreement that goods and services are ferried around the city before the tourists come out. It all seemed very genteel – maybe it's something about the water that keeps people so calm.

Dad and I had joked about gondoliering back in Ireland. He'd been a champion river punter in his day and I had threatened to fly him to Venice to show me how to do it. Gondolas have an offset keel which allows one oar to keep them going straight, and Dad told me it wasn't any more difficult than steering a punt. Sadly, there wasn't time for me to try, however; Mungo reminded me that we had to catch the hydrofoil across the Adriatic to Porec on the Dalmatian coast, where a couple of Croats had a car waiting for us.

It was more of a streamlined hovercraft than a hydrofoil but either way it was bloody fast: flat out on calm seas it could do forty knots. As we left Venice the captain invited us onto the bridge and I noticed he controlled the thing with the same kind of games console joystick as the ferry to Liverpool. It seemed a bit nerve-racking: we were on the canals; this was a big boat and there was a hell of a lot of traffic.

Maybe the nerves were of my own making, though: this was the last port of call I would be familiar with. From here on in there wasn't a country I'd visited before until we reached Australia.

We were heading for Croatia where less than twenty years ago there'd been a bloody war. I didn't know what to expect but had some ideas; poverty, smashed buildings, pot-holed roads . . .

I couldn't have been more wrong. Two and a half hours later the boat docked in a beautiful Mediterranean town where massive yachts were moored alongside traditional fishing boats. I was reminded of the south of France; balmy night air, pavement cafes and the most amazing sunset.

'So what's this car we're getting?' Russ asked.

'A Yugo: like a Fiat 127 only not as good.'

We carried our bags towards the car park where we had arranged to meet some guys who had agreed to lend us the car. Yugos aren't just like Fiats – they *are* Fiats, made under licence. This one was old and apparently nowhere near as good as the original. But it was local – the car of the masses in the days of Tito – and that was what we wanted. I'd heard it called 'disposable': drive it once and throw it away, the Bic razor of the automobile world.

'The transmission is like churning a baseball bat in a barrel of coconuts,' I said.

Mungo, weighed down under a mountain of camera bags, shot me a look. 'I hope it's got a boot.'

'It's a two-door hatchback,' I told him, 'hardly any room in the back seat and bugger-all boot.'

'I'll think positive. Maybe there's a roof-rack.'

There was, fortunately, and most of the gear fitted on it. Dean and Kristijan were waiting for us. They seemed like a couple of really nice, friendly guys. They showed us the car: it was compact as I knew it would be, but it was in good nick. They helped us pack the gear then invited us to stay with them in the hillside town of Motovun, about eighty kilometres away. We piled into the Yugo and eventually I found first gear. Soon we were bumbling along having a great time, following our hosts into the mountains, some good old-fashioned Croat music on the radio.

I pointed out of the window. 'Can you believe how clean everything is? Not a trace of litter; it's so pretty.'

None of us had known what to expect. Neither Russ nor I had been to the Balkans before. Mungo had been to Split briefly with the British army, but he'd not seen much of the country. Tonight we'd stay in the mountains and tomorrow we were heading for Zagreb.

'To get a bus to somewhere else,' Russ said. 'I can't remember where right now, we'll think about that tomorrow.' He laughed. 'That's how it's been, hasn't it? We can just about think from one day to the next. Any further than that and we get lost.'

He was right; we were covering huge distances and had planned for maybe thirty countries. To think much more than a day ahead at this point was too much to take in. And who wanted to anyway?

I loved the spontaneity of this trip. On a bike you have to concentrate on riding a lot of the time. Here I could kick back, and I was finding it much easier to get to know people along the way.

'Can you believe that fishmonger this morning?' Mungo piped up from where he was hunched in the back. '*Hey, Charles Boorman*: nobody calls you Charles, Charley, do they?'

'Venetians do,' I told him.

We stayed in a small house in a hillside town with bumpy cobbled streets. Leaving the main road we crossed a river, the croaking of bullfrogs following us all the way up the hill. We stopped at a local shop selling wine, cheese and grappa, which we imbibed of course; it would've been rude not to. Then we ate dinner and had a few beers with Dean and Kristijan, who told us about their country. They said that luckily the war hadn't really affected this area except in a few places, and that the young people in particular preferred to look forward, not back.

They put the three of us up in one room with only two beds. We stared at the beds for a moment. We were friendly enough, I suppose, for three blokes on the road, but not that friendly.

'So, Mungo,' I said, laying a hand on his shoulder. 'There's no way Russ and I are sharing . . .'

Mungo scratched his stubble. 'No worries. You two get your beauty sleep – you need it. Me, I'm pretty enough – I'm happy on the floor.'

In the morning we woke to a cloudless sky and the sound of cuckoos in the trees. We were overlooking a lush green valley and I was reminded of Tuscany: sloping hills, clusters of spruce trees and banks of olive groves. Russ came out and paused a moment to take it in.

'Beautiful, Charley, isn't it?'

I nodded and yawned. Very beautiful.

We drove six hours on empty roads right through the mountains. We crossed rivers and cut through massive pine forests back into open countryside dotted with old farm buildings and Friesian cattle. The Yugo was superb fun, the gearbox no worse than any other small car and unlike the Citroën the fuel gauge worked properly. Mungo rode up front some of the way, Russ in the back catching flies. We were beginning to think he had narcoleptic tendencies: car, boat, train . . . give him five minutes and he'd fall asleep anywhere.

It was after twelve-thirty by the time we reached Zagreb, which was later than we'd hoped. The bus was leaving for Vukovar at one-thirty but we had to be ready at one o'clock, which didn't give us any time to look around. We just about had time to cross the tramlines, say goodbye to our hosts and give them back their car. We wrote a quick postcard home and got on the bus; the three of us occupying a couple of rows of seats at the back.

Five hours later we pulled into Vukovar, which was very much the Croatia I remembered from the news. Most of the buildings had holes in them, sections missing as a result of shells or mortars; the stonework riddled with bullet marks. The city had a distinctive feel to it; uneasy, even a little dangerous. In 1991 Vukovar had been surrounded by what was the former Yugoslavian army. There was no Croatian army and two thousand 'defenders' took up arms and managed to hold out for eighty-seven days against tanks and mortars, trained soldiers. Ultimately they were massacred; eight hundred people went missing and twenty-two thousand were forced into exile. It was a stark reminder of what had happened after Tito died; how this region had crumbled again into the kind of warfare that had raged for centuries.

It was still beautiful, though, this city set at the confluence of the Vuka and the Danube; the water mirrored like glass. I stood at my hotel room window gazing beyond an inlet to the far bank shrouded by evergreen trees.

The following morning we were outside at seven-thirty. It was really warm, as if summer had arrived already. It did the old bones good after ten days on the road. We were heading for Serbia today, but first we were going to speak to a woman who survived the siege of Vukovar by hiding in her basement.

'You know the river pretty much surrounds the city,' Russ told me. 'A bit like the Serbians did in 1991. It's hard to imagine this city being attacked with tanks.'

I was staring at the hotel doors, the brown metal frames around the glass. 'See that,' I said. 'The door frame is riddled with bullet holes. Even this little hotel; God, nowhere escaped.'

Russ shook his head. 'The whole city was destroyed. When Tito died the states began to split up again. Croatia wanted independence and with it the piece of land that had been defined by Tito. The Serbs said they could have their independence but they didn't need all that land. The Serbs wanted access to the coast.'

'So they rolled the tanks in.'

After breakfast we met up with Natalia, the woman who'd spent three months in her basement. Echoing what Dean and Kristijan had told us, she said that since the conflict ended in 1995 the younger people in Vukovar had moved on. That wasn't necessarily true of the older generation, though. Some of their Serb oppressors had previously been their neighbours, some had committed atrocities and others held positions of power locally, particularly in the police force.

Natalia pointed out a water tower that we'd seen from our hotel. You can see it from lots of vantage points around Vukovar; it stands as a symbol of Croatian unity. When the Serbs shelled the defenders of the city, the water tower was hit six hundred times, yet still it remained standing. Every building around it was flattened but as if in defiance of the brutality, the tower refused to crumble. The Croatian people refer to 1991 as the 'Time of Hate': like a cancer they saw it consume individual people, communities, whole towns. When the fighting was over and Vukovar was overrun, the Serbs dragged two hundred and sixty-one wounded defenders and civilians from the hospital and brought them to an old building that is now a museum. There's a massive cross outside with lighted candles and smaller crosses draped in rosaries. Four people died from beatings that first night and over the next few days twenty people at a time were loaded onto a trailer and towed by tractor to a farmer's field. They were shot then dumped in a mass grave, all two hundred and sixty-one of them. The youngest was seventeen and three of them were women.

Natalia told us that so far two hundred had been identified, but seventeen years later the others are still to be named.

In a quiet suburban street across the road from a little petrol station there's a set of tall yellow gates that mark the site of one of the camps where the Serbs held Croat prisoners. Natalia's house is just up the road, a little place with pebble-dashed walls and a brown tiled roof. She told us how she and her mother hid in the basement with only raw potatoes to eat. They remained there for three months.

'It was terrible,' she told us. 'We are very afraid: every day soldiers come along the street tossing bombs into the basements.'

Russ was appalled. 'You mean grenades? They threw grenades into people's houses?'

She nodded. 'Every day we thought it would be our house, every day.' She had been a small child; her father hadn't fought as a defender but he'd been hauled off to a concentration camp anyway. He was a good man and believed they would survive, but he had no idea whether he would be shot and there was nothing he could do for his wife or daughter. He just had to hope and pray. In the end it was a Serbian neighbour that saved them, plucking them from the basement and taking them to safety.

I've always felt very strongly that war achieves nothing but suffering and misery. Listening to Natalia, the full horror of this conflict really hit me hard – perhaps because it happened so recently and most of the people killed were my age. Earlier we had paid our respects in a massive cemetery: it had beautifully paved walkways and sculpted trees, flowers everywhere. The headstones were black marble, and reading them I had realised that most of those who were killed had been born between 1959 and 1966. I was born in 1966: I have a wife, two beautiful children and a great life. These people hadn't made thirty; some of them not even twenty. There was one entire row where the victims had lost their lives within a few days of each other.

Feeling sombre we left Vukovar, hitching a ride on a maintenance barge to the town of Ilok further down the Danube. We could see the water tower from the deck; an everlasting reminder of Vukovar. At Ilok we'd cross into Serbia.

The crew of the barge were young guys who troll up and down the Croatian side of the river, fixing buoys and maintaining signposts that give vital information to shipping. The shore is thick with trees and part of their job is to clear dead or overgrown wood. Kitted out in hard hat, goggles and ear defenders, I had a go at cutting down some trees but kept jamming the chainsaw. When I did manage to make it work, I almost dropped a tree on Russ and Mungo. The bloke supervising me told me the Danube starts out in the Black Forest and runs all the way to the Black Sea: it's 1,774 miles long and has been a trade route and a supply line since before Roman times.

Downriver we came to a damaged buoy, the top bashed in by a passing boat. The crew hauled it on board with a crane then replaced the top and stripped the float of barnacles. After that it was repainted: on the Croatian side of the river the buoys are red and on the Serbian side they're blue.

Docking at Ilok we crossed into Serbia in a taxi. The cabbie spoke good English and was very chatty: he took charge completely, driving us across the bridge that spans the river between the two countries. We didn't have to do anything: he took our passports to the officials while we stayed in the car then drove us to the town of Backa Palanka and dropped us outside a carpet factory. I was due to drive a delivery van as far as Novi Sad. From Novi Sad we were taking a train, twenty-four hours to Istanbul. It was there we would have to overcome our problem of crossing the Black Sea. It had proved really difficult to get any kind of ship. We'd looked at containers, tankers, oil field tenders . . . but so far we had nothing lined up.

'It might be a case of being on the spot, instead of trying to organise it from London,' Russ said. 'We'll just have to see. If we can't get a ship we'll just have to drive across Turkey.'

We were waiting for the carpet to be loaded into the van. And here it came now, a massive thickened roll propelling its way towards us, end on. Raised slightly from the horizontal, it bounced up and down like a live thing on the prong of some kind of forklift. For a moment we just stared. Then we fell about laughing.

'Welcome to Serbia,' I said. 'Not as big as mine, boys: but it is pretty close.'

5
I See No Ships

About fifteen minutes from Novi Sad a community of displaced gypsies live in a camp known locally as 'Bangladesh'. Anna and Danka, a couple of girls who work with the people who live there, showed us around.

It's a miserable place; more like an old, abandoned army barracks than a place to raise a family. The buildings are single storey and built in terraced blocks with a string of concrete alleyways running between them. The walls are a grubby whitewash over concrete, the roofs corrugated iron. As we turned down a dirt road, a rubbish skip greeted us; beyond it rose piles of rubble, broken-down cars and bits of old iron. Even the impoverished highlands of Ethiopia weren't as derelict as this. The houses didn't seem to have any doors, most had plastic sheets for windows, and it didn't look as though there was any electricity. Dishevelled kids were running barefoot through the alleyways. We saw one man riding an ingenious contraption he'd made by welding the back half of a motorbike to a trailer, which carried his wife and daughter.

Gypsies – or 'Roma', as Anna and Danka called them – have always been outsiders in Eastern Europe, and since the Balkan Wars they have become even more marginalised. For these people life is very difficult: they've been shunted from pillar to post, nobody wanting anything to do with them. Finally, they ended up here. It was supposed to have been temporary but this place was fifteen minutes from just about anywhere and it looked to me as though they'd been forgotten. They're very poor and their traditional way of life is pretty much over. In Eastern Europe they've always had a reputation for being untrustworthy, and once you're the subject of that kind of prejudice life can become a downward spiral. Danka was clearly passionate about them, though, and she works tirelessly for their welfare.

I couldn't think of a worse place to live. There was rubbish everywhere; old fridges, chest freezers, beds. It was mad: a lot of stuff looked as though it had been brought back from trips to the city and just left where it was unloaded. But Danka believed that despite the seemingly hopeless squalor, these settlements – and the people who lived in them – had possibilities. It was just that the government couldn't see it.

She introduced us to a middle-aged man called Tomas, who collected scrap in Novi Sad in a homemade cart pulled by a mangy horse, which he kept in a makeshift stable. He hooked the animal into a harness he'd made from bits of old leather and wooden poles he'd cut straight from the tree. He made the seat comfortable and we drove into the city. Tomas didn't say much, but he seemed troubled – his family were in court in Novi Sad that day, for a reason I couldn't quite get to the bottom of.

Danka was determined to do her best to represent the people living in the camp. 'Serbia is a young democracy,' she said. 'We think we're strong but we're not. We don't really know how to deal with this.'

Once we got to the main road we said goodbye to Tomas and headed off to catch a bus from Novi Sad to Belgrade, the capital of Serbia. We'd originally planned to take the train but Anna told us the bus was much quicker, and we thought we would see more of the countryside. We showed our tickets to the driver, who tore them in two and handed the bigger halves back to me. Bad idea. Somewhere between there and the back seats I managed to lose them – something we only realised when we got closer to Belgrade and the conductor wanted to see them. We hunted high and low but there was no sign. There was a hole in the floor under my seat where you could see the road going by and it was more than possible the tickets were long gone. The girl sitting in front vouched for us and when we stopped the driver acknowledged we'd paid. With these two testimonies the conductor was finally satisfied. I decided I'd leave 'logistics' to Russ in future . . .

This mini crisis over, we were off the bus and back in a big city, the streets clogged with traffic, people hurrying about their business. It was a far cry from the shanty town we'd visited earlier.

We arrived just in time for lunch, and soon found a cafe with a pavement veranda, separated from passers-by with a knee-high glass panel, the tables sheltered by massive red parasols. It was good to sit outside and watch the world go by. It was a warm, close day, and I could smell a hint of rain in the air.

'What do we want to eat, then?' Russ asked as Mungo and I grabbed a seat.

We didn't get a chance to answer. A waiter came hurrying over and told us we had better come inside.

'Inside?' I looked up a little puzzled.

Nodding sharply, the waiter pointed. 'The storm is coming.'

Before we even had time to move, a gust of wind howled down the length of the street, billowing in like a hurricane and almost tearing the trees from their roots. I could feel my hair being dragged across my scalp. The table tipped over and, dashing for the restaurant door, we looked back to see parasols picked up and hurled across the street, blown around like skittles on their concrete bases.

I've never experienced anything like it – so powerful or so fast. It was almost like an explosion; one minute everything was calm and the next the street was chaos. The cafe's glass panel smashed into pieces, the metal frame buckled and the tables went flying. One parasol crashed into a nearby bus stop, another hurtled towards the road where the side of an empty bus only narrowly stopped it smashing into passing cars.

When the storm eased a little we rushed outside again and helped the waiters grab what they could. The wind was still incredibly strong: it whipped at us, tearing our hair and stinging our eyes as we hung on to one parasol, the canvas ballooning so fiercely it was all we could do to drag it closed. Once we'd got it folded we went for the one jammed in the bus shelter. There was glass everywhere; we were in danger of slipping over and cutting ourselves to ribbons.

Finally the wind seemed to blow itself out, leaving a heavy rain behind it. Hands on my hips I surveyed the damage. Miraculously, it seemed that no one had been hurt. Finally we sat down to some food (inside this time), and when the rain had lessened a little, we headed off to explore.

We soon found the tram that circumnavigated the city – a great way to get our bearings and experience this historic city. The Danube joins the Sava at Belgrade, making it an ideal trading centre and one of the oldest cities in Europe. Archaeologists have discovered earthworks dating back to Celtic and Roman times, the Slavs settling here in the seventh century. The city's prime strategic and political position led to a series of bloody sieges, occupations and street battles over the centuries, and we could only hope these days were now passed for good.

At seven-forty-five the next morning Mungo and I arrived at the train station: a large, sprawling building with a single arch door. We were on our way to Istanbul. Russ joined us – he had gone ahead to find Mr Popovic, the man with our tickets. 'I couldn't find him,' Russ explained, 'but I did find a friendly official. He really wanted to help but he kept taking me to all the wrong places.'

Remembering my experience with the tickets yesterday, I decided it was best to leave Russ to it. Mungo and I sat down at a coffee shop on the platform and ten minutes later Russ was back, tickets in hand.

'That's our train,' he said, pointing to a blue carriage tacked on to a couple of grubby-looking red ones. The green engine looked rusty and the track was overgrown with weeds. 'The blue carriage is the sleeping car. We've got a bed for the night but we stop maybe eighteen times.' He smiled. 'I love this. We're really on the move now, aren't we?'

'It's easier to get around Europe, though,' I said. 'Don't forget, after Turkey there's Georgia, then Azerbaijan.'

'Not to mention Iran,' Mungo added. 'That'll be an adventure in itself. We've heard nothing positive about the place in years.'

I thought about the countries to come: Iran, India, Nepal – all challenging in different ways. After that we had China to negotiate. 'I'm trying not to think much beyond Turkey,' I said. 'Though I must say, I'm really looking forward to riding through Georgia on a motorbike and sidecar. I love all the boats and trains, but that'll be *really* mad.'

Russ gazed around the station. 'There's a real charm to this,' he said. 'The whole place is worn down, but it feels exotic and evocative. Just the name – "the *Balkan Express*" – conjures up all kinds of images and feelings, doesn't it?'

'I can't believe we've only been on the road twelve days,' I said, shaking my head. 'It's only the twenty-third of April.'

'Twelve days since we left your dad's place,' Mungo said. 'We'll have travelled through eight countries by the time we reach Turkey. And it must be, what, twenty different forms of transport at least. A real whistle-stop tour of Europe.'

The cabins on the *Balkan Express* may have been evocative but they were also very small and functional. As well as the bed there was a table with a wash basin hidden underneath, a shaving mirror/cabinet and a window that didn't stay open. I propped mine ajar with a roll-on deodorant.

This was a good way to travel with a hangover, I decided. We'd tied a small one on last night, celebrating our arrival in Belgrade, and we were all feeling just a little bleh. The mood in camp couldn't have been better though: we were hanging out the windows like grubby schoolboys. Russ couldn't get the smile off his face. 'I love this train, Charley. It's got a faded charm.'

'Shabby,' I said, looking about. 'It's shabby, Russ.'

'But it's more real than the *Orient Express*.' Mungo was in the corridor. 'You can wear jeans and there's—'

'No piano, no champagne, nowhere to buy food.'

'We'll get food tonight,' Russ assured me. 'We stop for a while in Sofia to change engines and we'll pick up something there.'

We spent the day rattling through villages with wooden huts and larger towns where brick buildings had windows boarded up and grey apartment blocks dwarfed the railway line. We followed the river through sheer-sided cuttings and into deciduous forests; we climbed mountains where low cliffs punctuated huge grassy plateaus that reminded me of Mongolia.

Bulgaria's landscape seemed gentler and was very beautiful. Mungo said it reminded him of northern England, like the edges of the Lake District. Sadly, Sofia itself seemed shabby and rundown by comparison; the area around the station dominated by square, featureless flats; the kind of faceless blocks they built in the Soviet era. The train stopped for an hour while the engine was uncoupled and I dashed about changing money and buying bread and salami.

I could get used to this kind of travelling; it was so different from being on the bike where you really have to concentrate on the riding. Here we were jumping from one form of transport to the next; short hops and then long hauls like this one. Turkey was on my mind now, and the closer we got, the larger the Black Sea loomed. We still had no passage across. With nothing on the horizon we'd discussed the idea of a smaller boat instead of a container ship; one that stayed closer to the shore. That might be a lot of fun, especially if it stopped now and then: we might even get to see a few coastal towns. Settling down for a night's sleep, rocked by the motion of the train, I really didn't mind. That was the beauty of the expedition: everything was fluid. We'd figure it out when we got to Istanbul.

I was awake when we crossed into Turkey at two in the morning; a beautiful, clear moon hanging in the sky above. I'd dreamed of visiting Istanbul for maybe twenty years; in just a few more hours we'd be rolling into town. I couldn't wait – this was the city that had once been called Byzantium, then Constantinople . . . just those names alone conjured up a sense of romance and ancient history. At six o'clock, unable to sleep with excitement, I got up and hung out of the window, watching the world flash by.

We arrived three hours later. From my window, Istanbul looked modern, wealthy; low-lying suburbs with wide, sparklingly clean streets and small trees that looked like green lollipops.

Lucy was flying in to meet up with us to pick up the rushes for the television show. The team in London had spent three months trying to arrange a ship for us for the next stretch of our journey, but it seemed that for our purposes, they were all going the wrong way. Istanbul is divided by the Bosporus, a kilometre-wide strait that connects the Black Sea with the Sea of Marmara. Most ships were travelling from the Med beyond Gallipoli and into the Marmara. From there they cut through the Bosporus Strait to the Black Sea and on to the Ukraine and Russia.

'We've got a big day ahead of us,' Russ said when I bumped into him in the corridor. 'We're meeting a couple of guys who I hope will be able to help us get that elusive ship.'

'Hope being the operative word,' I muttered.

From the window we could see dozens of ships lying at anchor off the coast: surely one of them would be going east instead of north.

At the station we were met by Cenk and Jarus, two local guys we'd been in touch with in the hope of sorting out our transport problems. But the news on the ground wasn't any better. The first thing Jarus said was that our chances of getting a boat were pretty hopeless. 'We've tried seven hundred and forty different ships,' he said, 'and none of them will take you.'

Lucy met us at a hotel where we sat down with some thick Turkish coffee and tried to figure out what we could do. I'd been looking forward to seeing Istanbul more than anything, but as Russ pointed out it was in danger of becoming our nemesis. The expedition would grind to a halt right here unless we could find some form of transport to get us across to Georgia.

Jarus made a helpless gesture. 'I've been working on it all week, and the chances are very slim. Ships are sailing daily but the Turkish regulations and the international regulations say you cannot go unless you are the crew.'

Russ sat back. 'OK,' he said. 'At the moment we don't have any way forward with a ship, but, Jarus – you did mention we could take a lorry east, at least as far as the tea plantations.'

Cenk, the younger of the two Turks, spoke up. 'You know in Turkey there are buses called *dolmus*. The driver writes the destination on the front and drives around picking up people until the bus is full. Then he takes them to wherever he decided the bus was going. He has cologne on board so they can wash their hands and freshen up, and sometimes he has sweets which he . . .'

'That's it, then!' I interrupted. 'We'll buy an old bus, write "Georgia" on the front, buy some Turkish Delight and drive the thousand miles east, picking people up on the way. We'll just go for it, why not? We can call it the Love Bus.'

Cenk nodded, serious. 'You could,' he said. 'You know, it is possible.'

Ignoring us both, Russ continued: 'There's a ferry along the Bosporus, Jarus, isn't there?'

Jarus nodded. 'It's twenty miles.'

'And we could pick up the lorry from there to take us to the tea plantation?'

'It's possible, yes.'

'And that would be a fourteen-hour drive?'

Again Jarus nodded.

We decided to think about it some more. I still hadn't given up hope of a ship, so we left Jarus and Cenk to make further enquiries. I had no idea whether Cenk had been serious about buying a bus or not, but we headed into the old city to get Turkish Delight just in case. I'd only been in Istanbul a few hours but the place was living up to everything I'd expected. We crossed a bridge where men were fishing. We wandered along narrow cobbled streets with bright red trams running along them. I saw one young kid hanging off the back, grabbing a free ride and sliding down the road on the soles of his feet.

From my hotel room the skyline was a mass of buildings – the mixture of old and new strangely beautiful, the minarets pointing skyward like lunar rockets. Even the satellite dishes didn't look incongruous.

On the hunt for Turkish Delight, we found an old shop called Haci Bekir run by a woman called Hande. Turkish Delight is big business and Haci Bekir has a factory in Asia but some of it is still handmade at the shop. Hande's great-grandfather had started the business there, and his original oven was still displayed instore. Hande let us sample the goods: rose flavour, pistachio, walnut . . . she explained that sweets had always been a major part of Turkish heritage, but that Turkish Delight as we know it came about in the nineteenth century when corn starch and refined sugar first became available. That's all it is: starch, sugar, water and, of course, the flavouring; Hande told us that the Ottomans made sweets flavoured with honey and grapes, and she still sold some of the old recipes.

We bought bags of the stuff then headed deeper into the city. Passing through the old gates we found a covered bazaar, the air heavy with the smell of rich spices. Turkey is of course famous for sweets, tobacco and coffee; but it's also well known for tea and I bought some 'love' tea and 'lemon' tea from a shopkeeper called Turgut.

Man to man, Turgut told me that in order to keep his wife happy he'd developed his very own Turkish Viagra. He claimed to have twenty-one children and he looked very contented. 'You take a walnut,' he said, vacuum-sealing the tea, 'then slice a fig and press in the heart of the walnut. Twenty-five minutes later you're feeling very happy. Go ahead and try it.'

Leaving the bazaar, we wandered into a square where old women in head scarves were sitting at wooden tables selling brightly coloured cloths. I was having a great time enjoying the sights, but my mind kept returning to our transport problems. We were all feeling pretty weary: we'd covered a vast distance in a short space of time and were anxious to know how the hell we were going to get to Georgia.

'What about a Turkish massage?' Russ suggested. 'That'll unwind us for sure.'

'You think so?' I remembered the massage Ewan and I had endured on our Long Way Round trip, where I had been pushed and prodded to the point where I felt violated. 'We'll get pummelled, beaten to a pulp and then they'll tell us it was enjoyable.'

'It'll be different this time,' Russ promised, and he turned out to be right.

We picked a traditional Turkish hamam in the Tarihi Galatasaray Hamami, one of the oldest hamami in the city. It had been in the same family for about seventy years, and although the outside had been renovated in 1962, the inside had been a hamami since 1481.

An emotional goodbye with my dad at his house in Annamoe, Co. Wicklow.

The three amigos! Russ and Mungo would provide invaluable support.

Riding alongside John McGuinness, the Isle of Man TT record holder and multiple winner – a huge honour and a great way to begin the trip.

On the Q-Varl scallop vessel.
Not all our boating adventures
would turn out to be as fun . . .

The convoy down the M40. We'd hoped twenty might turn up . . .

On the fantastic Routemaster, getting ready to drive my family from London. It would be three and a half months before I'd see them again.

Crashing into the sea with the RNLI – a brilliant experience.

Me and Russ sailing a 12ft Laser dinghy across the channel. Not recommended.

The classic Citroën DS – the perfect way to arrive in Paris.

Paris has a great bike loan system. Onions and beret not included.

The *Orient Express* changing engines at Innsbruck. Definitely the most glamorous mode of transport we took.

Mungo, me and Russ with the Yugo in Croatia. Not quite as glamorous as the *Orient Express*.

Meeting a community of Roma in Serbia.

Heading back in to Novi Sad on a new mode of transport.

'Three little maids from school are we . . .'
In the hamami in Istanbul.

All aboard the Love Bus!

Our trip through Turkey in the Dolmus was unplanned but a definite highlight. Cenk is second from left, wearing his fantastic 'Borat' moustache.

Riding through Georgia in the Ural. We were very lucky to miss the conflict just a few months later.

An oil field in Baku, the capital of Azerbaijan. Locals fill their tanks with buckets of oil collected from the oil lakes.

It was stunning; thick marble walls, marble sinks, marble seats and a central dais where we lay on our fronts in the steam while the masseur, a fat and genial bald guy, worked our flesh. We were soaped, pummelled gently, pulled about and then scrubbed with flannel mitts.

'I could do this every day,' Russ said from where he was sitting next to a basin while another guy worked him over.

I lay on my stomach with a hot towel covering me. It was actually very pleasant: the room had a wonderful ambience; the lights changing now and then to enhance the atmosphere. I lay there thinking of 1481 and all the people who must have been through here since then. The guy massaging me was a sweet soul, and not at all heavy handed. Finally he sat me down and scrubbed me with a mitt. Just as I was thinking how enjoyable it all was, he soaked me with a bowl of freezing water.

6
The Love Bus

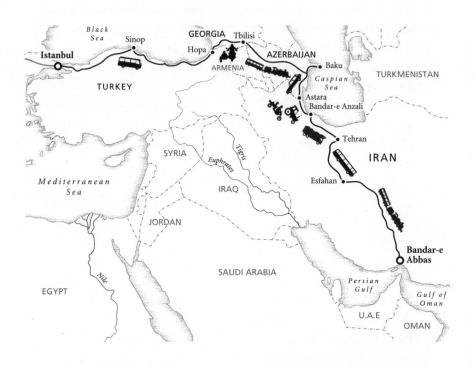

Cenk had been serious after all. With no ship available, a bus really was our only option. He managed to persuade a guy to rent us one, and by Friday night it was all agreed that we would drive to Georgia.

The buses – or *dolmus* – are minibuses rather than coaches, and there are red signs placed by the road denoting where they stop. Basically, it's an owner-operated, private service that takes people short distances – Cenk said about ten kilometres at most. Our destination was Hopa, near the Georgian border, 1500 km away – surely the longest route a *dolmus* had ever taken.

Waking up on Saturday morning I felt excited. Hopefully we'd pick up a few people along the way, offer them Turkish Delight and generate the kind of love I'd like our *dolmus* to be known for.

Even the rain – a grey blanket draped across the city – couldn't dampen my spirits. Apparently the temperature had reached thirty degrees the day before we arrived, but since then it had been overcast and now it was chucking it down. It was Mungo's fault: it was his birthday and it always rains on his birthday. We gave him a copy of *The Worst Case Scenario Almanac*.

'Thanks, boys,' he said, as we boarded the ferry. 'Stick with me and you'll be all right.'

We sailed up the Bosporus, which divides the two continents, towards the Black Sea, watching the eastern side of the city slip by. We leant on the rail, gazing across to the hillside where the buildings seemed to climb over each other.

'A beaten-up old truck,' Russ said. 'That's what it'll be. And Charley driving on roads where seven hundred thousand people are involved in accidents each year.' He shook his head grimly. 'Not an appealing thought.'

'It's only a thousand,' I said. 'It'll be fun, and this way we'll get to meet more people.'

'It's not meeting people I'm worried about.'

We stared into the water, aware that crossing the Bosporus was a key moment in the trip: when we left Europe behind and headed into less familiar territory.

'West to east,' I said to Russ. 'From Europe to Asia, Christian to Muslim . . .'

'We left riots behind us in Belgrade,' Russ reminded me, 'and yesterday the Americans fired a couple of shots from a ship in the Gulf. Bit of a set-to with Iran. I hope that's not significant, Charley.'

I stared pensively at the water again. Before we set off I'd toyed with the idea of swimming across the Strait with Lewis Gordon Pugh, who swam a kilometre at the North Pole and managed to come away with all his toes and fingers. He told me that people travel by their faces and that mine was such that it ought to keep me out of trouble. I realised now that I could never have swum across – the currents are too strong and the amount of traffic made the Grand Canal look quiet.

The *dolmus* was a large van – white, of course, what else when Boorman was going to be driving? GB stickers adorned the backs of the seats, contrasting with the traditional blankets the owner had thrown over them, and we'd written 'By Any Means' on the front. The owner was going to drive us out of the city because, as Russ said, seven hundred thousand people are injured on these roads every year. Once we were clear of the suburbs, I would take over.

'Charley,' Cenk said, 'there's a style to driving a *dolmus* – an attitude. You understand? *Every one driver* has their own style.'

'You mean you have to drive in a certain way,' I said. 'Shout, swear, yell at people to give you the money, that kind of thing.'

He nodded.

'No problem, Cenk: I'm a method actor. I can do *dolmus*.'

'OK. Give me *dolmus* driver.'

I looked at him for a long moment and then I curled my lip. 'Fuck you!' I threw out a hand in disgust. 'What is it, your mother teach you to drive, uh?'

'Fantastic,' Cenk said with a grin. 'You'll be fine.'

We were heading inland to a place called Bolu, a map pasted above the window to trace our progress. I checked to make sure the red stop light was working properly in the back window, and when the time came for me to drive I was ready with my *dolmus* attitude.

Cenk – who had long hair and a Borat-style moustache – was a fun guy to travel with. He sang (badly) and played the guitar (not quite so badly) but he kept me awake and entertained as we trundled through pastures and scrub hills, mountains capped by snow in the distance. Russ was in the back, eyes closed, and only waking up when we stopped for customers. We didn't get many: in fact the only people who got on all day were a bunch of school kids who didn't have any money. I gave them my best *dolmus* glower and Cenk chatted to them in Turkish, asking them what they wanted to do when they grew up. None of them knew. They should make a decision, he told them: before someone else made it for them.

I couldn't understand why we weren't attracting more people. There were plenty of stops along the way and although we didn't have any cologne, we had lots of Turkish Delight. Then I realised – it was Saturday. Nobody was travelling anywhere today, they were all at home. Tomorrow was Sunday and that would be even worse.

We reached Bolu at four o'clock and stopped for a late lunch in a cafe that had trained many famous Turkish chefs. Bolu is a peaceful town, nestled into a hillside and dominated by a large minaret. The houses are white, with arched windows and red-tiled roofs. Cenk loved the area: he explained that people skied here in the winter, and hunted during the season. It was also the perfect place for white-water rafting. When the snows melted the rivers were full and there were more rapids than you could shake an oar at.

Although we weren't attracting any customers, I was enjoying the drive – the roads were wide and clean, and clear of traffic. We were heading north-east now, back towards the coast, and we stopped for the night in Safranbolu, a town on the old Silk Road. It was hard to find a room so late, but at last we were directed to an ancient hotel in the old quarter. It was eccentric but beautiful: from the outside it looked like a fort, with windowless walls and a chimney pot for each room. The rooms were built in a quadrant around an open courtyard, with a first-floor balcony running all the way round. It was very atmospheric, especially when the call to prayer lifted from a minaret somewhere close by. The only thing that worried me was that my room was right off the quadrant, with my door opening out on to the courtyard. This was Saturday night and I had a feeling the place would be heaving.

The hotel was situated in a labyrinth of steep cobbled streets. We found a sprawling bazaar that filled one side street and sold just about everything you could imagine: food, clocks, T-shirts, leather, copperware . . . Right outside the hotel a woman wrapped from head to toe sold fruit from balsa wood boxes laid out on an ancient rug.

Sure enough when we got back from dinner the hotel was jumping; not just with diners but traditional Turkish music. It was right on top of me and it was deafening. I was exhausted but there was nothing I could do except lie on my bed and laugh. Even downstairs in my cellar bathroom the walls echoed. What was it about me and this trip? A marching band in Northern Ireland, the ding dong of a station announcer outside my hotel in Calais and here I was on the Silk Road plagued by a Turkish folk singer.

I wasn't in the best of moods the following morning: I'd really hoped for a good night's sleep but there had been no chance of that. It didn't last long though. Cenk was so funny that no one could be in a bad mood around him: Mungo only had to look at the guy and he'd start laughing. He had our *dolmus* destination board ready: today we were aiming for Trabzon via Mengen, Yenigaga and Gerede. We left the noisy, four-hundred-year-old hotel behind and headed up the coast.

I moved the map from above the window to the dashboard and penned the route in black felt-tip. Cenk was up front beside me with Russ straddling the back seats, strumming Cenk's guitar.

'OK,' I said. 'Don't get us lost, Cenk, we have a schedule to keep.'

'I promise, Charley. I promise not to get us lost.'

'You did yesterday, more than once.'

'But not today,' he said.

I was joking. We'd taken the odd wrong turn yesterday but you could hardly call it lost. We didn't want to lose time however, and were aiming to cover 450 km today. But it didn't take long to realise we'd be on dirt roads a lot of the way and our speed would drop off considerably. There wasn't much traffic about but the roads were narrow and twisting, cutting a path through domed hills, banks of wooden houses and rusting tin roofs. Russ moved up behind me and gripped the back of the seat.

'We've got to be in Hopa on schedule so we can meet Hari the Austrian and get the bike across the border. Georgia and Azerbaijan are less stable countries than a place like Turkey and you know what those kinds of borders can be like. We could be held up for hours.'

'I know,' I said. 'We'll push on as far as we can today and then make a really early start in the morning.'

We were climbing all the time now, higher into mist-shrouded mountains. Coming through one village we saw an old man standing by the roadside, wearing a thin jumper and sports jacket, a flat cap pressed to his scalp.

'Our first customer, Cenk,' I said. 'Get the cologne ready.' We had cologne now; maybe it was the lack of the full *dolmus* service that had been our undoing yesterday. Or maybe it was the bumbling blond driver that made people nervous.

The old guy got aboard happily enough, Cenk offering him Turkish Delight and cologne. Rinsing his hands he sat back, not bothered by the cameras. He told us he was going to the street market in the next village, just a few miles up the road. He was a lovely old guy, chatting away about his life. He said his village was fine to live in during the summer but not in winter: it was too cold in winter, it was too cold now; it ought to be much warmer. He spent the winters in Istanbul with his daughter. When we reached the next village he wanted to pay his fare, but of course we wouldn't take any money. Instead he insisted on buying us a cup of tea, so Russ and I sat outside a cafe listening while he told his mates about us.

Back in the bus Cenk told me that we should ask for money; we could hardly say we were really in the *dolmus* business otherwise.

'I don't know,' I said. 'I feel the love, Cenk . . . The love bus, A to B for free.'

'OK,' he said, picking up the guitar. 'It's up to you. You know the *Dolmus* Blues, Charley?'

'No.'

'You sing alternate lines.'

With a twang of the strings he started. '*I got the* Dolmus *Blues.*'

'*And my feet are aching.*' OK, not great, but I was put on the spot and it was the only line I could think of.

'We drive no place, we got lost.'
'And there's no one to pick up.'

We climbed further into the mountains, the mist coming down thickly now. The narrow roads had no run off, and there were shale cliffs on the near side.

'Fuck,' I said, looking round at Russ. 'I can't see anything.'

'The road would be good, Charley.'

We made it over the top at last and slipped out of the mist once more into rich-looking fields, hillsides dense with pine. An hour or so later we came upon our second customer of the day, a young guy in his twenties, with black hair. He was carrying a shopping bag and he was going our way. His name appeared to be Farti: I apologise for the spelling but that's how it sounded and Cenk couldn't enlighten us.

From the moment he sat down and Russ pressed a box of Turkish Delight on him, Farti looked like a rabbit caught in the headlights. He washed his hands self-consciously, sniffed them and sat there fidgeting. Maybe it was the fact that the ride was free or that a mad Englishman was driving and talking about love. Maybe it was Russ on the guitar or the way I overtook a lorry and missed out on a couple of girls hitch-hiking: no card-carrying *dolmus* driver would ever do that. Maybe it was Mungo sticking a fucking great camera in Farti's face that made him think he'd been kidnapped. Whatever it was, the poor guy couldn't wait to get out; as soon as we hit the next town he dived for the door.

'Can I open the door?' he babbled. 'I want to open the door.'

We were barely beyond the outskirts and I hadn't even braked. Pulling over I stopped the bus and he was gone in a flash.

'Was it something we said?' Russ wondered.

I felt bad about it, though admittedly not until we'd stopped laughing. Farti, if you read this I apologise, we meant nothing by it; I suppose we just got our wires crossed. I'd hate to be put in a situation where I had no idea what was going on: it must have been terrible, stuck in a *dolmus* with Borat and a couple of camera-wielding Brits.

'We're not very good at this are we,' Russ admitted sadly.

'The whole point is to meet people and all we do is scare them off.'

'We should charge,' Cenk decided. 'They'll feel better if we take their money.'

We ended the day a long way short of where we intended to be, but we'd had a lot of fun on the way, including a brilliant lunch eating a strange soup with cheese and rice, that tasted like pizza. We'd skirted the Black Sea and I'd been glad we were driving rather than bobbing along, seeing some of the country instead. By the time we found a hotel (my room way up on the top floor and facing the back) we'd been on the road for twelve hours. We would start early tomorrow so we could hook up with Hari the Austrian, who was bringing us the motorbike and sidecar we'd be riding through Georgia.

Our last morning in Turkey, we sat down to breakfast and discussed the route in detail. We did this every couple of days: we had so much ground to cover, so many borders to cross and so many different forms of transport we had to stay on top of it all.

'We have to really push on today,' Russ stated. 'Make up some ground.'

I nodded. 'I've loved Turkey, though, haven't you?'

'Oh yeah, it's been great. The *dolmus* was a brilliant idea. And Cenk's hilarious.'

I sat back for a moment. 'I really missed Olly last night. That's the one problem with this trip: being away from home for so long. The enormity of it all really hit me, you know: how far we have to go.'

'It's a long way,' Russ nodded. 'But we've made it this far OK. So long as we get to Hopa today we'll be on time. Now everything depends on Dubai. Miss that container ship and we have to wait a week. We can't afford that: a week lost and everything else we've set up could fall to pieces.'

I sighed. 'And we've still got to find a way of getting in to China.'

'Never mind China – there's Iran to think about first, then the dhow across to Dubai.'

'Dhows get attacked by pirates,' I said. 'Some of them *are* pirates. That'd be nice, sailing out for half a day only for some guy to put a knife to your throat, rob you blind and toss you over the side.'

Behind us the TV was showing last night's news: there had been a football match between rival clubs in Istanbul and the images showed riot police with tear gas and batons trying to break up the fights.

'Bizarre,' Mungo said, joining us. 'The last two cities we've left – Belgrade and Istanbul – a day later they're rioting in the streets.' He shook his head. 'If this carries on no country will let us in.'

We placed a new sign in the *dolmus* window: Ordu, Trabzon, and our final destination – Hopa.

Russ had been picking away at Cenk's guitar and he'd come up with a song. 'Are you going to sing it then?' I asked him.

'Yeah, why not? It's called "By Any Means".' He cleared his throat, hit the chord and started singing:

By any means of transport we're rolling down the road
By any means of transport we will go
By car and boat and truck and train, down under Sydney is
our aim
By any means of transport we will go.

You probably had to be there.

Tipping a bottle of water down my neck I swallowed too much and gagged. Mungo was sitting beside me and found it particularly funny. 'Don't you ever get that?' I asked him. 'Drowning when you're drinking water? It wouldn't happen with a beer. Was it Hemingway who said he doesn't drink water because fish fuck in it?'

We picked up another passenger and this time we were determined he wouldn't suffer the same fate as Farti. His name was Amin and he was just fifteen. As he took his seat I looked round anxiously.

'Are you OK?' I asked. 'Is he all right, Cenk? Is he relaxed? I want him to be relaxed.'

Cenk had dispensed with the Turkish Delight and the cologne: he spoke to Amin in Turkish.

'He was a bit scared when he saw you, Charley,' he joked. 'But he's all right now.'

Amin was a religious student studying the Koran: he told us that one day he hoped to be an imam – what Cenk called a *hodja*.

'Your mother must be very proud,' I told him. We'd heard the call to prayers throughout the country, five times a day, the first before sunrise and the last after the sun had set. It was particularly atmospheric hearing the calls ring out in the darkness.

We got to where Amin was going and wished him well. He got out and that was it, only four passengers in three days all the way to Hopa.

Hari, a tall Austrian guy with cropped hair, was waiting for us on the sea front, dressed in a denim jacket. Square apartment blocks overlooked a two-lane carriageway with a grassy median between: beyond it was a stony beach. Now we were close enough we could see that the Black Sea was patchy with oil. Hari was from Ural, the Russian company that had been making fantastic motorcycle/sidecar combinations since the 1940s. They were incredibly sturdy – so good, in fact, that the invading Germans made their own version of them.

Hari had towed one on the back of a trailer all the way from Austria. It was painted camouflage green and looked very functional, with a chunky front wheel and fender; oversize fuel tank and two individual seats on the bike; the rear one with an oval handgrip for the pillion. There was a kick start on the left and a two-wheel-drive facility for rough roads. The side car carried a jerrican; the seat was covered with a faded leather tarp and there was a luggage rack on top of the spare tyre. This was it, our transport for Georgia and maybe Azerbaijan as well.

As I took a tour round the bike, Russ took a couple of phone calls. When he came off, he look perturbed.

'What's up?' I asked him.

'Two problems. First off, we can't get Iranian visas in London.

We thought we could but we can't. We have to try and get them in Georgia, but I'm told there's no guarantee.'

'So what do we do?'

He shrugged. 'If it comes to it, we dump the camera gear and try to go in as tourists: get our passports stamped at the border and hop on a train. Hopefully it won't come to that, but have to plan for it, just in case.'

The second problem was easier to solve. Apparently we couldn't buy crash helmets in Georgia: we'd have to buy some here in Hopa. Helmets sorted, and still mulling over the visa problem, we headed for the mountains and the tea plantation we'd promised ourselves we'd see before we crossed the border.

It was quite a trek, the road a switchback and narrow as hell as it climbed into the mountains. This was very pretty country, very lush; there was lots of water here. The tea was grown by individual owners on little plots of beautifully green terracing. They sold collectively as Caykur but it was a tough living. Pulling over beside a humpback bridge, we were introduced to one of the growers. The bridge, which spanned a shallow, boulder-strewn river, was like something from *The Lord of the Rings* – there were steps up to it, steps along it and down the other side and it was overgrown and slippery with ivy.

The grower told us that the tea-growing season in Turkey lasts only six months in comparison to the full twelve that planters get in Kenya, India and Sri Lanka. With only half the harvest, they were only able to produce three crops a year. They cut just two leaves and the bud off each plant using a special tool that hoiked the leaves into the bag at the same time. It was very labour-intensive, and the only advantage they had over their twelve-month competitors was that they were able to grow organic tea economically because the insects that needed pesticides were killed by either snow or beetles. The big problem had been getting the bags of picked tea down the sharply sloping mountain to the road. Someone had come up with the ingenious idea of running a cable from the road to each of the houses; the bags of tea were hooked onto it and slid down to trucks waiting below.

I could see entire families working the terraces and I don't think the growers made much money, but their houses, half hidden in rich, dark foliage, looked beautifully kept, with white walls and tiled roofs. I'd never given much thought to the tea we buy at home but now I vowed it would be Fair Trade or a similar cooperative from this point on.

Back in Hopa, Russ took another phone call from London. Apparently we should wait until we got to Azerbaijan to try and get the visas. We were certain to get them in Baku apparently. I wasn't convinced, but there was nothing we could do about it. We would just have to wait and see.

7
Born to Ride

The following morning we were up at six-thirty. It was 29 April – we had left Wicklow eighteen days ago. It felt like a lot longer. We said our reluctant goodbyes to Cenk – he had been great fun and his idea for the *dolmus* had been inspired. Meanwhile Hari the Austrian had gone ahead with the Ural yesterday and was waiting for us on the Georgian side.

We arrived at the border at eight-forty only to find it already backed up with trucks waiting to cross. The officials ushered us away. They couldn't deal with us yet, they said: we had to come back later.

'No way,' Russ muttered. 'We've had experience of these kinds of crossings before: we'll stand our ground and wait.'

We stayed where we were, sitting in a queue of cars that didn't move for hours. Finally things began to happen and we made it through around midday. There was a mass of vehicles all bunched up and when they started to move there was no order, no queue, drivers just piled in from all over. At the checkpoint we waited our turn with everyone else but were barged out of the way by five women who ignored the queue completely and pushed their way to the front. The officials seemed to know them and they were dealt with first: I assumed they must cross every day.

At last we were through and into Batumi where the Ural was being unloaded. I couldn't wait to get going. I was really enjoying travelling on all the different forms of transport, but when you get right down to it, motorbikes are where it's at.

Russ was talking to Nick; a local guy we'd arranged to guide us through Georgia. It seemed like a good idea, given that the country was so unknown to us, and that we didn't speak a word of Georgian.

'Nick's just been telling me that a spy plane was shot down,' Russ said. 'Part of Georgia is disputed territory. Apparently the plane was keeping tabs on the Russians and they shot it down. It's tense, I had a feeling it might be. We'll have to be careful.'

'Riots,' Mungo muttered from behind the camera. 'Everywhere we go there are riots.'

It was 450 km to Tbilisi, the capital of Georgia, and we had hoped to make it in one day. But with the border crossing and an hour lost in time-change it was already one p.m. Originally we had planned to ride all the way to Baku, the capital of Azerbaijan, but poring over the maps and train times now, we realised this would never work if we wanted to get our visas for Iran in time. We decided to ride as far as Tbilisi then take an overnight train to Baku and camp out at the Iranian Embassy. As long as we made Tbilisi by four-thirty tomorrow we could jump on the five-fifteen and all would be well.

With Russ already in the sidecar I got on the bike and fiddled around, getting a feel for everything. It started first time which is always a good sign, and Hari told us it was more than reliable. The gearing was one down and three up and the brakes seemed pretty sound. I'd driven a Royal Enfield with a sidecar for half a day but that was the limit of my experience – cornering, especially the right-hand bends, could be interesting to say the least. Also, the Ural's sidecar was on my right whereas the Enfield's had been on the left, so everything I'd learned was now the other way round.

'I've never done this,' Russ said. The rain was coming down and he had pulled the tarp up to his chin. 'I suppose the trick is to trust the guy who's driving.' He looked up with a mock-nervous smile.

'You'll be fine, Malkin. We're back in my territory. I was born to ride, remember?'

With my case strapped on the rack and Russ's bag in the little boot, we headed out of town past blocks of pink flats that reminded me of Russia. It looked run down; the buildings with that stark, Soviet influence Ewan and I had seen on Long Way Round.

The pitted, bumpy roads weren't good either, and the weather was horrendous, the rain lashing down. It was hard to see properly and I only just missed a pedestrian who stepped out from behind a lorry. At last I got my bearings, sorted out my position and we rode out into the grey, wet countryside.

The Ural was never known for its speed, and soon we had trucks overtaking so close we were almost forced into the trees.

'Hey, Charley,' Russ yelled from the sidecar. 'I asked Nick what the Georgians would think of two guys hurtling across country on a Russian military motorcycle.'

'What did he say?'

'That we'd be OK so long as we weren't packing a Kalashnikov.'

Black clouds hung low and dreary over the mountains, the trees dripped water and the potholes filled with rain. I could feel my suitcase jiggling around on the rack and Russ was telling me the sidecar had no suspension.

This was absolutely nothing like Turkey. I've noticed before that each border crossing is different, and it takes time to acclimatise. This was weird though; it was so like the Russia I'd seen it was incredible.

Climbing the hills we were at last overtaking the slower traffic while I tried to make sense of the steering: the bike juddered a bit under braking and I got one right-hander completely wrong. The rain was coming in almost horizontally and visibility was down. I overcooked the bend, missed the steering and swung viciously across the road.

'Whoa!' Russ cried out from the sidecar.

'Sorry, mate, sorry.' I got the bike back on line and wagged my head. 'Fucked that up, didn't I? Thank God nothing was coming or we'd have been squashed tomatoes.'

We stopped off to meet some of Nick's friends who lived in a small house with narrow doors that opened on to a large living area. They couldn't have been more hospitable, feeding us meat, strong cheese and a sort of vegetable curry. Through Nick, they asked us about the expedition. We told them how far we'd come and how far we were going. We told them our fears about Iran and getting into China and they wished us the best of luck. They were like people the world over, happy to open their doors and welcome us, to feed us and show us pictures of their families.

Outside again, I got the bike going while Russ called London.

'Everything all right?' I asked, when he came off the phone.

'We won't know for sure until we get to Baku. We keep getting told different stories. Thursday morning we'll have to get straight down to the embassy. It'll be a fiasco, I can see it already.'

'Have a little faith.'

'Faith: right, sure. I tell you what, Charley, I'll believe we'll get the visas when I see the stamp in my passport.'

I felt for Russ – it was easy for me to trust in faith while he and the team back home organised everything. We were on the road because we loved it, a couple of mates trying to get to Australia by any means we could. But we were also filming, and although we were doing a lot on the hoof, circumstances change all the time and there was no way we could leave everything to chance.

That night we stopped in a town called Kutaisi. While I took a shower Russ wandered down to the River Rioni. It was here that Jason and the Argonauts were said to have sailed in search of the Golden Fleece. Standing on the stone bridge, Russ thought the river current looked far too vicious, but that's how the story went. According to the legend, Jason sailed up the Bosporus from Greece and across the Black Sea to Georgia. It is only a legend, of course, but then most legends have some basis in truth. And even to this day miners use sheep's fleeces to attract the gold from their pans, which is one of the many theories of where the idea of a golden fleece came from.

The next morning was still overcast, rain spattering the puddles, and it didn't make the same old grey apartment blocks any more inspiring. Conscious of our afternoon train from Tbilisi, we set off early. As we left the city a police car pulled alongside: it seemed to linger in the middle of the road, the two cops looking long and hard at two guys on a Russian army motorbike.

En route to the capital we passed through Gori, the sombre-looking city where Stalin was born. After Lenin died he had systematically set about destroying anyone who didn't agree with him; scientists, writers, artists, poets. During the great purges of the 1930s he murdered six million people and sent millions more to a living death in the gulags. It can be strange how a famous person's home town remembers them, especially if they were a brutal dictator like Stalin. In Gori there is a massive statue of Stalin in front of the Town Hall, and his old railway carriage – green with a black roof – is on display behind a set of ornate iron railings, as part of the Stalin museum. Instead of the usual five tons it weighs around eighteen because he had it reinforced so nobody could shoot him or blow him up when he was travelling around the country.

As we had arrived in good time, we stopped to take a look round, even stepping aboard the carriage. It was strange to think the man who'd been responsible for so much suffering had eaten, slept and drunk vodka on this carriage. There was a small kitchen at one end with a metal hotplate and a metal sink, and the corridor was wood-panelled, reminding me of the *Orient Express*.

'Take a look in here.' Russ pointed out one of the two bedrooms Stalin had used. There was a bunk on the left and a desk and table, velvet curtains tied back from the windows, ornate light fittings and an air-conditioning system and beyond it was a conference room with a large table and eight chairs. There was something macabre about the opulence – knowing he must have made life and death decisions for thousands and thousands of his countrymen here, living in luxury while they starved.

The old brick house where he was born had been preserved too. It seemed to have been part of a terrace once, but it was hard to tell because it looked as though all the other houses had been torn down to make way for the museum. It was covered by a sort of concrete mausoleum that had been built to protect it from the elements.

We had been hearing explosions for some time – on the bike,

while we were in the carriage and again outside Stalin's house. We could only assume that the army, on a state of alert, was practising with big guns somewhere. It was a strangely appropriate setting; the city is overlooked by a medieval citadel, an ancient fortress with holes in the walls from decay and from battle.

'Hey, listen to this,' Russ said. He had just received a news text from Lucy. 'Georgia–Russian tensions: Russia claims Georgia is massing troops in the break-away region today. It warns that it will retaliate if Georgia uses force and Georgia has reacted angrily to the statement. The EU urges caution in this area.'

Again we heard the sound of guns in the distance.

Russ was still studying his mobile. 'Bloody hell. It's all kicking off. Two people have been killed in Tibet: a Tibetan and a policeman. China announced thirty people have been jailed and many people are worrying that they weren't given a fair trial.' He lifted his eyebrows sharply. 'That's still to come, China and Tibet. The closer we get the less it looks like we're going to find a way in.'

We'd had enough of Stalin and back on the Ural we quickly drove the last eighty kilometres to the capital. I was loving the bike; it was great to ride and I'd got the right-hand bends figured out now. The country was flatter and less rocky here, and the tarmac a lot smoother. The rain eased and we made good time to Tbilisi. There was no need to go straight to the station so we climbed to the Metekhi Church that overlooks the curve of the river and gives a great view over the ancient city. In front of us was a massive statue of Vakhtang Gorgasali, the King of Georgia in the fifth century, dominating the city on horseback. It was an atmospheric spot, the muddy brown river flowing under an old stone bridge and beyond it the city with its tree-lined streets and medieval churches. After the minarets and mullahs of Turkey it was a jolt to be back in a Christian territory.

'It doesn't look like Kutaisi,' I said, 'or Gori for that matter. No Russian flats overshadowing everything.'

'The Russians were here, though,' Russ said, leaning on the ramparts. 'They wandered in uninvited just as they did the other Soviet territories. They'd been influencing politics here for centuries. They insisted the Georgian royal family relinquished their power way back in the 1780s. Then when they invaded in 1921 the royal family went into exile. Now Georgia's a democracy the people want them to come back but it seems they don't want to.'

I'd loved riding the Ural, and it had been great to have the wind in my face again, but now it was time to catch a train. I left the bike outside the station, and managed to have a quick phone call with Olly and the kids before it was time to board. They seemed to be OK and I promised Olly I'd phone her from Baku when we could have a longer conversation.

It was our third night on a train, and I've got to say this was the shabbiest yet: first the glamour of the *Orient Express*, then the faded grandeur of the *Balkan Express* and now the 'Baku–Tbilisi' – we were going downhill rapidly. It was an ugly train, the carriages shunted up against a stark concrete platform that had all the charm of a Soviet dictator. The train was painted green and blue and the paint was flaking badly. The corridor looked OK and there were even some nylon curtains at the windows, but it wasn't clean and our cabins were pretty smelly.

'It'll be all right,' Russ encouraged me. 'When we get going and the wind comes through some of the mustiness will blow away.' He opened the door to the toilet. 'Bloody hell.' There was a hole in the floor to pee through, the ground visible below: the pan was stained aluminium with no seat and no toilet paper. The flush was a pedal but when you pressed it all that happened was a hole appeared in the floor and again you could see the tracks.

'Dumped straight on the ground then,' Russ said. 'Nice.'

'I thought I needed to go,' I said, 'but I reckon I can hold it till we get to Baku.'

We crossed the border in darkness, a couple of hours on the Georgian side and again on entering Azerbaijan. Our passports were taken off for inspection – I really hate that moment, especially when you're on a train. It's your life, your identity, all you have. I kept thinking, what if the train goes and I haven't got my passport back?

We were allowed to get out and stretch our legs, but had to stay close to the door of our carriage and not wander off anywhere. Georgian officials in army uniform marched up and down with the kind of sour-faced demeanour only border guards can muster. At Azerbaijan they wore those massive Russian-style caps with wide brims and peaks that scrape the bridge of their noses. They strutted the length of the corridor and searched every inch of my carriage using a camera on a pole before poking through all my stuff.

Finally they gave me back my passport and I joined Russ in the corridor.

'That was different,' I said.

'No worries, mate. Only Iran to come.'

8

Passport Stamps and Oilfields

Riding the Ural through Georgia had been fun, but I'd been absolutely knackered when we got on the train at Tbilisi. Even so, I don't think I slept a wink.

Perhaps it was the noise of the train, the rocking motion, but I had a feeling it had more to do with our visa hassles, and the problems we could be facing in Baku. Thoughts of Olly and the kids kept going round and round in my head too, and when the sun came up I was more tired than when we had boarded the train.

Russ came into the cabin, looking apprehensive about the day ahead. From the window Azerbaijan seemed a desolate country, grey and flat. It seemed as if there was nothing out there apart from telephone lines stretching out into heavy skies.

'It's like the Russian steppes,' I said.

'That's what I thought.' Russ shifted my case along and hunched on the other seat. 'Just like Russia.'

So much for my theory that borders always revealed a new kind of landscape.

An hour or so later the steppes were behind us and we approached the coast with the train hugging a peninsula. Across the bay we could see what we hoped was Baku rising out of the hillside as neat sandstone buildings. It was strange to think it was the first place in the world where people drilled for oil – over a hundred and fifty years ago.

Our local guide, Zaur, was waiting for us on the station platform. He was a young, good-looking guy with a shaggy mop of black hair. As well as being a guide, he'd done some work as a model, and later we saw his picture on the back of a bus.

Zaur wasted no time in introducing me to the military-green UAZ-469 jeep I was going to drive to the border. It was Russian built, left over from Soviet days. It looked pretty sturdy, and I suppose it had a kind of charm, but the Russians – they build tanks and weapons, but when it comes to cars . . .

This one had a set of Mercedes roo bars on the grille and a canvas roof, part of which was loose and hanging over the windscreen. The gear stick was elongated and bound with string, the dash a handful of single dials. What looked like the entire car's electrical innards dangled underneath.

Getting behind the wheel I hunted down first gear; like the old Land Rover from Brighton I had to double declutch. 'Oh well,' I muttered. 'If you can't find them, grind them.'

We took off into Baku. Gone were the sandstone houses we'd seen from the train; this place was high rise, office blocks and apartments, many of them under construction. Zaur told us the city was split into the downtown area and what they called the inner city, the old part with historic palaces and mosques. We hoped to see them later – once we had the visas.

Zaur jumped in next to me, throwing out directions as we sped off on our way to the embassy. It was a manic city, the roads choked with everything from ancient Ladas to oil tankers to top-of-the-range Mercedes. The brakes on the UAZ were spongy, which was worrying given I was driving it for the first time in a strange city of two million people. They didn't bite until the pedal was almost on the floor, and to add to that the steering was vague, to say the least. You had to turn the wheel almost halfway before the thing responded.

I glanced at Zaur. 'How far is the border?'

'Six, maybe eight hours.'

'And the road, is it a good road?'

He shook his head. 'Mostly it's bad.'

Russ was in the back looking pensive. This was the pressure point. In a couple of hours we would know if those elusive visas would be stamped in our passports. I was pretty nervous myself – there was no back-up plan and I had the UAZ to contend with after a sleepless night on the train.

At last we made it, and without killing anyone, pulling up next to a grimy-looking building in a small side street. The embassy was basically one room with a piece of glass in a wall and a round hole in the piece of glass. The officials perched behind looking out. It was busy and chaotic – no orderly British queue – with everyone trying to shove their applications through the hole at the same time.

Zaur discovered that they stopped processing applications at eleven a.m. and it was already ten-twenty. He also found out that once we'd handed the applications in we had to go across the city to pay the fee at a particular bank. You had to come back with the receipt before they would do anything further about the application.

'Jesus,' I muttered. 'How far is it?'

From Zaur's reply I worked out it was like going from Fulham to Soho and back again in rush hour. Leaving Zaur at the embassy we piled into a cab.

The traffic was dire, blocked lanes, deliveries, cabs and buses; a million and one other vehicles on the road. The driver was doing his best but it was past ten-thirty and we knew there was no way we were going to make it.

'This is crazy,' Russ said from the back seat. 'Stop the car,' he said. 'Stop the car, I'm going back. You go to the bank, Charley; I'm going to see if I can get Zaur to persuade the embassy staff to stay open. I doubt they will but you never know.' He jumped out, and phone in hand, headed back on foot through the bustling streets.

At last we got to the bank, and, asking the cabbie to wait, Mungo and I jumped out and signed our forms. I kept looking at the clock and thinking – we'll never do this in a million years. Even with Russ's powers of persuasion, it's unheard of for a bureaucrat to hold the door open past the appointed hour.

At ten-fifty-five we were back in the cab and heading towards the embassy. I phoned Russ and let him know where we were.

'Make it as fast as you can,' he said. 'We've explained the problem and been on the phone to London. They've been on the phone to our contacts in Iran and they've been on the phone to the officials here. There's just a chance so get here as quickly as you can.'

At a little after eleven a.m. we were stuck in traffic with cars blocking us in; all I could do was sit there and take in the hubbub of the downtown area. There was an enormous amount of work going on, buildings being thrown up on every corner. It was a crazy, hectic mix – cars hooting, the rattle of massive drills, ships' horns blasting down by the docks. Finally we got moving, but we didn't get back to the embassy building until eleven-twenty-five. Amazingly the hole in the glass was still open and Russ was still there. Thrusting all our documentation together with the bank receipts into the officials' hands, we had no choice but to wait outside. They still hadn't said they would be able to process everything in time.

On the street we had a chat about what to do next. There was no point in us both hanging around, so while Russ and Mungo waited for news on the visa, I went to sort out some paperwork of my own.

In order to drive the UAZ to the border I had to be notarised on the owner's insurance. Zaur phoned the owner, a guy called Edabar. On arrival he immediately jumped up on the bonnet and set about tearing off the bit of canvas roof that was dangling down. It was nuts; there I was by the side of a busy road in Baku with this Azerbaijani jumping about on a Russian UAZ ripping bits off the roof.

Satisfied, Edabar got in and drove me to the documentation place. He told me he used the old jeep to go hunting. Halfway across the city the brakes packed in and we pulled over.

This wasn't looking good: a six- to eight-hour drive on dodgy roads in a jeep with even dodgier brakes. Edabar, however, was used to this: with a shrug he grabbed a pair of pliers then hunched down among the pedals with his legs sticking into the road and set about the mass of dangling wires.

I wasn't sure what he was doing but could only assume the brakes were pressurised electrically somehow, because after a few minutes he was back behind the wheel and they seemed to be working again. We drove along the front, where the Caspian Sea lapped low stone walls and ahead of us massive derricks were unloading container ships. The place reeked of oil. Later I found out that over the decades a hell of a lot of oil has seeped directly into the ground, making Baku the most toxic city in the world.

I was having serious reservations about how far this old jeep would manage to take us. I called Russ and he agreed we'd try to find an alternative just in case.

'Any word on the visas?' I asked him.

'Nope, I'm still waiting.'

Half an hour later at the licensing office, my phone rang.

'Russ?'

'Hello, mate.'

'Well?'

'We got them.'

'Fantastic.' I breathed a massive sigh of relief. 'I can hardly bloody believe it.'

With the paperwork complete we could now afford to chill out a little, so we asked Zaur to take us to Icheri Sheher or inner city – a fortress surrounded by high walls and beautifully paved walkways. It feels as if you're entering another world and yet you're still within the confines of the city. Zaur showed us Shirvanshah's Palace, a self-contained structure with a mosque and minaret as well as a family mausoleum. It's thought the Shirvanshah dynasty built the palace as a shrine to Seyyid Yahya Bakuvi, a Sufi mystic, in the fifteenth century.

'Bakuvi,' Russ said. 'That must be where the city gets its name then. You know, Azerbaijan is one of the most ancient countries on earth. Apparently every stage of man's evolution is represented in this country.'

I glanced at Mungo behind the camera. 'And some are more evolved than others, aren't they?'

'It's the land of fire,' Zaur said. 'Azer means fire. Before Islam the people worshipped it. Come on, I'll show you.'

He took us above the city to a hillside where a fire, twenty metres across, burns; flames leaping from fissures in the rock. They're fed by natural gas and have been burning constantly for hundreds of years. No wonder the locals used to worship it – in the old days it must have seemed supernatural.

Zaur said there was an old Hindu temple in Surakhani, not far from Baku, where a fire just like this had burned continuously. The buildings, which were constructed in the 1700s, are still there, but the flame itself went out in 1969 when Soviet drilling knocked out the natural gas that fed it.

Thankfully I had a good night's sleep, and the next morning – 2 May – we were ready early. We had been able to locate an alternative to the UAZ just in case, but I'd start off in it and see how it went. Outside and still yawning I was trying to work out how many different forms of transport we'd been on so far: motorbikes, a fishing trawler, a ferry, taxi, train, a London bus, a lifeboat, an old Land Rover, a dinghy and then a Citroën. In Paris we'd jumped on bicycles then the *Orient Express* and a water taxi. After that it had been a hydrofoil then a Yugo and another bus. The *Balkan Express* to Istanbul and then three days across Turkey in a *dolmus*: was it yesterday we were on the Ural? No, the day before . . . it was hard to take it all in.

Russ and I spread the map over my suitcase and pored over it.

'The UAZ bothers me,' I told him. 'It drives like a pig, the brakes are crap and when you're idling you have to keep one foot on the clutch and flap the accelerator otherwise it conks out.'

'Give it a whirl as far as the outskirts at least,' he suggested.

I looked at the map, tracing a line south from Baku to Astara where we would cross into Iran. 'The ship for India leaves on the twelfth of May; is that right?' I said.

'Yeah, from Dubai. It's the only one we can get and we can't miss it.' He smiled with relief. 'We've got five days to get through Iran, and then we cross the Gulf.'

'Great,' I said. 'Maybe we can relax a little.'

I had a guy called Bilal with me now, a middle-aged man who worked for an oil company, driving in and around Baku. He could fix the UAZ if it went wrong. He told me he had lived in Baku all his life and up until a couple of years ago it had been very hard to get work. He said the place was better when it was governed by the Soviets.

'I've got a job now,' he said. 'But it's hard; nothing is stable. When the Soviets were here we had jobs and everyone had an education. Everyone had medical care. Most of the people I know preferred life as it was back then.'

It was an interesting perspective; it's easy to assume people were automatically happier after the fall of communism, even with the economic troubles. Yesterday I'd visited a memorial – one hundred and thirty-seven marble graves laid side by side all the way to a flickering eternal flame, housed in a stone pagoda. On the night of 19 January 1990, twenty-six thousand Soviet troops stormed the city following a series of Azerbaijani independence demonstrations, firing on the crowd. The shooting didn't stop for three days: the graves I had seen belonged to the one hundred and thirty-seven martyrs who died.

It became obvious very quickly that the UAZ wasn't going to make it: as we left the hotel I noticed oil seeping from the hub on the near-side back wheel and the brakes were definitely shot. It was a shame because I liked driving it. But when I nearly clattered up the arse of another car, that was that.

Our back-up vehicle was a restored 1964 Volga – a proper Russian four-door saloon first designed in 1956, which had undergone many changes since. It was manufactured by GAZ, the Gorky car company; and instead of a winged lady they had a leaping deer on the bonnet. This model had been put together from bits and pieces gathered together by its owner, an enthusiast called Telman, who had owned the car for about three years. Not all the bits he'd used were original: the dash, for example, had come from a series 3 BMW. I didn't care; the brakes worked, the seat was comfortable and we had a long way to go.

Outside Baku we stopped at the oldest and probably most neglected oil field in the world. Hugging the coast, it was seriously ugly, the ground a mush of rock and sand and seeping oil; the whole area littered with rusty derricks and weary, nodding donkeys. Russ reckoned the first oil had been drilled here around 1846 and some of these pumps were still tapping the dregs of the really old wells. By chance we'd met an English guy called Robert Ashford, who worked in the oil business. He told us that the donkeys might produce twenty barrels a day but no more. At today's prices though, that was still a couple of grand.

'Hitler wanted to come to Baku,' Robert said. 'Did you guys know that? This place has been the hub of the oil industry for ever and he had his eye on it. There's a famous picture of him with a "Baku" birthday cake: if he'd made it here he'd have had all the oil he wanted and who knows, he might have won the war.'

We pulled over next to what was basically a lake of oil; a huge expanse in the middle of the nodding donkeys and rusting equipment. Two workmen in cheesecutter hats and heavy coats were maintaining an old pump. One of them, a cheerful soul called Tahir, with chipped gold teeth, told us the lake was filled with crude oil pumped directly from the wells: it formed this lake and was then pumped elsewhere. He didn't seem to know where exactly, but he was paid $200 a month to keep the pump working. I think oil was about $115, maybe $118 dollars a barrel, so that gives you an idea of how little the state oil company was paying him.

While Tahir was talking we saw a couple of cars pull up, the drivers jumping out and opening the bonnets. Taking a can apiece they climbed down to the edge of the lake, scooped up the oil then poured it straight into the engine. Bonnets closed, they turned around and headed back to the city.

Further south we stopped to take a look at a natural spring with gas bubbles in the water: it had been piped into a fountain for drinking but if you put a match to it the water would appear to catch fire. It was just about the weirdest thing I think I'd ever seen.

We followed the coastline, the Caspian Sea on one side, the other flat and featureless save for the massive burning oil towers in the distance. Russ was in the back-up van, checking that Mahmood, our Iranian guide, was going to meet us in Astara. I was looking forward to Iran; it was just so different, and as Mungo said we'd heard nothing positive about the place in years.

Azerbaijan, meanwhile, had seemed such a strange, incongruous place – the oil industry with its massive cranes and drilling platforms set against a historical walled fortress, and natural flames bursting out of the mountainside.

We arrived at the Iranian border just as it was about to close at six p.m. We decided to make a go for it, and leaving the cars we hefted our gear and walked up to the Azerbaijan checkpoint. It was one of the weirder crossings; we had to make our way on foot through a labyrinth of narrow outdoor passages. Mungo said it looked like some kind of strange toilet complex. Eventually we came out between two bricked-up derelict buses that served as offices. We presented the immigration people with our passports but they were the ones stamped with our Iranian visas and not the ones that had been stamped as we came into the country. That threw them. We always travel with more than one passport, as some countries don't like you visiting others and a spare passport is back-up if anything goes wrong.

'Here we go,' Russ muttered, 'confusion is going to reign after all.'

I've said it already – I hate going through border controls. Your life is in the hands of people who could confiscate your documents, detain you, lock you up and throw away the key. I've seen the maddest things. Right here there was a woman wailing and screaming because the contraband she was smuggling was being taken off her. In Turkey we witnessed a driver and a cop bitch-slapping each other; at another crossing we'd seen a car bumper ripped off when the driver decided to argue with an articulated lorry.

The different passports really didn't sit well with the officials in the derelict buses. We explained as best we could and they had a bit of a conference. Luckily, our late arrival worked in our favour for once: in the end I think they just wanted to go home. They made a decision, stamped the passports and we walked out of Azerbaijan and crossed the river heading towards Iran.

On the far side a soldier with a Kalashnikov slung over his shoulder was waiting, watching us every step of the way. Russ was alongside me, Mungo a little behind. 'Here we go, boys,' Mungo muttered. 'Get ready for Iran.'

But as we got to him the soldier just smiled. 'Where are you from?'

'London,' we said. 'England.'

He nodded. 'You're welcome here. Welcome to Iran.' And stepping aside he ushered us into his country.

9
A Mass of Contradictions

Mungo talks about the buzz when you cross a border. We all felt it then; it had been a tiring day but now the adrenalin kicked in and we looked around with a renewed sense of curiosity. After all the hassle – the changes in plan, the dashing around in Baku – entering Iran was as simple a crossing as I've ever experienced; a couple of minutes with customs and immigration and we were in. Russ said we were due a smooth passage after all the hoops we'd had to jump through and finally we got one.

We were in the border town of Astara, walking along a puddle-soaked street into a new country. All I could think about was that this was a religious dictatorship and I had no idea what to expect. But as we crossed further into the town, there was a sudden sense of energy, people smiling and nodding. It was quite a change from the rather dour atmosphere in Baku.

We met our guide Mahmood, a short, friendly guy in his late forties, a little chubby, with greying hair and a twinkle in his eye. He flagged down the driver of a Lajvar, a kind of tuk-tuk with a motorbike front and a trailer, only you sit side by side and there's a steering wheel instead of handlebars. The owner – a young, good-natured guy called Ahmed – let me up beside him. Two minutes in Iran and I was driving one of the vehicles they used to carry goods back and forth between the check-points.

Ahmed showed me how to drive, warning me to be careful with the steering because it was easy to tip the whole thing over. I asked him about himself, and he explained that he'd been a wrestler who hadn't quite made the grade. Apparently wrestlers have a high social standing in Iran and this guy had narrowly missed out on his dream. He had a wife and a little boy of five and had been out of work before he started doing this. He'd forked out the $2,000 to buy the rig and now he carried goods back and forth across the little stretch of river.

'Do you like the job, Ahmed?' I asked him.

He shrugged. 'It's my job,' he said. 'It's what I do. I have to like it, don't I?'

The countryside was damp and very green; not at all what I had expected. After saying goodbye to Ahmed we left Astara on a rice-grower's tractor and made our way south towards Bandar-e Anzali through paddies interlinked by raised walkways. I'm embarrassed to say I had no idea Iran grew rice or that this part of the country was quite so green and beautiful. It contradicted everything I'd thought about the place, a sea of rice fields set against grey, almost misty, mountains.

This was our twenty-first night on the road. I desperately wanted to call my family, but the phones were playing up and I hadn't really been able to speak to them properly for a long time. Instead we headed into Bandar-e Anzali where we found a hotel, dumped the bags and ate dinner. We talked about preconceptions based on selective news bulletins. Our news was governed by commercialism, Mahmood's by the state. It's so easy to judge a nation by what we see on the news; it's only when you go there yourself and meet people that you can even start to make sense of it all.

Mahmood agreed. 'Take the fighting in Iraq,' he said. 'I would think that how we see it is not how it's reported in your country. We believe the British and the Americans will never leave. Always there will be a battlefield and it will always be close to us.'

'Why do you say that?' asked Russ.

'Because it's better for them to fight here. They know that if they leave, the fight will only follow them. They will be chased home and nothing will alter except the battlefield. They would rather it was Iraq than Britain or America.'

The town of Bandar-e Anzali is a busy port on the southern shores of the Caspian Sea. Several interested countries have been caught up for years in an international dispute over the Caspian, and Iran and Azerbaijan have both claimed ownership of certain oilfields there. Perhaps even more confusingly, Iranians call the Caspian a lake, whereas the Azerbaijanis think it should be defined as a sea – which has further implications in terms of fishing rights and general shipping access. I got the impression that this was one problem that was not going to be solved overnight. It's borders again, isn't it? Never my favourite subject.

Anyway – forget the Caspian, I couldn't even really get my head around the fact we were in Iran at all. Just crossing the border you can tell it is very much its own place. It has its own calendar, and there's even a half-hour time difference with Azerbaijan. It's a massive country, with a population of over seventy million people – about fifteen million of whom live in Tehran. The Iranian president, Ahmadinejad, has been in a slanging match with George Bush over the possibility of Iran going nuclear. But the ultimate power in Iran is the Supreme Leader, currently Ali Khamenei – he rules the country, and is what Mahmood called a 'clergy'.

I was very conscious that we were travelling through a religious dictatorship, but my first impressions of Iran were of an upbeat – and in some ways surprisingly modern – country.

It felt like a huge milestone to even be here; especially after all our trouble with the visas. So many people had told me it was not a good idea to come here, but then they'd said the same thing about Libya and other parts of Africa. My personal experience has been that people are just people the world over and their main ambition is to have a happy life; it's the politicians who make it difficult.

Outside the hotel the next morning Russ and I spread out the map, which had become something of a ritual each day. Today we were heading south to Tehran.

'I had the biggest cockroach you've ever seen in my room last night,' Russ said. 'It was as big as my palm. I'm not kidding.' Squatting down, he looked at the map. 'We're doing all right, aren't we?'

I had to agree. We were travelling at a good pace, but still seeing a lot of each country. And amazingly we were still on course to arrive in Dubai as planned.

We set off as early as we could in Mahmood's van – though we were hoping to flag down a truck further along the route. Our first stop was a village that looked as if it had been carved straight from the mountain. It was very steep and shrouded in trees and the buildings were linked by steps and stairways, and old stonework bridges that criss-crossed a mass of streams and waterfalls. The stone was a sandy-grey colour, the same as the mountain, and from a distance the buildings were almost camouflaged.

Long ago Ewan and I worked out that the best places to eat when you're on the move are the places where the truck drivers stop, and today we were looking for a truck anyway. Heading south again and feeling hungry, we came upon a couple of old Mercedes trucks parked outside an open-fronted cafe in the town of Rasht. Inside, two guys were squatting on a piece of carpet, eating their lunch. No table, no chairs, just a bit of Persian rug laid with plates and bottles of soft drink.

Lunch looked great – a combination of meat and rice cooked in lots of rich spices. Sitting down on our own bit of carpet, we ordered the same. Mahmood introduced us to the two men, explaining that we were from England. The young man seemed a bit shy, but the older guy – who was slightly built and wiry, with black hair and a thick, black moustache – was more than happy to chat. His name was Asadollah and he'd been driving a truck for seventeen years. I asked him if we could hitch a lift to Tehran, not sure how he would respond. He just grinned and said he'd be happy to have us aboard.

It was a fabulous old truck, a bull-nosed 1973 Mercedes with a white cab and the Iranian flag painted on each wing. It was carrying cement today but Asadollah said he'd haul pretty much anything and he'd haul it anywhere. Recently he'd been to Turkey and Syria: sometimes he was away for three weeks at a time, he and his buddy taking it in turns to drive. The cab was very personally decorated, done out in a blue button fascia with pictures of Asadollah's family dotted here and there and prayer beads hanging from the rear-view mirror. He told me he loved the old Mercedes and that he had covered almost a million kilometres in it.

Sitting high up in the cab, trundling through the mountains, I felt like a little boy in a candy shop. Asadollah seemed a kind, relaxed man, perfectly in tune with his vehicle and where he was going. Driving half on the highway and half on the hard shoulder so other people could pass, he told me about his family, his life on the road and how much he enjoyed it. I began to fancy the job myself. Maybe if my career as an Irish scallop diver didn't work out . . .

Heading further south, we moved from the dirt road to the motorway, the terrain becoming drier and the valleys less green. We entered a long tunnel that led through the mountains and when we came out the other side it was like driving into another country altogether.

I was gobsmacked. Gone was the grass, the damp feel, the richness of the land; now we were in a harsh desert with sand edging the road, stark hills in the distance and no foliage or greenery whatsoever. Asadollah explained that Iran is split into three very separate areas: the northern climes where it's wet and cold and they grow rice, then this area where the desert begins and it starts to get warmer. South of Tehran it really was the Iran you think about and could become blisteringly hot.

We stayed that night in the capital: a crazy place with fifteen million people and at least fifteen million cars. We'd thought Azerbaijan was busy but this was ridiculous. We weren't allowed to film anywhere official, including petrol stations. I worked out there was some kind of smart-card system in operation and the government was effectively rationing fuel. No wonder; any more vehicles on the road and this city would grind to a standstill.

There was a different feel here; we all sensed it. We were still made welcome, and nobody gave us any grief, but this was the capital and the sense of repression was much more evident. There were far fewer women out on the streets, and when we went out to dinner we saw only men in the cafes. The women we did see were covered head to toe in traditional clothes, their hair tied up in scarves. There were even special police cars with women officers who made sure women were covered up. Perhaps most shocking for me was to see how women had to sit at the back on buses. I suppose this was more like the Iran I had been expecting, and it was not a comfortable experience. Mahmood explained that very few women had jobs. They weren't allowed to touch any man other than their husband; not even to shake hands.

The next morning we worked out a route to the bus station, which was across the other side of the city. We were going to take a subway (we hadn't even realised there was a metro system until we saw the signs) to the station, but first had to find a taxi. I was keen to find a female taxi driver, but in a city of God knows how many taxis, only a handful of women were allowed to drive them.

I was quite eager to leave Tehran. My initial impressions of Iran as a whole had been positive, but the closer we got to the capital – the seat of power – the more the reality of the dictatorship began to hit home. There were so many rules, so much you weren't allowed to do. And while individuals made us feel welcome, I could sense a lot of anger. Many of the locals we spoke to were very angry with Britain and openly sided with the Taliban, and there was a lot of talk about creating a state of war in the Middle East.

Russ went out to pick up a copy of the *Iran Daily*, a newspaper published in English. When I appeared with my suitcase he was sitting on the kerb with his cellphone in his hand. 'Have a look at the paper,' he said. 'There's quite a lot of mention about Britain. They're saying that Labour was mauled in the elections and Boris Johnson is now mayor of London . . .'

Meanwhile, Mahmood had managed to locate a female taxi driver. I was really pleased because this would be my first and probably only opportunity to meet an Iranian woman. I wasn't sure whether she would be talkative, but there's nothing like driving a big city taxi for seeing life and I didn't see why Tehran should be any different.

The taxi driver's name was Fariba. She was dressed all in black, but she was also wearing designer sunglasses and seemed an upbeat, confident woman. Through Mahmood I asked her how many women drivers there were in Tehran. She said that there were only four or five working for a regular agency.

'There are women driving taxis that are only for women, though,' she said. 'Private taxis. But I have been with an agency for two years. Before that I used to be a women's driving instructor. Actually as far as some of my family is concerned, I am still a trainer. I cannot tell them I drive a taxi because they will not comprehend it.' She said that she had never experienced any trouble from her male passengers, and that business was very good because many men felt more comfortable if their wives were driven round by another woman.

Fariba, who was in her thirties, told me she wasn't married because it was hard to find a good man. She was joking: the truth was her father was bankrupt and he was old, her mother cared for her father, and it was down to Fariba to provide for the family.

'Is it difficult being a woman in Iran?' I asked her.

She thought for a moment. 'Women here have the same problems as women everywhere,' she told me. 'Mostly the pressure is from the economy.'

We were deep in the heart of the city now, the traffic four lanes wide and inching forward bumper to bumper: it was ten times worse than Baku. People swapped lanes, honked their horns. Mopeds carrying outrageous loads skipped between the cars. Fariba said motorbikes were particularly dangerous, and that riders would barge between the cars and clip them, using their feet to lever off and carry on.

'Do you mind the customs?' I knew my questions might be awkward, but this was my only chance to ask. Fariba seemed so modern and open, she was bound to have an opinion, although whether she felt able to express it was another matter. 'Do you find it difficult having to wear traditional clothes all the time?'

She looked at me in the rear-view mirror. 'Customs are not limitations,' she explained. 'They are the customs of society and we live with them. If you drive in India, for instance, the women there wear different clothes. We try to live with it: it's not difficult.'

Mahmood pointed out a brick building with green doors marking the entrance to the subway. Pulling over we got out and I grabbed my bag.

'Thank you so much, Fariba,' I said. 'You're an amazing driver and what you're doing for women is terrific. That's the safest I've felt so far in Iran. Thank you.'

'You're welcome,' she told me.

We made our way down the escalator. The station was very clean, with cafes and newsstands in the foyer. It reminded me of the metro in Paris. *Mr Bean* was playing on a widescreen TV above the platform, which seemed incongruous, to say the least.

'I'm a bit tired today,' Russ admitted as we hung on to the overhead grips. 'Tehran's at altitude; four thousand feet. And we've done nothing but rush around for days.'

'We can chill out on the bus,' I said. 'It's six hours to Esfahan.'

Rattling into the tunnels, I looked at the other passengers, mostly men, apart from a couple of groups of women. Nobody was saying much to anyone – just like the underground in London or Paris, I thought. I was struck again by how lucky we had been to speak with Fariba. What a fantastic woman – so friendly and spirited, despite all her country's restrictions.

The bus to Esfahan was the kind you find in any major country; very modern with air-conditioning, TV and reclining seats. I sat back and chilled, letting my mind wander. South of Tehran the landscape changed dramatically. We were in a world of rock and sand: no trees, no bushes, just the odd bit of scrubby sagebrush clutching the side of the road. It was a vast red emptiness, broken only by the occasional village or truck stop.

On the bus we met a girl who had travelled from India to see her father. She told us – in very good English – that she lived with her mother in Mumbai, where she was finishing her education. We would be in Mumbai in about a week, so we bombarded her with questions, eager to know what to expect. Apparently it was about forty degrees there at the moment, and incredibly humid – hard to imagine in the dry heat of Iran.

The six hours passed very pleasantly, and were easily better than any coach travel I'd experienced in Britain. As soon as we sat down, a waiter brought us a drink and a little piece of sponge cake – they brought water whenever we asked for it and there were nuts and snacks to buy. Maybe that's how we should have stocked the *dolmus*, instead of the Turkish Delight and cologne . . .

Esfahan was spectacular. It is the second largest city in Iran, and yet there didn't seem to be any high-rise buildings there – it just spread across the desert floor under the slopes of the mountain. Apparently it was established over 1,500 years ago. The wide river flowing through the middle of the city was called the Zayandeh Rood or 'life-giving river'. It was a city of trees and flower gardens, of bridges – an incredible contrast to the red desert we had just driven through.

We stared in wonder at the Seeyo-Se-Pole, a massive red-brick bridge that spanned the river on two levels. On the second level, people sat watching the boats pass underneath. It was very beautiful, and nothing like Tehran, with its modern industrial blocks and high rises. I loved it.

We stopped for tea at a massive C-shaped plaza. The terraces bordering the plaza were two storeys high, with shops at ground level and a sprawling mosque facing us. The entrance was formed by a pair of intricate portico turrets with slim spires, and the domes of the mosque itself were painted blue.

We wandered the length of a bazaar, open-fronted lock-ups selling clothes and second-hand goods, kettles and gourds, leather plates and Persian rugs. One store had the most enormous twin-headed battle-axe and a shirt of chain-mail. 'Ewan would love this place,' I said. 'He'd buy up everything.'

Strangely enough, seeing the axe made me suddenly homesick – for Annamoe, my dad's place. A week before we left, we'd taken the kids to see him, and some of the props from *Excalibur* are on his piano, including the golden mask I'd worn as Young Mordred. I'd been about fourteen. Dad put me on a horse and told me to ride through the woods down by Lough Tay where our neighbour Garech Browne lives. 'Just hold on,' he said, 'and gallop. You'll be OK, the horse won't run into any trees.'

We grabbed a cup of tea in a narrow cafe with glass tables and carpet-covered benches. A line of interlocking battle-axes hung on the walls and the ceiling was choked with masses of lamps and lanterns. There wasn't an inch of clear space, the walls covered in tapestries and photos of famous wrestlers. The tables were laid with tobacco bongs, and a few men were gathered around smoking.

The tea was served in a glass with sugar crystals on the side, and a plate of crystallised honey, which we ate like biscuits. I decided to try a hubble-bubble, but just had a couple of tokes – a sheesha pipe full of the stuff is like smoking a whole packet of cigarettes. The tobacco in mine was apple-flavoured.

The people in Esfahan were very friendly: they asked us where we were from and told us how much they loved the English. A country of contradictions, for sure. By the time we left it was dusk and with the city lit up we could see just how flat it was. The place just unravelled under the shadow of the mountain, as if the lights were strung together for decoration.

We spent the night in Shahr-e-Kord, a small town of sandstone buildings in the middle of the desert. The next morning we rose and set off to meet a group of nomads who would be taking us into the desert. The weather was as contradictory as the country: yesterday had been boiling hot but this morning the rain was crashing down and I shivered in my jacket.

Leaving Shahr-e-Kord we headed into the desert. The red rock and sand had been replaced by scrub, quite green in places but rocky with shale slopes and – strange as it may sound in the pouring rain – very dry.

Along the way we picked up our guide, an old man who pointed out the sights as we passed, including a glimpse of sheep being driven along a ridge. He told us the people were Baluch, a generic name for a number of different nomadic tribes who speak a western Iranian dialect called *Baluchi*. We found them camped beyond a shale rise, a handful of tents set up in the shelter of a natural gully. There didn't seem to be any men around, only women and young children, girls mostly. A donkey was tethered in a pen made from wooden poles and chicken wire; a couple more tied to stakes in the ground.

A woman sat cross-legged on a mat outside her tent wearing a black headscarf and a shawl over her robes. Her two daughters crouched behind her. The tent was large and square with a sloping roof and when we got closer I realised it was made from lots of pieces of cloth all sewn together like a quilt.

It reminded me of Mongolia; the tents, the sheep and goats,

little children running around. These people were very poor but the woman had a strong face, she looked proud and was more than happy to talk to me. I asked her about nomadic life and whether it had changed much in recent years.

'It's very hard,' she said. 'It used to be better, our people were more together. Now the rain is not coming as it should and many leave to go to the city.'

'Where's your husband today?'

'He is working with the sheep – he is looking for water.' She gestured to a small lean-to kitchen, made from poles and canvas. A large kettle was hanging from a piece of twine, yellow jerricans sitting under a work surface fashioned from a couple of poles. Mahmood told us that for the last two years it hadn't rained as it should and if it carried on this way the people would have to sell their sheep and move to the city. The woman had eight children (her sons were off working with their father) and all ten of them slept in the one tent.

We were high up here, the mountains orange and pink stone. The whole place looked thirsty. These people had a tough life, but a proud one, and it was a shame to see it being lost to the cities. The kids were great fun, of course: kids are kids no matter what the situation. I messed about with them, getting them to creep up on me and chasing them away like an ogre, the kind of game children play all over the world.

It made me think of my own kids. I really missed them, and with the phones still playing up it was even more difficult. Back in Esfahan, waiting at the station for our next train journey, I managed to get through to them briefly. They all seemed in fine form. I tried to explain to Olly how I felt about Iran – it had been such a weird experience. There are pluses and minuses everywhere you go, of course, but here the differences seemed much more pronounced. The segregation of the women had particularly upset me. I had enjoyed the north more, where the people had seemed more relaxed and the rules and regulations weren't so clearly in evidence. There was plenty of water, the weather was less oppressive and of course it was further from Tehran.

On the platform, Russ was inspecting the train. 'This is our fourth train,' he said. 'The fifth if you include the one from Liverpool. The *Orient Express* was the best and the Tbilisi–Baku the worst: we'll have to figure out where we rate this one.'

I studied the military green engine and the pink and blue carriages. The cabins looked pretty small. The train was packed, and the four of us (Mahmood was coming with us) would be sharing one cabin, along with all our gear.

We watched the world go by for a while. It was sandy and flat again, the mountains just hazy shadows in the distance. The cabin was compact, to say the least – Mungo was on the top bunk on one side with Mahmood on the seat below. Russ would be sleeping on the other seat two feet across from Mahmood, and I was on a bunk above Russ. Our gear was strapped on a third bunk above me. But despite being cramped, the train was air-conditioned and the service was fantastic, way better than anything we'd get in Britain. They served dinner on metal plates with real knives and forks: chicken kebab on rice with yoghurt and a lime. The food had been amazing everywhere in Iran – though the meal we had at the transport cafe with Asadollah was probably the best.

In the next carriage along from us, four very attractive sisters were travelling south with one of their young sons. They were in and out of our cabin all the time – we guessed because we were foreign and filming. They were wearing plenty of make-up and only just about wearing their obligatory headscarves. They were full of fun, and one of them just loved the camera. Sitting down next to Mungo, she made sure she was in every shot that Russ was filming. Poor old Mahmood had to keep translating; he talked and talked to the point where his brain was fuddled and he finally said, 'no more'.

The girls were from Esfahan and were on their way to Bandar-e Abbas for a week's holiday. They wanted to know if we were married. Mahmood immediately told them we were single, but we explained that I was married and Russ was in a relationship: it was only Mungo who was actually available. That didn't bother them: they wanted to know if we were happy to have second wives. Marry us, they said mischievously, and take us out of here. They were vivacious, attractive and the way they were dressed was pretty rebellious for Iran – so much so that every now and again someone would pass in the corridor and scold them about it.

After dinner we chatted for a while with other people who joined us from the corridor, but in the end even the energetic Mahmood really couldn't do any more translating and descended into silence.

I got my bunk ready for bed, using the sheets and pillow cases the steward had provided. Then I unrolled my sleeping bag liner.

'You've got sheets, Charley,' Mungo said.

'I know, but it's what's *under* the sheets, isn't it?'

'Under the sheets, right . . . Give me a nod later and I'll come and give you a cuddle.'

Tugging a three-day-old sock from my foot I shoved it into his face.

10
Smugglers and Submarines

Russ was looking bleary-eyed when I slid down from my bunk and folded it away.

'Morning, Russ. Did you sleep well?'

'Yes, I think I did, actually. This train's pretty comfortable. Not like the one from Tbilisi, eh?' He yawned and looked out of the window. 'We're in the desert,' he said. 'In fact we've been in the desert all night.'

I shook my head sadly. 'Russ, we've been in the desert since we left Tehran.'

We wandered down to the dining car and ate a breakfast of tea and crispy naan bread with a sticky sort of grey peanut butter. It was OK, but nothing like the dinner we'd had the night before. I was thinking wistfully of a creamy latte and a bacon roll when an old guy came in with a meal he'd brought from home. Sitting down, he unwrapped a cloth containing walnuts and without hesitation offered some to us. It was a typical, generous gesture: he didn't know us from Adam and seemed to have very little, but what he did have he was more than happy to share.

Back in the cabin Russ and I laid out the plastic-coated map and I hunted down the felt-tip to go through our plans. Once we arrived in Bandar-e Abbas we would find the docks and try to get a dhow to sail across to Dubai.

Russ nodded. 'As soon as we get settled I'm going to check with Lucy about the container ship we want to take on from there. And we really need to keep abreast of the news now. The situation with China and Tibet could change at any time.'

Outside, we'd passed beyond the sand dunes and it was mountainous again, the peaks white as if they had been coated in salt. Below them mud-coloured settlements were springing up all over the place. Iran was a vast country and the seventy million people seemed thinly spread. Russ pointed out that no matter what the religious leaders said, no matter the political disputes between our government and theirs, the welcome that soldier had given us in Astara had been pretty much echoed all the way south.

Russ spread his fingers to measure distance across the map. 'You know, when you look at the map we've actually done a third of the trip already.'

I checked the GPS. Russ had suggested that if we couldn't get a dhow, we could sail a dinghy across the Strait. I wasn't sure about that. 'OK. A direct line to Dubai is a hundred and fifty miles. I reckon we're maybe forty or so out of Bandar, which makes the straits at least a hundred miles of sailing.'

Russ had moved on. 'Our nemesis is still China,' he mused. 'Somebody said we can actually go in to Burma and then get a plane to fly us to Laos.'

'What kind of plane?'

'Cessna.'

'Great. I can take off and land then.' I demonstrated how to ease back on the stick. 'The Thailand Cessna club said they'd pick us up if we wanted; they'd fly us across Burma to Laos. We could do that if it comes to it because a Cessna doesn't count: it's a small plane, not a commercial airliner. We'll just have to see how the land lies when we get there but if we end up in a Cessna, that's fine with me.'

It was only nine in the morning when arrived at Bandar-e Abbas, but it was already stiflingly hot. We said goodbye to the four girls from the next carriage and went outside where the sun was beating down on the pavement and the sky was a shimmering blue with not a hint of cloud. The street was wide and dusty; a commercial district with a line of yellow taxis. I was looking forward to a shower. Sleeping on the train is fine and that particular train had been pretty fabulous but there were no showers. I realised then that this would be our final day in Iran – we had walked into the country from the north and now we'd be sailing out from the south.

In the hotel I washed my socks and undies; my wife would have been proud of me. It was already past ten, and we needed to do something about finding a dhow. Mahmood said it was so hot down here that everything closed between twelve and four p.m.

Mungo came in looking agitated. 'Have you seen the news? There's been a cyclone in Burma. They think something like fifteen thousand people have been killed.'

I switched on the TV and we sat down and watched pictures sent by a BBC reporter based in Thailand. Burma has to be one of the most secretive regimes in the world: a British colony until 1948; after independence democracy only lasted till 1962. That was when General Ne Win led a military coup and since then the army has been in control. The journalist said that most of the casualties reported so far seemed to have been from one town in the south. Houses had been blown down, trees uprooted and roads blocked. There were fears for the rice crop – the cyclone had created a huge wave which swept across the Irrawaddy Delta.

Russ had seen the news too and we were all a little quiet when we met outside to grab a taxi.

'I hope to God the military let foreign aid in,' he said. 'And fast. They're really going to need it.'

I nodded. It was horrendous, and it sounded as though the number of casualties could go even higher. It was strange to think that just earlier that morning we had been talking of travelling through Burma, and now just a few short hours later there was this terrible tragedy. It was an unsettled region but we could never have predicted this. I couldn't stop thinking about all those people suffering so badly. Of course it could have a big impact on our plans – and along with the crisis building between China and Tibet, our road to Laos was gradually being cut off. But that seemed like a very tiny, insignificant problem in the face of such a tragedy.

As we approached the docks our confidence was flagging: it all looked much more organised than we'd envisaged: large white buildings, lots of construction work going on and lots of security.

Russ shook his head. 'I was hoping for an old quay with boats tied up but it's all quite official-looking, isn't it?'

Mahmood took us into the shipping office and immediately struck up a conversation with one of the officials. It was cool inside after the heat-blasted pavement. Breaking off from the conversation Mahmood turned to us.

'There is only one desk, one shipping company that goes to Dubai.' He pointed to a glass booth with no one behind the counter. 'One ship that goes every other day. They don't carry passengers. He is very sorry but those are the rules.'

Quite a few people had gathered now, officials from the port and from various shipping companies, their chatter echoing across the empty room. Mahmood deliberated with them for a bit longer but finally he turned to us. 'They are sorry,' he said, 'but they are really restricted and not allowed to take any passengers. I've asked them again, but there is nothing they can do.'

We decided to take a walk and see if we could make a private deal with one of the captains. Mungo wiped the camera lens and Mahmood lifted a finger. 'If they see the camera they will take it,' he said. 'It is best to put it away.'

We wandered down towards the water where massive berths were cut in concrete to accommodate the big ships like the glimmering cruise liner we could see moored in the distance. Crossing some cleared ground we saw a wire fence and a gate; beyond it, tied up to the dock, was just the sort of battered old wooden dhow we were looking for. It was flat-hulled and painted a dirty blue with an open foredeck, the stern covered by an upper deck with a chipped balustrade like an old pirate ship.

We got Mahmood to ask the crew if they'd take us to Dubai.

They laughed.

'They don't take passengers,' I muttered.

Mahmood shook his head. 'No,' he said, 'there is no way they can do it.'

The next thing we knew a security guy had appeared in a white shirt with epaulettes and a baseball cap. He looked pretty pissed off.

'What're you doing?' he demanded. 'You're not supposed to be here.'

I apologised, and Mahmood explained quickly who we were, where we were from and what we were trying to do. The security man chilled out then: he explained that two years ago a law had been passed forbidding not just the dhows, but any cargo boat from taking passengers. It was all to do with smuggling – not only contraband, but people – and the Iranian government had cracked down hard. He told us to go to the government office and speak to the head of security; see if he could help us.

The head of security was in his office by the shipping company and he was as helpful as he could be under the circumstances. He looked almost apologetically at us. 'I'm sorry,' he said, 'but there is no way: there is no place on a dhow to sleep.'

'We don't need a bed,' I told him.

'It doesn't matter. They do not take passengers.'

We asked if there were any other more traditional vessels we could take, rather than the regular ferry.

He shook his head. 'No, nothing. It is impossible. Only the ferry will take passengers because of the people-smuggling. Dhows don't come in to the customs area. They have no passport stamp; they come to a different place than where the customs is. They just unload their goods and reload. Even if one would take you, you might not get your passport stamped and they would take you to a different place in Dubai other than where the customs office is and then you might not be allowed in.'

We realised it was hopeless. It was a pity because it would have been very cool to cross the Strait of Hormuz on a dhow. Instead we had to rush to the ferry's booking office, hoping desperately there were still places free. We were in luck – we managed to get four tickets for the next ferry, which sailed on Thursday morning – the day after tomorrow.

That night I was up and down like a jackrabbit: like an idiot I'd left the balcony door open in my room and I'd been fighting mosquitoes ever since. I'd been bitten on my fingers and on my back; I'd killed one so engorged with my blood it spattered all over the pillow.

The following morning – our last day in Iran – Mungo and I headed for the docks and a boat to Qeshm, a small island just south of Bandar where Iranians like to go on holiday, just for a look around. Mungo was complaining about the badger strapped to his chin. He likes his stubble; he's never clean-shaven but he never lets the full beard grow either. The girls in the office had made him promise he would let it grow, however, and see how long it was by the time we got to Sydney. But we were in thirty-eight-degree heat now and it was only going to get hotter: he'd picked up a shaver and tonight the badger was coming off.

We took a speed boat to the island; a big old cheap tub with a canvas roof to keep the sun off. This was one of the most controversial stretches of water in the world: with what was going on in Iraq and Afghanistan the British were here as well as the Americans. The nature of the place was clear, with tankers and oil rigs and warships all clearly in evidence – and not all of the warships were Iranian. Sitting there with the breeze in my face I saw a periscope break the surface of the water. I couldn't believe it. 'Mungo look,' I said, 'a fucking periscope.'

We watched as it lifted, like three metal struts sticking out of the water. It clearly wasn't a buoy because it was moving. Then it just disappeared again. 'Jesus – that was a submarine,' I said. 'It makes you realise just where you are. It's probably American. Or maybe one of ours, even.'

'It could've been Russian,' Mungo said. 'Mahmood told me he thought the Russians were here as well.'

To be honest, neither Mungo or I were very impressed by the holiday island. There wasn't much there save for a rather dirty-looking beach with a few pagoda-style huts on the promenade. It felt very downbeat and we'd been told that smugglers in speedboats picked contraband up from here and tried to get it back to the mainland.

Mahmood had gone a little quiet and neither of us thought much about it. But later he said how much he liked Qeshm and he planned to bring his family here for a holiday. Mungo and I felt terrible for voicing our opinions earlier – we couldn't believe we'd been so insensitive. We felt terrible and it really brought home the differences between our cultures. We were used to such a high standard of living, had such high expectations. The reality is that Iranians have little choice as to what they do or where they can go and to a man like Mahmood, Qeshm was pretty cool. Sometimes I forgot we were in a religious dictatorship and that choice is pretty limited. There are loads of young people in Iran – something like 70 per cent of the population is under thirty – and there's nowhere for them to go. Apparently people would often just jump in their cars and drive around because there is nothing else to do. Mungo and I agreed we should be much more careful about voicing our feelings from now on, not just in Iran but in any country. It was bloody rude, and if we'd heard anyone slagging off our country we'd pretty quickly tell them where to get off.

The reality was that despite all the hardships, the Iranian people had been very kind and generous to us. I've been to a few places now around the world and I've come to realise that the less people have, the happier they are to share.

At last we managed to secure a trip on a dhow, even if it was just to get back from the island to the mainland. There were a bunch of the old boats tied up at the docks, some for passengers and others for cargo; exactly the kind of thing we'd wanted to sail to Dubai. The passenger area was fenced with wooden planks to make sure no one fell overboard. Under the low roof, rough tables were fixed to the floor and all sorts of people were sitting at them: women in scarves – some with red masks completely covering their faces – men in long shirts and loose-fitting trousers, and lots and lots of kids.

I wandered up to the wheelhouse and in sign language asked the captain if I could have a go at driving.

This was a proper boat, the kind the Persians had used for centuries – although this one admittedly was powered by diesel and not a sail. The wheelhouse was narrow with a long padded bench and a massive old wooden ship's wheel instead of the games console joystick I was becoming used to seeing on this trip. I perched next to the captain, who was barefoot and steering with his toes. We couldn't say much, he had no English and I had no Persian and he was concentrating on the boat. The dash had a radar screen as well as a radio, but that was it apart from an old ship's compass floating in a wooden box. I reckoned there were 120 souls on board and I took my responsibility seriously, negotiating the buoys and a massive oil platform, not to mention tankers and warships. OK, that's not quite true, I steered a bit of a course, the current trying to push us starboard, but all the time the captain's toes were right there in the wheel spokes.

Back on deck I was leaning on the rail when a speedboat flew by, hopping across the waves with an intermittent scream as the propeller lifted clear of the water. Two young guys were holding on to their smuggled goods while another guy was steering. I waved to him and with a mischievous-looking grin he waved back. The speedboat was maybe twelve or thirteen foot long – we'd seen a few of them in the harbour at Qeshm. They'd more than likely have to deal with the navy when they got closer to Bandar-e Abbas; we'd seen a whole bunch of military speedboats back there. Mahmood told us it was an occupational hazard and if the smugglers were approached they'd just dump the contraband overboard and plead innocence.

Back at the hotel I left Mungo to his electric shaver. Later he told me it took him three attempts to get rid of the badger, the batteries packing up twice before he could get the mains to work. He went from mountain man to moustachioed seventies porn star before finally arriving at the stubble he likes to think is cool.

At twelve-thirty a.m. battle resumed in my room. Two mosquitoes this time: one cocky little sod and his friend. The cocky one had been doing fly-bys right under my nose and I was buggered if he'd get away with that. Finally I caught him trying to hide out at the top of the curtains and without any compunction whatsoever I squashed the little bastard.

11
Die Really Hard on a Boat

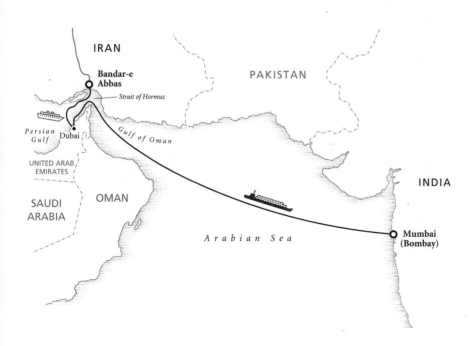

On 8 May we left Iran and caught the ferry to Dubai. I'd visited once before when I was training for the Dakar Rally. I'd planned on spending two weeks sand training on a Honda but I'd crashed only a couple of days in and broken my collar bone.

This time, Dubai was great, a few days in paradise; fabulous room, great pool, you know the kind of thing when you're knackered. The most daring thing I did was head for the shopping mall. I was supposed to buy DVDs for the crossing to India plus some shorts and maybe a couple of T-shirts. I came away with a dress to send home to my wife and a Leatherman. Oh, and a rubber ball.

By Sunday afternoon I was itching to get moving. Another country was beckoning, somewhere I'd never been before, and to arrive on a container ship would be fantastic. We'd received a news text telling us that India had fired a nuclear test missile while we were crossing the strait to Dubai but I tried not to let it bother me: just another bit of political agitation in a politically agitated area.

Russ had to fly back to London to take care of some business, which just left Mungo and me. The ship didn't leave until early Monday morning, but customs worked differently here – the paperwork had to be sorted well in advance and they wanted us on board today – so we arrived at the Jebel Ali Harbour in plenty of time.

This was a whole new experience for me. We had seen a lot of container ships on the strait – massive floating hunks of metal weighed down by hundreds of containers – but I'd never been on one and I didn't know the drill. I spent most of the afternoon repacking my case, getting rid of heavier clothing, which I wouldn't need now. Everywhere from here on would be pretty warm, I reckoned. I'd take my waterproofs, but if it got cold in Nepal I'd try to buy something locally.

We were travelling with Maersk on the *Nedlloyd Tasman*, a ship registered in London. It was enormous; black-hulled, it sat high in the water with the deck miles above us. We stood there for a few moments just taking the whole thing in; not just the enormity of the ship itself but the activity, the hubbub all around us. Truck after truck was pulling up, each loaded with containers. Then cranes known as split grabbers would swoop down and pick one up then swing it across the deck and set it down. It was like watching a movie: so state-of-the-art and technical that it appeared almost computer-generated. This was probably the wackiest bit of transport we'd travelled on so far.

I climbed the rope-sided gangplank, lugging my suitcase which still seemed to weigh a ton. On deck we were met by Dave the boatswain, or third mate, who took us to the ship's office to be registered. Already I was tingling from the noise of the docks and the bustle. Dave introduced us to Kevin the captain, a really nice guy and so laid-back he was about to fall over. He told us we could have the run of his ship and film anywhere we wanted just as long as we followed the rules and wore the requisite clothing: pale blue boiler-suits, hard hats and safety boots.

Dave explained that he was in charge of maintenance. Each day the chief mate Jim would tell him what needed doing and he'd organise the crew to do it: anything from painting, splitting wires, fixing lifts . . . you name it.

They only carried a crew of twenty-three. Dave told us that 'back in the day' his first ship had been a thirty-year-old rust-bucket. He had spent the entire fourteen-week passage painting it. Those were the days when alcohol was allowed, the crew was a complement of forty-six and every night was party night in the bar. This ship was dry: company policy. It seemed to be a bit of a deal for the crew. The captain explained that when he had been responsible for dishing out a few cans, the officers and crew used to unwind together. Now it seemed life on board was more fragmented.

Our cabins were on the fourth deckhouse deck, where the officers and apprentices slept. Carrying my heavy case four flights up left me panting for breath, but the cabin itself was a welcome sight – air-conditioned and spacious with a TV and DVD player strapped down for rough weather. David apologised for the view from my window – basically a wall of containers – but I could hardly expect anything different from a ship carrying five thousand of the things. On the plus side, David said that the weather forecast was good, and the sea should be calm all the way to Mumbai.

After that we were introduced to Alistair McLean, the Scottish chief engineer. He informed us there was an engine problem. That was a good start; only just on board and we'd broken down even before we'd set sail.

We followed him down to the engine area. There was no air-conditioning here and the heat was intense, the steps so hot you couldn't put your hands on the metal rail. Alistair explained that the lube oil pump, probably the most important pump in the whole engine, had an electrical problem; one of the connectors had exploded, compromising the insulation. Three technicians were working to make the switchboard safe while they waited for parts to be flown in from Ireland and Denmark.

I commented on the heat – I was sweating and the control room was so humid it was almost misty.

Alistair smiled wryly. 'You think this is hot, Charley – just wait till you see the engine room itself. It's fifty-seven degrees in there.'

He explained that the ship used massive amounts of electricity and generated its own supply. The switchboard looked relatively easy to understand: a wall panel with black lines linking each section, green lights to let you know everything was in order and red to tell you when an area had been compromised. They needed power to supply the bow thrusters which enabled the ship to turn. It was a huge ship – 40 metres wide and 276 metres long – and the rudder alone wasn't powerful enough to turn it.

Alistair took us into the engine room and 57 degrees is bloody hot, believe me. The sweat was pouring as we picked our way through miles of lagged pipes to look out over the massive engine casings. The engines burned heavy oil, which is the waste from crude after the components of petrol or diesel have been taken out. It was a lot cheaper than diesel but had to be heated up so it was viscous enough to use efficiently. At full speed the ship burned between 760 and 770 tonnes of fuel a day. A year ago the price had been $260 a tonne but now it was up to $500 and every second cost them roughly a dollar: over a 24-hour period that's $86,400. Alistair showed me a piston. I tried to hug it – my dad's into hugging trees – but it was so big I couldn't get my arms around it.

'That's a spare,' Alistair said. 'There're ten of those in the engine.'

It was too hot to spend any length of time down there so we made our way upstairs to the bridge. I'd expected lots of buttons and twirly things (that's a technical term, you know) but instead the stairs led up to a glass-panelled corridor, spanning the full width of the ship – in fact it overhung the sides with panels in the floor so the officers could see all the way to the waterline sixty feet below. There were two consoles and two helms, one on each side. The helm itself was a separate block, like a lectern with a proper wheel to steer by – Jim told us that the ship had one of the most advanced autopilot systems in the world and it could follow the red line of a plotted course to the letter: the problem with that, though, was it meant the rudder was moving all the time and that burned huge amounts of fuel. There were also chart tables with dividers and rulers as well as a computerised chart plotter, two different radar systems and – most importantly – a kitchen area with a kettle and coffee maker.

As well as generating its own electricity (which, amongst other things, was used to power some five hundred refrigerated containers), the ship created fresh water with a full-on desalination system that mashed up all the poop and pee and got rid of it. Once at sea it was self-sufficient; a village, a little slice of Britain popping up anywhere in the world complete with Marmite, HP Sauce and Branston pickle.

The wheel intrigued me. I hoped to be steering the ship myself once we'd got beyond anything we could bash into and Jim told me that after ten hours' practice I'd be competent to bring the ship into harbour.

With my hard hat in place and feeling very much at home, I followed the mate down to the dock where fresh food, fruit and veg, cans of soft drinks and cartons of cigarettes were being loaded – lifted from the van onto a wooden pallet then tied with netting before being hoisted aboard. The officers were all British but the crew was Filipino. The head chef was also Filipino and his galley was immaculate. He cooked English food for the officers and his mate Wilfred cooked Filipino-style food for the crew: mostly fish and rice, and chicken wings – spicy stuff. Mungo and I ate Filipino for lunch.

By the time we'd got going we'd already been on board for more than twenty-four hours. The scheduled departure time of early Monday morning came and went and after that there seemed to be delay after delay. The ship was bound for China ultimately and time was money, but there was nothing anyone could do about it. First there had been the electrical problem, then various other issues: towards evening a container that was supposed to weigh 27 tonnes was found to be nearer 40. The split grabber that tried to lift it couldn't, so another one had to be brought in. We were told we'd be off around four p.m. but, things being what they were, at six-thirty we were still on the dock.

I asked Dave if he got ashore much but he said as this ship had a small crew he was a watch-keeper, which a boatswain normally wouldn't be. He kept the watch from eight a.m. to midday, then again from eight p.m. till midnight. During the afternoon he organised the ship's maintenance, which meant he didn't have a lot of time to himself.

'I get ashore when I can,' he said. 'Especially in Singapore and Hong Kong because the terminal is close to the city. The trouble is that these days the ships are getting so big most of the terminals have to be built miles from anywhere.'

'But you enjoy it though?'

'Oh, yeah, I love it. Not as good as back in the day, but there you go.'

They weren't just loading containers but sections of deck: you could only load so many containers on top of each other before another layer of decking had to be laid down. It all fitted together like a massive jigsaw. Everything was monitored by computer, the refrigerated containers plugged in and checked daily: they could be carrying anything from frozen food to medicine and even blood products – sometimes the value in one container alone could be astronomical. Walking the gangway on the starboard side I noticed the name of the company that made the sections of deck. 'Macgregor,' I said, pointing it out to Mungo. 'See, Ewan's never very far away.'

The main trunk of the ship was the cargo section. Behind this, towards the stern, the deckhouse rose up, seven storeys high. The bridge and the wheelhouse were at the top, and below that came the instrument room. The fifth floor housed the ship's office and the senior officers' cabins. We were sleeping on the fourth, and on the third level there was a recreation room and the laundry. The rest of the crew kipped on the second deck and below that were the mess rooms and galley.

On the lower level we were greeted by a poster depicting knife-wielding bad guys slipping over the side. 'Be Vigilant in Pirate Areas', it said.

Vigilance was right: at night everything was locked up and no one was allowed outside in case some pirate took a pot shot from a speed boat. The Horn at the Strait of Hormuz was a particularly dodgy spot, and tonight we'd be steaming right through it.

Still our departure was put back; another hour slipped by then finally we watched from the deck as the tugs came alongside. The organisation was extraordinary. How everyone knew what they were doing and when to do it, not just on the ship but the crane operators and truck drivers, just baffled me. It worked like clockwork: on board some people worked during the day and others at night and because of that there was a code of conduct; quietness in the corridors and no slamming doors. There was a hierarchy here but everyone knew their role and every role was respected.

It was getting dark now, the water black and the dock glowing with orange lights. Mungo and I walked more than a quarter of a kilometre through an open-sided corridor of steel arches to the bows, where we watched the crew make ready to bring in the bowline. The rope was as thick as my thigh and it took two guys to cast off before it was winched aboard. It had a breaking strain of 120 tonnes and cost $1200: the only way it might break was if a winch didn't pay out correctly or jammed altogether and the full weight of the ship was suddenly on it: if one did snap, though, it would be bloody dangerous.

The tugs were ready at eight-fifteen. They were tiny compared to our great hulk of a ship, but were very powerful. Jebel Ali Harbour covers fifty-two square miles and over a hundred different companies operate out of it. There's a thirteen-mile sea channel that has been dug especially for the big ships that need the draught and the pilots accompanied them until they were beyond it.

A pilot joined our ship from the harbour, instructing our guy at the helm. The captain oversaw everything: the ship was ultimately his responsibility and the pilot only instructed, he didn't take the controls. Kevin told us that the only place where you hand over totally is the Panama Canal: there the pilots steer and if they mess up it's their responsibility. He'd seen a pilot take a ship through closed lock gates, and another time crash the ship into the side walls. Kevin was mate on that ship: the captain was about to jump in and grab the wheel but Kevin physically dragged him away.

Interfere with the pilot at all and as far as the insurance company were concerned, the accident would have been their responsibility.

There is no gearing on these big ships; once the engine fires up the propeller turns, so they don't start the engines until the ship is out of the channel and the pilot is about to get off.

We stood on the bows watching the tugs tow the ship out towards the open sea. The lights of Jebel Ali were strung across the water and the dark of the night gathered about us now, though it was still thirty-five degrees. As the harbour slipped away, I was thinking – our next stop would be India, and Mumbai. The thrill of this trip still took my breath away sometimes.

On the bridge the pilot had done his job and he was heading below. We watched through the glass floor, the water churning as his boat rocked up alongside, pressing against the ship. The pilot climbed down a ladder and dropped onto the deck. The tug peeled off and we were under way: ahead of us the Strait of Hormuz, maybe pirates, terrorists even. I swaggered back to my cabin in coveralls and hard hat feeling like Bruce Willis in the little-known movie *Die Really Hard on a Boat*.

I now know how tennis shoes get from China to the shops, or how a small grower can get blueberries from South America. Container ships are fast and efficient and it's not expensive for a bunch of small companies to get goods shipped. New markets were being opened up because of it. Most stuff is brought to us in the UK rather than us shipping it, mind you. All we really ship is stuff like scrap metal; India takes a lot of scrap metal apparently.

I woke up feeling a little bit down: this was great fun and I was really privileged to be here but I missed Olly and the kids: I'd spoken to them and they'd been doing stuff I'd normally do with them. Mungo and I were getting on really well, though, he's great to hang out with and like me he's not much for being by himself. Russ doesn't mind, he's pretty self-sufficient but I like company. It was a pity Russ wasn't here; he would really have loved this – the engine and navigation, all the technical stuff.

Back in Dubai he and I had sat down and sorted out our route forward. We'd be on motorbikes again soon – Royal Enfields coming up in India – with bikes again in Cambodia and the last section in Australia. I can't be away from bikes too long, any more than I can be away from my family . . .

It was fascinating talking to the crew, people like Dave and Jim and another guy called Chris who we'd been hanging out with. He and I formed a team on fire drill that morning. We mustered in the control room and the chief mate told us we had to put out an imaginary fire on deck. I followed Chris and grabbing the hose we hauled it to the 'affected' area between two massive banks of containers. We took up four corners, two guys on each one. I held the nozzle while Chris helped with the weight: the hose bucked and kicked in my grip but we blasted those crates with enough water to sink the ship. 'Hey, Chris,' I yelled. 'This is the first time I've let off a fire hose when I wasn't drunk.'

He told me that if a fire breaks out in any of the really delicate parts of the ship such as the engine room, the area can be sealed and then pumped full of CO_2, ensuring nothing gets damaged further by water or powder from extinguishers. We did another quick drill on the poop deck where I had to let off an extinguisher, then we all piled into the covered lifeboat which sits ready to launch, right over the stern. It carried thirty people, though a few more could hang off the sides. If it had to be launched they would also throw out the fold-away lifeboats and lash the whole thing together to make it more visible. There were rations on board and water, and enough fuel to steam for twenty-four hours at six knots. Dave told me more people had been killed by the boats than saved by them though, which wasn't very comforting. On some ships they weren't maintained as they should be, or the hooks were released too early or released themselves when the 'shock load' as he called it, was still on them. The boat would hit the water then from a great height and potentially break up. Fortunately, none of this crew had had to use a lifeboat for real and this one was maintained properly. I noticed they carried the same kind of distress beacons we'd taken on the bikes when I did the Dakar: if you were really buggered you'd set them off and someone would hopefully come and get you.

I followed Jim, the chief mate, touring the ship from end to end as he always did, seeing what needed maintenance. From the stern we made our way forward, down miles of cramped, narrow corridors with pipes lining the walls and ceiling like something from *Alien*. Jim told us we were walking on various fuel and water ballast tanks. He explained that tonight he'd fill the tanks with sea water then gradually let it drain. As the water drained it would drag in fresh air. In the morning we'd take oxygen meters down into the darkness and check it. If the ship lost containers or got out of balance these tanks could be partially filled with sea water to redress the change in load.

There was so much to learn. There were no engines or ventilation fans in the bows, and we stood there in the semi-quietness, just the noise of the sea echoing against the hull. Jim showed us what happens to the ship in rough weather, pointing to where the slapping waves had taken their toll – chipped paint and buckled surfaces. Another thing for Jim to keep an eye on.

Up on the bridge we sat down for a chat with the captain, Kevin, in the 'Big Boss' chair. Between us was a console with dials and switches, and in the middle a little knob to steer the boat. You didn't need the wheel after all, you could steer sitting here with your feet up. We mentioned the minor damage we'd seen in the bows and Kevin told us how in really bad weather you could look the length of the ship and watch the superstructure twist and buckle. It was designed to be flexible, he said, and move with the water a little – the way tall buildings are often designed to move with the wind.

I asked him how long he'd been at sea.

'Forty-one years, almost,' he said. 'I started on the fifth of November 1967.'

'It must be a huge responsibility, this job.'

He nodded. 'The crew first and foremost, of course. And then there's the value of the cargo: it's phenomenal. Never mind the cost of the ship itself.'

Last night he'd mentioned that he'd been in New York on 9/11. I asked him what happened.

'We were five miles out at anchor,' he said. 'Back then you could see the twin towers from miles out at sea. We watched it all unfold, we knew what had happened with the first plane and we watched the second one hit and then the towers collapse. It all seemed to happen in slow motion. It didn't seem real until the towers were gone: there one minute then just an enormous cloud of dust. That was when the realisation hit. We were there for days; they thought the next terrorist threat would be someone on a ship like ours determined to ram Manhattan.'

I asked him about life on board. Most trips took ten weeks, and I was curious to know how his wife coped. It was the sort of question I could have asked myself, and I could really identify with being away from home for so long. He told me he had been married for thirty-two years and had two grown-up children: he'd always done this job and his family were used to it.

'My wife says I break up her routine when I come home,' he said.

'Oh yeah, I know how that feels. When I get home from a trip Olly says it's like the third child arriving: everything runs like clockwork when I'm gone and then in I come and it's chaos. Did you always want to be a captain?'

'No,' he joked. 'I wanted to be an admiral.'

'Would you recommend it as a profession?'

'Being diplomatic – it's not what it was. The ships used to be a quarter of the size with twice the number of people on board. You'd be on three- to four-month trips and you'd spend three or four days in port. You could go ashore and see the sights. Nowadays it's all go-go-go. But for a young man the pay's not bad and you get qualifications that you can take ashore. There're plenty of jobs around in the shipping business after you get off a ship.'

I asked him about pirates.

'We're out of the area now. The worst places are the Malacca Straits, parts of China and off the coast of Somalia. A passenger ship went in a little close to Somalia and was boarded. Yemen can be bad too, and the Indonesian islands.'

My stomach dropped a little – we would be sailing that way later, from Singapore to Borneo and East Timor. I told him as much and he sucked his breath like a car mechanic about to tell you your engine's fucked.

'Tankers are a target,' he said. 'They're slow-moving compared to us. A lot of tugs are taken in the Malacca Straits – the strip of water between the Malaysian Peninsula and Sumatra. It's the main shipping channel linking the Indian and Pacific Oceans. The tugs push barges, Charley. You have to be careful there.'

'Not quite Jack Sparrow, are they?'

He shook his head. 'No, they're more like armed robbers. That's all piracy is, really: armed robbery.'

After dinner I went outside the bridge to the little gantry. We were 770 miles from Mumbai. The cross wind was blowing at 25 mph and I could see the waves rolling and crashing in the wake of the ship; the sky was pitch-black and cloudless, stars glittering high above. Through the windows the bridge was in darkness apart from the soft glow of computer lights, radar screens and dials. It was like something out of *Star Wars*. I half-expected to see Ewan at the helm, guiding some spaceship home.

In the morning we inspected the ballast tanks down below. With the manhole unscrewed you could see an oval hole descending into darkness. Jim checked the atmosphere for any oxygen/fuel mixture which was potentially explosive. When he was satisfied we climbed down the vertical ladder into the dank, very hot, pitch-black tank to make the inspection. We used high-powered torches to check the walls, floor and ceiling for corrosion or leakage. It was really close, tight and airless and if you suffered from even the slightest bit of claustrophobia you really wouldn't want to be down there.

I'd really enjoyed my time at sea: it had been like a mini-adventure within a great big adventure. I took a walk to the front, my favourite part of the ship, and looked down at the bow cutting through the water. The containers are stacked so high that they block out almost all of the wind, and without the engine noise or fans here, it's surprisingly peaceful. The views are fabulous, with the matt blue of the sea spreading in all directions. I decided I could do this job, for a while at least anyway; ten weeks on and ten off, so that when you're home you really are at home. When you're on the ship the hours are long but the food is good and there was good camaraderie among the crew, both British and Filipino.

Driving a lorry through northern Iran – a country that defied all our expectations.

Riding a motorbike/trailer hybrid. The owner looks a bit nervous for some reason . . .

With Fariba – one of the very few female taxi drivers in Tehran.

In the desert outside the city of Shahr-e-Kord in Iran, visiting a group of nomads.

I spent a week on the container ship Nedlloyd Tasman, sailing to Mumbai, and had a fantastic time.

Hanging on for dear life on a train in Mumbai.

The inevitable tuk-tuk in Delhi.

Poor old Mungo gets the bad news.

In Agra, with one of the seven wonders of the world. (The Taj Mahal that is – not me!)

On the way to Ramnager on the Tata truck.

On the Ganges.

The bustling river bank at Varanasi – a truly spiritual place. I really fell in love with the city.

Once in a while I even had to walk . . .

The Ambassador – the iconic car of India.

Tractoring through Nepal. Actually one of my favourite modes of transport on the whole trip.

Betty the elephant.

In the foothill of the Himalayas, and *walking* again. Sadly I didn't get to ride on the yak.

Mothers awaiting the 'cold chain' vaccines in the remote town of Chaubas, Nepal.

Delivering the
vaccine for UNICEF
in Chaubas.

Yes, I could definitely do this as a job. After I'd spent some time as an Irish scallop diver and Iranian truck driver, that is. I was getting quite an imaginary CV together on this trip.

I took a moment to cast my mind back to 12 April, leaving Dad's house and riding up to Kilkeel. After that it had been the scallop boat, the Isle of Man, the ferry. God, I'd driven a lifeboat, a Land Rover, we'd sailed a dinghy, I'd driven a Citroën that secretly ran out of petrol, sat with the driver of the *Orient Express* and been on the bridge of a hydrofoil from Venice to Croatia. We really were traversing the world by any means possible. A Yugo, an overnight train from Serbia, then right across Turkey in the Love Bus, then the Ural through the city where Stalin was born and where the Russians and Georgians were still flexing their muscles, another train, and then the mad dash for visas in Baku: driving around the most toxic city in the world in a UAZ with no brakes and very little steering. I thought of Asadollah in Iran and his Mercedes, and now here we were on this massive ship where the generators that powered the refrigeration containers were bigger than a double-decker bus. Oh yes – the double-decker bus. I'd driven one of those, too. I couldn't believe how lucky I was to be doing this, and couldn't wait to get moving again; India was beckoning, and I had high hopes for Mumbai – surely one of the most exciting cities in the world.

My excitement was tempered though; we'd just heard that there had been a terrible earthquake in Sichuan, China. It had been so violent that the after-shocks were felt 1000 kilometres south in Vietnam. The first casualties had been nine hundred students but they reckoned closer to ten thousand people might have been killed and thousands more were missing. What with that and the awful cyclone that had ripped through Burma, it didn't seem to matter any more whether we ever got to Laos. It's a strange, unfathomable world, really; poverty and privilege, hope and disaster. I thought of all those people in China and Burma, suddenly homeless. Parentless children; childless parents. I thought of Fariba the taxi driver in Tehran trying to feed her family because her father was bankrupt, and the gypsies in Novi Sad, Tomas with his mangy horse and handmade cart. And here I was on this ship about to land in India. It was humbling: there seemed no rhyme or reason to any of it.

I could only be thankful for the gifts I had been given – my wife and children, and the privilege of being able to travel the world like this. And I'd made some friends on the *Nedlloyd Tasman* – Kevin and Jim, Chris and Dave. It had been an honour travelling with them, and while Mumbai came ever closer, I was sorry to be leaving them behind.

12
Dial 1298 for Ambulance

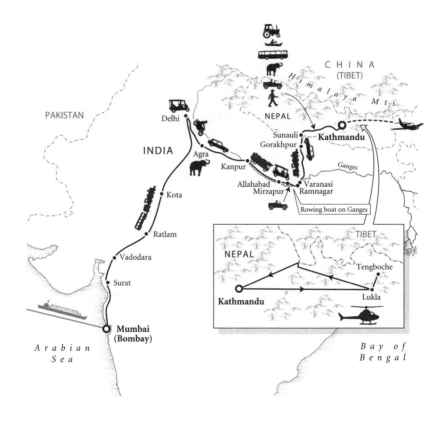

The next morning we waited for the pilot to guide us into port. It was a beautiful day, and we could see Mumbai's skyline stretching like a mini Manhattan along the coast.

The pilot had been due to arrive at eight a.m. It was now ten and there was still no sign of him. Mumbai is a tidal port and high tide was midday; if we didn't dock by then we'd have to wait until midnight. My heart sank at the prospect; the city was tantalisingly close, but now I had visions of sitting here twiddling my thumbs until the early hours of the morning.

At last the tug came alongside, bobbing up against the hull. Once the ladder was secured the pilot, a little guy with a moustache, climbed on board. Then he saw our camera and wagged a finger at us.

He was not happy. On the bridge he told us we weren't allowed to film and he was contacting port security. We explained we were making a programme for the BBC and that we had a permit. He was having none of it though, even after Mungo had gone to fetch the documentation. We decided there was no point in arguing, so we put the cameras away and let him get on with it.

As it turned out there was no problem with security or customs. I got the Indian seal stamped on my suitcase and within an hour of docking we were in the back of a taxi.

Driving into Mumbai was a mind-blowing experience. They say the smog is so bad it's like inhaling two and a half packets of cigarettes. We bumped along roads lined with ramshackle open-fronted shops selling fruit and vegetables, behind them apartment blocks and flats scraping the sky. Crowds of people crammed the pavements and the roads were chock-a-block with trucks, cabs, cars – even oxen-pulled carts. I saw an entire family on one motorbike: two little girls on the petrol tank and Mum and Dad on the seat. It was everything I'd thought it would be, vibrant and buzzing and a huge contrast from the calm of the container ship.

Some of the newer buildings looked only half built, whereas others were old and beautiful: banks of apartments from the days of the Raj, beautiful stone balconies with balustrades strung with lines of washing.

I couldn't stop grinning. We had the entire country ahead of us and a whole variety of different forms of transport planned – from ambulances and motorbikes to trucks, trains and boats; perhaps even elephants.

Our first stop, however, was R.K. Studios in Chembur, an area of the city where a lot of film production companies are based. We had a new guide with us called Rina, who could also translate for us when necessary, though luckily for me a lot of people spoke English. Rina had discovered that I had been acting since I was three, and thought I might like to see the studio that had been established by Raj Kapoor, a very famous Indian actor and film maker. It wasn't quite Bollywood but it would certainly give us a flavour. Bollywood produces more movies a year than anywhere else in the world and I couldn't travel through India without having a bit of a look.

When we got there they were filming a family singing contest; a bit like the *X Factor*, I suppose. We took up position in the walkway close to where the audience was sitting, boom-mounted cameras swinging above our heads. There were banks of lights and the set was pure kitsch – all bright pinks and gold. The presenter was a beautiful Indian woman and it looked as if her co-presenter was up there singing with his mum. She seemed very nervous, tripping over her words and breaking off before starting again. It was the final song, something of a finale, and the audience loved her. When at last she got through it they were on their feet cheering and clapping, it was a brilliant atmosphere. I knew then for sure that India was going to be fun.

Driving to the hotel, I peered out of the window, soaking it all in; the crowds, the old weathered buildings, the sights, sounds and smells of this huge city. Mumbai is the capital of Maharashtra state and has a population of about twelve or thirteen million. If you include the suburbs it's more like nineteen million, the fifth-largest metropolitan area in the world. At one point we pulled up alongside one of the city's famous black and yellow Fiat taxis and saw three adults and ten children all squashed inside.

In my hotel room I switched on the TV and caught up with what was going on around the world. We'd had 'Ocean News' on the ship, a computer printout that was updated every day, but now I was able to see just how devastating the cyclone in Burma had been. Thousands of people had been killed and thousands more were homeless. There seemed to be real difficulty getting aid into the country and foreign aid workers weren't allowed in at all. It was heartbreaking. According to the reports much of the aid that had managed to get through had been stolen by the army.

Then there was the terrible earthquake in Sichuan Province in China. It seemed that the epicentre had been in Chengdu, pretty much where we'd planned to travel. Our journey wasn't important though, not when I saw what had happened to so many poor people. One report described how a school had been flattened and the body of a child brought out still clutching a pen. It really brought home China's one-child policy: the earthquake had destroyed whole families. It showed in the faces, despair, incomprehension; survivors hunched in the rubble, their stares vacant in shock or filled with impossible grief. I thought of Olly and the kids, and once again I was struck by how fortunate I was.

I woke the next morning with a sense of real anticipation and headed downstairs to meet Rina, who was waiting to take us to a Mumbai slum. I'd been to slums in Swaziland, and also in Brazil when we had been filming in the Amazon. In fact, Mumbai reminded me a little of Belem: the heat of the place, the colour and noise; the way humidity marked the walls of the old buildings.

But the slum we were visiting today was different from any I'd seen before. There were no open sewers and the air was quite fresh. In fact, the place was generally pretty clean, and you could see the inhabitants took pride in their homes and their work. They were pottery makers, a cottage industry that has existed in this part of Mumbai for generations. The car pulled up in a busy street and I skipped between trucks and taxis to the other side, narrowly avoiding a guy on a bike piled high with trays of eggs.

Stepping into a narrow alley that ran between two ramshackle shops piled with terracotta pots, I passed a woman carrying a massive bowl of clay on her head. She wore a beautifully coloured sari and wrapped cloths round her head to form a flat surface for the heavy bowl. The strong smell of clay being fired hung in the air. Ewan and I had seen bricks from the Nile being fired in Sudan but this was different; here the air was thick with it, as strong and pungent as a large bonfire.

I was in the heart of a cluttered enclave. Secondary alleys – little tributaries from the main alley I was walking down – led off at all angles. Flowerpots and bowls were stacked in piles waiting to be collected. The smoke drifted, catching in my throat, and I tried to imagine what it must be like living with that all the time. The houses were a real hotchpotch – some of the walls were made of tin, some from stone, some of the doorways had proper doors while others had nothing more than a quilt hanging over a length of string. My first impression had been right – the place was clean, and while there was no doubt that these people were poor, I could feel the spirit of a real community.

The alley opened into a series of wider yards where the buildings were less oppressively close and the floor was set with massive stone kilns – great boxes steaming away. We were told that the clay pieces were made by hand then stacked in the bottom of the kiln. After that a great pile of shredded cotton was dumped on top and set alight. The cotton smouldered and burned very slowly, keeping the heat in and firing the clay. Ingenious and inexpensive, this was the way that the kilns had traditionally been used.

Rina explained that the community had been here for at least a hundred years, generation after generation making clay pots which sold for forty or fifty rupees – about sixty pence. Others believed it had actually been there for a thousand years but whichever it was, this was a slum where the residents had created their own way of life.

It was really hot, though, and – sorry to lower the tone – I was getting a sweaty arse. I was wearing my favourite light-green combat trousers. They're very comfortable, but unfortunately when they get wet the colour changes and I was getting a wet patch around the crack of my bum.

'Are you OK, Charley?' Rina asked. 'What's wrong with your bottom?'

It was so embarrassing: there I was in the slums of Mumbai and a woman I barely knew was asking me what was wrong with my bottom. Red-faced, I explained that there was nothing wrong, I was just a little hot and sweaty. Mungo was laughing so hard he could hardly hold the camera.

Moving on quickly, I stepped aside to let a guy wheel his bicycle past, two massive milk churns hanging off it. Kids were taking jerricans to get water, some were playing with footballs or cricket bats; it didn't look as though any of them went to school, though it was hard to be sure. Groups of white-haired women squatted on their heels, working the clay into different shapes and sizes.

We went into a house littered with pots ready for firing and mounds of malleable clay. A guy was sitting on a stool with a manually operated wheel between his legs: he was lining a mould with clay prepared for him by two women working alongside him.

'Wow,' I said. 'That's really cool. Tell me, how long have you been doing it?'

'Since this morning,' one of the women piped up.

I fell about laughing.

Smiling wryly, she sat on her heels and studied me. This was her business; she ran it with her husband who was in the next room making smaller pots with lids. He could put out thirty-five a day, he said; and the guy with the hand wheel could make fifteen of the larger ones. They had had the business for fifteen years and the guy I'd spoken to worked for them. He'd been making pots all his life, as had his father before him and his father before that: a long line of potters going right back to his great-grandfather.

There was a real buzz and sense of purpose to this area, and a lot of good humour, too. People took pride in their homes – there were flowers and neat lines of washing. Some streets were more established than others, as if the people there had a little more money; in fact one was quite wide with lean-to porches over the doorways and even the odd low-walled yard. In other areas great banks of homes were strung together, made from a mixture of cloth and banana leaves. Above them the electrical wiring that powered the place was a mass of tangled plastic. If that lot sparked the whole place would go up.

Strongest of all was the sense of community and respect. I moved out of the way as a woman carrying a bowl of clay passed it to another woman who met her halfway along the alley. A little further on the second woman was met by a third. Teamwork: it was all around us.

At the same time, the divide between rich and poor was probably clearer here than almost anywhere I'd visited. I spoke to one young guy who lived in a couple of rooms with his brother, his brother's wife, his sister and his mother. While they made pottery, he worked in a shopping mall selling luxury goods none of which he could afford himself. When he was finished for the day he came home here.

Leaving the slum we headed back towards the hotel where we were due to meet up with an ambulance crew. Up until about five years ago there were no ambulances in Mumbai, an amazing fact given it's a city of twelve million people. But it was true, if you were in an accident or collapsed for some reason there was nobody to call.

This all changed when a wealthy man's mother collapsed with a heart attack, and he realised that he had no idea what to do. Thinking that this was an unacceptable situation, he started an ambulance service with a few friends. Initially they funded the service themselves with just five vehicles, and enlisted the help of the London Ambulance Service (reputed to be the best in the world) to organise the logistics of a city-wide operation. They discovered early on that they could spend their lives begging government bodies for grants, so instead they decided to self-finance everything. With the support of an American NGO and some big business sponsors, 'Dial 1298 for Ambulance' was born.

This non-profit organisation is run by an energetic and enthusiastic CEO called Sweta. She explained that they have converted thirty small vans into ambulances, many of which are first-responders. There are also twenty much larger and fully equipped Mercedes ambulances, crewed by a driver, a helper and a doctor. The ambulances responded from all over the city and there was a payment tariff, charged only to those who could afford it. It was a great system, with the rich helping to pay for the poor.

Sweta told us that there were five hundred accidents on the railways alone every month. I was gobsmacked. She explained that the railway system is the oldest in Asia, with three major lines that the people refer to as 'locals'. She said that people just weren't conscious of their lives. The trains were massively overcrowded, the doors were always open and people hanging out of them would be hit by oncoming trains. I still couldn't get my head round the numbers – six million travelling by train every day and five hundred serious accidents a month. Sweta said that each train driver in the city kills as many as seventy people during his career. She also told us that many of the ambulance doctors had tended the victims of the Mumbai bombings. On 11 July 2006, Islamic Jihadists attacked a set of commuter trains. Two hundred and seven people were killed, seven hundred more were injured and these ambulances had been in the front line. It was hard to imagine what would have happened if the service had not been operating by that time. Undoubtedly they had saved many lives.

Next Sweta introduced us to Dr Rujuta, who showed us round the Mercedes ambulance we would be travelling in. It was as well equipped as any ambulance in the world: heart monitors, oxygen, defibrillators and suction gear as well as every drug under the sun. The stretcher was collapsible and the back of the ambulance was soundproofed and sealed against infection, which was something I'd never thought about. Then again I'd never been in the back of an ambulance before – every time I've had a bike accident it's been in the desert somewhere and I've had to get myself to the hospital.

Dr Rujuta explained that they attended anything from a heart attack to a road traffic accident or the trains, where the injuries could be really grisly. Her primary objective was to stabilise the patient and manage that stability until they were at the hospital. The patient's emotional state was also very important – accidents could be terrifying, and Dr Rujuta was very concerned to keep the patient calm.

Jumping in the back, we headed for the local station. We parked quite close to the terminal, and after the soundproof journey I was struck again by just how busy the city was. The main road was heaving with traffic and people walking in the road, ducking between the vehicles. All we could hear were car horns. The place was alive with pigeons, so many it made Trafalgar Square look like a bird-free zone; they were everywhere, like a grey cloud swarming the street. The shops were crammed side by side selling anything and everything and the variety of smells was just amazing.

In front of the shops, individual traders had goods laid out on the road: anything from magazines and books to flowers, spice and incense. It was mental, and I loved it.

Something caught my eye and looking again I saw an old beggar lying in the road with his arms sticking up as if he was dead and rigor mortis had set in.

'Is that the kind of person you deal with?' I asked the doctor.

She nodded. 'Rich or poor, our policy is the same. We treat the patient, it doesn't matter who they are.'

While she went over to see if he was all right, Mungo and I headed for the station, picking our way across the road before taking an underpass to a rickety old footbridge. I realised we'd not seen many tuk-tuks in Mumbai, and Rina told me that the government was trying to phase them out because of pollution. The old Fiat taxis chucked out a lot of CO_2 as well, and over the next few years they would also be replaced. Looking down, we could see that the streets were full of rubbish, the railway sidings caked with so much it encroached on the tracks. It wasn't just papers and stuff people had thrown away, but piles of dust and rubble, as if bits of buildings had fallen down and the debris had just been swept to one side.

It was incredibly hot, pushing forty degrees and the sweat was pouring off us. Mungo was dripping so much the camera lens was soaked. In the end he tied a home-made sweat rag round his forehead.

From the bridge we could see the station and now I understood how so many people could be involved in so many accidents. The platforms were quite narrow, and packed solid. Trains were coming and going constantly – I counted one every three minutes – and even as they were pulling in people still walked across the tracks. And I mean lots of people, crowds of them, well dressed people, poor people, old people with sticks and women carrying babies: it was madness. The trains themselves had so many passengers hanging from the open doorways it would be easy to get hit. The really scary part, though, were the trains that didn't stop: they came steaming in at a rate of knots and it was all too easy to imagine what would happen to some unsuspecting soul ambling across the tracks.

'Imagine being the driver,' I said to Mungo. 'Jesus, how traumatic is that?'

We would be taking one of these trains to Mumbai Central Station tomorrow, and from there we would board an overnight train to Delhi. We'd originally thought we might go via Jaipur, but given our commitment to UNICEF in Nepal we'd changed the route. Perhaps it was just as well – a couple of days ago six bombs had gone off there in the space of fifteen minutes – Islamic extremists. The attack had been smack in the middle of a crowded tourist area and had killed eighty people.

The next morning we were reunited with Russ, who was just back from London. He was looking forward to Delhi and picking up the Royal Enfields. Our train left at four o'clock, and we spent a rather luxurious morning in the hotel swimming pool. We figured we deserved a chilled-out morning – we had a challenging route ahead of us.

The humidity sucked the breath out of you and I'd just been for a dip when this older guy came over.

'I keep seeing you with cameras,' he said with a smile. 'What are you guys doing, exactly?'

I explained about our trip, and how we were filming it for the BBC.

'Oh right. I get it. So are you doing one of those Charley Boorman shows or something?'

I laughed. 'Or something: I am Charley. Nice to meet you.'

Before we left I took a last look across the Mumbai skyline: a mixture of old and new; the city and the sea. The downtown area was all skyscrapers whereas the residential districts were older, with sloping tiled roofs and arched balconies: there was a hint of the old world still about them. Right on the waterfront was the 'Gateway to India', a massive arched monument. It had been the first thing we had spotted when the ship steamed in. A couple of old women with straw brushes were sweeping the rubbish from around this little fragment of empire.

Bags packed, we were on a local train by one-thirty p.m., though Russ almost didn't make it. I was on board with Mungo, talking about how hot it was, how I was sweating so much I felt as though I was in a shower. Russ was still filming on the platform when the train began to pull away.

Looking round I saw him grab the rail at a run. 'Jesus Christ,' he said. 'That caught me a bit by surprise.'

Standing at the door I realised just how easy it would be to get clipped by an oncoming train; they really did pass very close and you couldn't hear them coming above the noise of the one you were on. You could be looking the other way or talking to someone and the next thing you'd be under the wheels and chopped to pieces.

Mumbai Central was an old-fashioned-looking station with the train timetables written on paper and clipped up on boards just like the old days. People were lolling on chairs, some lying asleep on the tiled floor, kids milling about everywhere. I wasn't feeling great, it was really hot and that seemed to be sapping my energy. The Chinese earthquake was on my mind, and the situation in Burma. Being so close brought home the reality of other people's lives in a way that watching TV news in Britain never could.

The Delhi train was clean, but cramped: the carriages open-plan with seats and bunks in a C shape on one side of the passageway and single seats that folded down on the other. Each area could be curtained off but it was right on top of the others and the carriage felt a little sterile, a bit like being in a hospital. Rina was travelling with us and she squatted cross-legged on the single seats she'd already folded down.

I was not having a good day: Russ told me I'd lost my sense of humour. I lay on the top bunk with the air-conditioning vent directly above me, so cool it was actually chilly. Before I settled down for the night I taped a piece of the *Herald Tribune* over it, though not until I'd read that more than 75,000 people had been killed so far in Burma. The country seemed to be falling apart and yet their military president was quoted as saying the crisis was under control and they were already rebuilding. Yeah right; less than two weeks after the cyclone had hit.

Lying back I closed my eyes and thought about home: Olly had sent me a video text on my mobile phone and she was wearing the dress I'd sent from Dubai. Kinvara had finished her SATS and had been delighted to tell me she'd got the part of the caterpillar in the school production of *Alice in Wonderland*. Doone had just finished a tough first year at secondary school. I missed them, and it would still be quite a long while before I saw them. But we had already covered close to seven thousand miles and tomorrow we would be in a new city – Delhi. I fell asleep thinking of my girls back home. They were a long way away.

13
Oiled Up and Knee Down

I woke up on another train. It's a great way to cover long distances but I'm not a fan, you never sleep properly and the next morning you feel as if you've got jet lag.

We were a couple of hours from Delhi and it was much drier here, the earth dusty and the buildings tattered and run down. The people were waiting for the rains, every inch of land sown with crops.

As the scenery flashed by, I wondered what we would do after we'd met up with UNICEF in Nepal. Our original route would have taken us in a fairly straight line from the eastern side of the Black Sea across Turkmenistan, Afghanistan and Pakistan, but the political turmoil in those countries had forced us to come south. There was no chance now of taking a Cessna from Burma to Laos, and with the Tibetan border still closed and the tragedy in Sichuan, we might have to accept defeat and take a commercial air flight from Kathmandu to Hong Kong. It was against the spirit of the journey, but that morning I couldn't see a way around it.

Perhaps it was just my general mood that left me so pessimistic. The damp heat in Mumbai had overwhelmed me and I'd not felt well at all last night. Part of it was some kind of heat exhaustion, I'm sure, but part of it was an intense feeling of homesickness.

Olly had told me that the girls were really missing me, especially Kinvara, and for the first time I wanted to jump on a plane and go home. Stupid I know: I was so lucky to be doing this in the first place, but there's always a moment on any long trip when you feel like that and there is no point in denying your emotions. If you do, your feelings can fester, and in a team as tight as ours that would bring everyone down.

In Delhi a porter came for our bags, a cloth wrap tied round his head similar to what I'd seen the women use in Mumbai. With no trouble at all he hefted not only my heavy suitcase but Russ's bag as well, and balancing them both he led us down the platform and over the footbridge to where tuk-tuks were waiting in the busy street. Suddenly I was energised; I'd never been in a tuk-tuk before and after the confinement of the train it was just what my flagging spirits needed.

The streets were crazy, even busier than Mumbai, and boy do the drivers love their horns – they were blaring out so often and so loudly you could barely hear yourself think. Mungo and I jumped in one tuk-tuk and Russ got in another and off we raced to the Imperial Hotel, first down narrow side streets and then a three-lane black top where our respective drivers really put the hammer down. The driving was nuts, and almost immediately we had to brake hard for a motorbike. The guy on the front was wearing a crash helmet but the little girl hanging on behind him wasn't, which didn't seem to make much sense. I remembered we would be riding Royal Enfields tomorrow. We really needed to get new crash helmets.

We blatted across the city, first us in front then Russ, overtaking, dropping back: all that was missing was Murray Walker's commentary. Russ's driver was so enthusiastic he forgot to brake and rammed the back of another tuk-tuk, sending Russ flying chest high into the meter.

Delhi is the second-largest city in India and sits on the banks of the Yamuna River, which used to be a trade route with Rajasthan. It has a population of around seventeen million and I think most of them were out and about on the streets that day. Hundreds seemed to be thronging a park where there was a massive World War One memorial to Indian soldiers.

We arrived at the Imperial Hotel almost simultaneously and a debate broke out about which tuk-tuk actually turned in first: while we were arguing I noticed the security guard checking under cars for explosives.

The hotel staff knew we were on our way to Australia and we were met by a woman who dabbed a bindi – a red dot – on each of our foreheads. I'd only seen women with them before, but she explained that on men they're called *tilak* and generally they only wear them on festive occasions. The other time, though, is when the man is about to undertake a long voyage, so for Russ and me it was not only appropriate but very thoughtful.

After a quick shower we jumped in another tuk-tuk. Sitting back with the canvas sides open and the breeze in my face, I decided this was my favourite form of transport so far. I was looking forward to learning more about Delhi and this was a great way to get around.

We stopped at a massive red fort called Lal Qi'lah, which strangely enough means 'red fort'. There were thousands of tourists milling about, but fortunately we bumped into a guide called Raijpal, who agreed to show us around. The fort had been completed by the Mughal Emperor Shahjahan in 1648 and it only took ten years – not bad at all considering its size. Shahjahan not only built the fort but also what is now Old Delhi, what he called Shahjahanabad. It was the capital of the Mughal Empire from 1649 until 1857.

The colour of the sandstone is natural and every piece was shipped up the Yamuna River from Agra. Shahjahan built the place as a palace but designed it like a fort; the four sides of the exterior wall are one and a half miles around and the height varies from about sixty feet where it borders the river to over a hundred where the wall faces the city. Much of the art work is marble and Shahjahan's centrepiece, the Peacock Throne, was inlaid with a hundred kilos of gold. It's not there now though; Raijpal told us that the Persians carried it off in 1739.

There's a mosque in the grounds as well as a separate palace Shahjahan used only in the monsoon, and a place on the river where he liked to fish. He had thousands and thousands of servants, acres of ornamental gardens and a hundred and twenty fountains that were pumped by hand.

There's a poem inscribed in the wall of the room where the Peacock Throne used to stand: 'If heaven is on earth it is here, it is here, it is here'.

The fort is still one of the most important landmarks in the country and each year on 15 August – Independence Day – the Prime Minister makes a speech there.

After the magnificence of Lal Qi'lah we searched for some decent crash helmets but without much luck. I'd stopped earlier at a roadside vendor but the helmets were of such poor quality you could bend them, and on these roads they'd be useless.

The next morning I was woken up at six-fifteen by music blaring, and had to call down to reception. After the luck I'd had with hotels, I was beginning to wonder whether I should just find a nice quiet park to sleep in in future.

It was Monday 19 May, our thirty-eighth day on the road, and the rains had come to Delhi. While Russ went out to buy crash helmets and wellies, I did an interview for Indian TV about Long Way Down. I took the opportunity to recount how the Lord's Resistance Army stole children as young as seven or eight in Uganda and forced them to become killers, how if one of their comrades escaped but was recaptured the others would be made to beat them to death. Some of the stories Ewan and I heard in Africa still have the power to move me to tears of sorrow and anger. I knew there were more stories waiting for me in Nepal.

By the time I was finished the Royal Enfields had arrived, parked out of the rain next to the owner's beautiful old Jaguar. They were sit-up-and-beg Bullets, silver tanks with a black frame, and one of them had two holes in the seat. Looking at the rain coming down hard and fast I knew those holes would quickly take on water and the seat would get soaked from the inside. Sitting there in a pair of jeans wouldn't be much fun. When Russ came back with a couple of lids, I took the matt black one and bagged the bike without the holes by hooking it over the mirror. Sorry, Russ.

The bikes were built in India and a few years back Russ had

been to the factory at Chennai. He told me they were assembled entirely by hand and there wasn't a computer in sight. No CNC machinery, the old lathes were turned by hand and the workers wandered around in bare feet: an iconic British marque produced on the subcontinent then sold back to Britain.

It was midday before we got going. Jo had flown in from the office in London to pick up the next batch of film rushes and she would be with us all the way to Varanasi. Mungo was going to film from the back of a battered old pickup, and Rina was still with us to help with the language. It was still chucking it down and at the gates I reminded Russ that we needed to be careful, the roads were thick with traffic and as this was the first rain they'd had in months, they would be like glass.

Just as I had predicted, it was very scary, the cars all bunching up behind one another; trucks, buses, tuk-tuks. It reminded me of riding in Cairo – that had been pretty mad too. One guy came alongside on a scooter, controlling the thing with one hand while texting with the other. Another scooter had an entire family on board, two kids together with Mum and Dad. I saw another with three kids, the youngest hunched goggle-eyed on the petrol tank.

Russ and I were riding along with vehicles coming from both sides, cutting across in front of us and weaving back again. Buildings lined the road and pedestrians crossed back and forth relentlessly. There was not a moment's respite from the madness all the way to Agra. Every driver seemed to have one hand permanently on the horn and the rain was making the tarmac treacherous. I had to laugh – it had been raining as we crossed the Wicklow Mountains, raining in Georgia when I was on the Ural, and it was raining here in India now I was on an Enfield. Every time I got the chance to ride a motorbike it was fucking raining.

I was really enjoying myself though, the bike was quite powerful and the brakes weren't bad. They were new bikes but they looked exactly like the originals; in fact if you put them side by side the only thing to differentiate them would be the electric starter.

Once out of Delhi the land spread out and there was the odd hint of greenery, but the entire way was lined with homes and shops; homespun markets that spilled into the road. I saw horses and bullocks pulling carts, and one enormous load being dragged along by a camel.

The traffic lights were particularly mad: when they changed to red the vehicles would bunch up and squeeze into every gap imaginable. Then as soon as they went green again they'd all just go for it. It was chaos, but somehow it worked. I guess if you lived there and rode those roads every day you just got used to it.

Thankfully the rain stopped but by about two o'clock it was searingly hot, so we pulled into a car park packed with bikes and went to find some lunch. We had a little bit of a drama when Russ couldn't find his key – after much alarm and self-recrimination, he found it in his back pocket. I could hardly blame him as riding along these roads was enough to frazzle anyone's brain – even one as organised as Russ's.

About two thirds of the way to Agra we pulled over to pick up some water and take a breather from the heat. Mungo was in the back of the pickup, where he'd been alternating between standing up and leaning on the roof of the cab and kneeling by the tailgate. He was kneeling as we pulled in and, shouldering the camera, he shifted his weight to hop down. As he did he cried out.

It didn't sound good: it didn't sound good at all. We went straight over. 'Are you all right, mate?' I asked him.

Mungo didn't reply right away, just let go a little breath as he lowered himself to the ground.

'I'm not sure,' he said. 'I think I've done something to my knee.' He tried to straighten his right leg and a line of sweat broke out on his face. 'Fuck,' he said, 'that hurts.'

'Maybe you've bruised it or something.'

'I don't think so, I felt something go. It's really painful.' He tried to put some weight on it and winced. 'Jesus: that feels like someone's stabbing me.'

This wasn't good: he couldn't walk, couldn't put any pressure on the leg at all. Putting down the camera, he reached for the tripod that was lying in the flatbed and used it as a crutch to move around. I took a good look at his knee – the joint was already swelling.

'That's not a good sign,' I said. 'Sorry, Mungo, but swelling so much and so soon: that's the joint trying to take care of itself.'

'There's no way you can film,' Russ added, concerned. 'You'll have to ride up front, mate; try and keep the weight off it.'

'Fuck,' Mungo said. 'I'm sorry. I've had injuries before, done ligaments and stuff, and this feels bad. I'm really sorry, guys, really; I'm gutted.'

We tried to reassure him, and said we'd check it out when we got to Agra. I suggested it might be OK after a rest, but Mungo didn't look convinced. I knew from my own experience that when you really do have a bad injury, you just know.

'My brother-in-law is an orthopaedic surgeon in Newcastle,' Mungo told us. 'I'm going to try and get hold of him and see what he thinks.'

'Good idea,' Russ said, and between us we helped him into the cab.

Russ rode on ahead, which is never a good idea. I've always thought that when you're riding in a group you should stick together; you ride to the level of the slowest rider – that's the unwritten rule. I remember in Siberia on Long Way Round, Ewan and Claudio were ahead of me when my back tyre blew. I pulled over, expecting them to stop, but Claudio wasn't checking his mirrors and they rode on for forty-five minutes before they realised I wasn't with them.

But Russ was determined to see the Taj Mahal in the sunset, and with the injury to Mungo we'd stopped longer than expected. I'd hoped for a little respite from the traffic between Delhi and Agra, but we weren't getting any. I hung back with the truck while Russ weaved between the cars, and that was the last I saw of him until later that evening.

An hour or so down the road I could feel movement at the back wheel of my bike. Looking down I saw oil on the exhaust. That meant there was oil on the back tyre. I pulled over immediately. Stripping off my helmet I took a closer look. The bike was definitely leaking oil. I thought the most likely explanation was that the Enfield technicians had overfilled it. Unhooking the air box, I saw the filter was black.

I rode it a little further down the road and pulled into a petrol station so I could figure out what to do. The oil must have bubbled up when I cracked the throttle and soaked the filter, before spurting out onto the exhaust and the rear tyre. I imagined the little overflow tank would be choked as well.

At the petrol station I had quite a crowd around me as I took the filter out and tried to give it a clean: one big guy in a brown shirt was talking away nineteen to the dozen. I explained to him, as best I could, that there was too much oil in the engine. He kept on though, pointing at the bike then pointing down the road. Finally Rina came over.

'Charley,' she said. 'He's telling you there's a Royal Enfield agency a hundred yards down the road.'

I couldn't believe it – here I was with my bike leaking oil and there was a dealer literally just down the road. I thanked the big guy and rode off. Sure enough, not a hundred yards on the right we saw a shop front with a black and red sign: 'Choudhary Motors, Royal Enfield agent'. An enclosed passage ran alongside the shop front and I could see a few bikes lined up. Riding the Bullet straight in, I stopped beside a smiling, bearded guy in a green shirt and explained the problem. He told me they could sort it out right away. Together with another chap he stripped the filter and cleaned it; then they cleaned the air box and the overflow tank. The bill came to about £1.50. For good measure they also tightened the chain.

In the meantime I'd been trying to get hold of Russ. I called him from the shop and walking out to the roadside I called again, but all I got was an answer phone.

'Russ,' I said. 'If you get this message you need to switch manually to another network. We've got an oil leak on my bike and we're trying to sort it out.'

Mungo was no longer limping – he was hopping. It looked very bad – he couldn't even put his foot on the floor now. With his arm around my shoulders I helped him get to the toilet.

'I spoke to my brother-in-law Steve,' he said. 'He reckons it's a classic torn cartilage: you know, kneeling down for a long time then giving it a twist as you get up. The cartilage catches between two bones and when you try and stand it tears.'

This was exactly what I'd feared. A torn cartilage would take a lot more fixing than an overfilled engine, and if Mungo was out of action we had a real problem. 'What did he say you should do?' I asked him.

'Give the knee a day's rest and take anti-inflammatory tablets: if it's still bad after that I'll have to get it seen to.'

'What does that mean?'

'It's not too bad: Steve reckons with keyhole surgery I can be back to normal in a few days.'

'But you'd have to fly back to London?'

He shook his head. 'Not necessarily. He knows a really good surgeon in Delhi he can hook me up with.'

We carried on with no sign of Russ and no answer from his phone. We really did need to stick together in future; there hadn't been a disaster with the bike or anything but you never know. Mungo was there, but if we had been in a bad accident there was nothing much he could have done to help.

The roads didn't get any clearer and the driving got considerably worse. I passed a tuk-tuk with about ten people in it, another with people on the roof. Swinging into the outside lane to pass a couple of bikes I was almost mown down by a huge great truck coming the wrong way. I just about avoided him and he barrelled on down our fast lane without slowing and without looking back.

It was dark when we got to Agra; we'd missed the Taj Mahal at sunset but if we were up early enough we might catch it at sunrise. Finally we made it to the hotel. By this time Mungo was pretty sore: he was pretty down too and I felt for the poor guy. There's nothing worse than being injured on an expedition; you feel like shit because you're in pain but you feel worse because you think you're letting your mates down. By the time he sat down in a chair he was really pissed off and the pain was excruciating. I knew then he'd need some kind of surgery. That meant I had to start thinking about alternatives: there was Anne, maybe, a really good freelance camerawoman from Denmark. If Mungo was out of action perhaps she could fly to Kathmandu.

We met up with Russ eventually at the hotel; he came bounding into the lobby with a grin on his face. 'That was an amazing ride,' he said, 'fast and a bit scary, but amazing.'

'You should've waited,' I said.

'Why?'

'I had an oil leak on my bike. We had to get it fixed.'

'I got behind an ambulance that had its alarm bell going; it was clearing all the traffic so I just stayed with it. I thought that you were bound to get caught up so there was no point stopping because I'd have to wait for half an hour at least. I figured the best thing to do would be to just get there.'

I looked at him a little sourly. 'So you didn't think something might've happened?'

'Where?'

'Well, behind you.'

He shrugged. 'You were all there to deal with it. I'd only have been waiting for you. If anything had happened you wouldn't turn up and . . .'

'You should've waited,' I said. 'We should stick together.'

'All right,' he said. 'We'll make that our plan in future.'

Mungo's injury was the real issue, however. We decided to go to the Taj Mahal at dawn and leave him resting in bed. If there was no improvement by midday we'd have to find a doctor.

It had been a long day, and when we got up at six the next morning, the news wasn't any better. Instead of easing off, Mungo's knee seemed to have seized up completely and the poor guy was devastated. There he was on the adventure of a lifetime and he was really worried now that he wouldn't be able to finish it. We asked Rina if she would try to set something up with a doctor as soon as one was available, while Russ and I rode out to the Taj Mahal. The thought of losing him now made me feel nervous – I'd woken up with butterflies in my stomach and I wasn't feeling any better now. I tried to remain hopeful, but it was hard.

I really felt for Mungo, he was having a very hard time. Back when we were with the ambulance in Mumbai he found out that his grandfather had died. He was an old man and he'd had a good life but it hit Mungo hard. His grandfather had been a World War Two Spitfire pilot, and throughout Mungo's life he'd been something of a mentor. The poor guy had to deal with that and now his knee had given out on him.

Strangely enough the city was almost deserted. It was probably the only time of day when you could ride a motorbike without your heart jammed permanently in your mouth. I loved it – just a few bicycles and rickshaws, horses and carts; a handful of people walking. Riding through the empty streets of Agra, I tried to chill out a little. Regardless of how things panned out with Mungo we had a big day ahead of us – we needed to cover another three hundred kilometres today to rendezvous with a truck that would take us to Varanasi.

Agra was full of old, weather-beaten pink buildings. Some of them looked as though they'd been painted that way; others were built from the same sandstone we'd seen at the fort in Delhi. We rode for half an hour, weaving around the few vehicles before turning into the car park for the Taj Mahal. This was as far as we could ride. The buildings are beginning to crumble and there is a pollution exclusion zone around them: the only way you can get close is by taking one of the electric tuk-tuks. However, one of the locals told us if we crossed the river we could view the Taj from the far side.

We both fancied riding a bit further, so back on the Bullets we headed towards the water. This was the same Yamuna River that flowed past the Red Fort in Delhi, and I was reminded of my dad's description of the Avonmore flowing through our property. India is one of those countries that really gets under your skin and funnily enough I'd spoken to Dad about it only last night: he'd spent a lot of time here and always knew I'd love it.

We cut through a poor residential area where dogs were running in the road and the houses were little more than hovels. I could hear people laughing, and saw young kids sitting in bowls of water while their parents poured more water over their heads.

We carried on between the buildings seemingly going nowhere, then took a right and a left and came out on a narrow, two-tiered bridge. It was a lumpy old ride over pitted tarmac, and the wonderful chaos had returned – rickshaws, horse carts, tuk-tuks . . . and every time a vehicle passed we were forced right to the side.

We came off the bridge, hit a road of white cobbles and there at last was the Taj Mahal rising from the mist in front of me. It just appeared like a mirage, marking the horizon with its magnificent white domes and minarets. It was more beautiful than I ever thought it would be.

We got as close as we could then parked the bikes in a run-off overlooking the flat, dusty banks of the Yamuna River. I couldn't believe it; from my home town of Annamoe all the way to the Taj Mahal, early morning mist bathing the walls, no sound except the distant voices of children down by the water. It's a Mughal tomb, the burial place of Shahjahan and his favourite wife Mumtaz Mughal, built on a plinth with a maze of basement chambers underneath. A local man explained that these were built on hardwood pilings over the water, which sounded like the buildings in Venice. He said that the architect designed it that way so that if an earthquake hit the region the water would move rather than the earth, thus keeping the building from collapsing.

Built between 1631 and 1653, it took twenty thousand men working day and night to complete. The buildings are inlaid with precious and semi-precious stones, and at varying times of the day the ambience is completely different. At night the place glows red in the moonlight. In the early morning it's a sort of sky blue, and in perfect sunshine it is milky white. Legend has it that when it was finished Shahjahan decided to cut the thumbs off his workers, all twenty thousand of them, so they could never build another Taj Mahal. That's gratitude for you.

While very conscious of pollution, we were keen to get as close as possible on the bikes: Ewan and I rode right to the great pyramids and that had been a fantastic experience. The closest we could get here was an old brick road where a group of policemen were gathered. When we explained what we were doing they let us take the bikes almost as far as the water. The view was amazing; the road fenced with spiked railings on one side and a canopy of trees on the other and between them, across the low-lying Yamuna River, one of the great wonders of the world.

It was just such a pity that Mungo wasn't there: we'd come so far together on so many different forms of transport and it was one of the iconic moments of the expedition. But I suppose that's life. Some injuries happen so unexpectedly – just standing up from a kneeling position and that's it, you're out of the game. As we stood there the clouds began to gather. We could hear thunder rumbling in the distance.

Russ came alongside me. 'The bullocks are lying down in the fields,' he said. 'That means the monsoon rains are coming.'

Below us a woman in a long skirt drove half a dozen cows across the muddy river.

Back on the bikes we headed for the hotel. The main road was heaving again and we were bimbling along between the tuk-tuks and taxis when we saw an elephant on the far pavement. It was just standing there with its keeper, salivating over a stack of fresh watermelons that another man was selling by the side of the road.

It had to be done: all this way and all these forms of transport, this might be my only chance. Parking the bikes further up the road we walked back to the young guy and his elephant.

'Hello,' I said. 'My name's Charley and I'd like to ride your elephant.'

He just looked at me.

'We don't have to go very far.' Russ pointed back to where we'd parked the Enfields. 'Just from here to there by those motorbikes. Is that all right?'

The young guy held out his hand. 'Five hundred rupees,' he said.

He showed me how to grab the elephant by the ears and climb onto his trunk. Then the elephant lifted me up and I clambered over his head to a bunch of blankets strapped together as a sort of harness.

With the keeper leading and Russ looking on I rode about thirty yards to where we'd parked the bikes. Not the longest journey I've ever taken but definitely the most exotic. I would have liked to have carried on, but we had to get Mungo to the doctor so, journey completed, I climbed down again using the elephant's raised foreleg as a step.

As we pulled up at the hotel Mungo came hobbling out on a crutch. Rina had found an orthopaedic surgeon so we grabbed a cab. Mungo sat in the front, his face grey with pain.

'How are you feeling, mate?' Russ said.

Mungo made a face. 'Not too good to be honest. The knee's no better. I feel like a dead weight. I'm bitterly disappointed. I hope it's something that can be sorted quickly. I don't care what it is: I just want to get on with it.'

We looked at him.

'You know,' he said, 'if you're on an expedition and you get dead weight you have to cut the rope: kind of how I feel at the moment.'

We got to the clinic and helped him out of the car. There was a short flight of steps up to the doors of the LIC Medical Examiner, a dirty white building in the middle of Agra with a guard carrying a double-barrelled shotgun.

There were a few people in the waiting room, a handful of women who looked a little suspiciously at us, together with a bunch of kids clearly intrigued by three Englishmen with a camera. The receptionist ushered us up the narrow corridor to Dr Arun Kapoor's office. The door was open but he wasn't there. Mungo perched on the examining table.

'This looks all right,' I said, pointing to a display of plastic bones. 'He's got lots of knee joints and stuff.'

Mungo was in no mood for jokes but someone had to lighten the atmosphere.

'I think the best thing to do would be to chop it off,' I went on. 'I'll use the Leatherman, which is always a good tool. It's got a saw and I can cut through the tendons.'

'You'd be better blowing it off,' Russ suggested. 'Dynamite.'

I shook my head. 'No, that would be too messy.'

Fortunately the real doctor came in at this point. Mungo explained what he'd done and the doctor examined the knee, working it this way and that and asking Mungo what hurt. Side to side was OK, but trying to press the knee flat and straighten the leg was agony.

'I think you've twisted the patella,' the doctor said. 'But we had better take an X-ray to make sure.'

That sounded quite positive, a twisted knee wasn't so bad, surely? We accompanied Mungo along the corridor to the X-ray room, where he was laid on the table and his knee twisted round so the radiographer could see it properly. A few minutes later we were back in Dr Kapoor's office looking at the pictures.

The tendons on each side of the knee seemed to be all right and nothing was cracked or broken, but Dr Kapoor couldn't see the ligaments.

'The X-ray won't show them,' he explained. 'The only way to

see the ligament is with an MRI.'

'Can we do it here?' Russ asked him.

'Not here. You have to go about three . . .' I thought he said 'hours' down the road and my heart hit the floor. But he'd actually said three kilometres. Thank God. He marked the referral 'urgent' and told us we could get the scan done right away.

Russ was trying to encourage Mungo, who was looking even more deflated by this inconclusive result. 'Don't worry, mate,' he said. 'There's still a whisper it could be bruising.'

Back in the taxi we discussed our options. 'Depending on what it is, you and I could ride on today if we wanted,' Russ said to me. 'If it's just bruising, Mungo could follow later.'

I shook my head. 'I don't want to do that. I think we should keep the group together no matter what now. Especially after what happened when you went racing ahead yesterday.' I wagged my head at him. 'What if you'd been in an accident, eh?'

He shrugged. 'I'd have been fine. I was behind an ambulance. No, you're right,' he added more seriously. 'We should stick together.'

It felt like the right decision for another reason – by the time we left it would be getting late and it would take us hours to get to the rendezvous. Most of it would be on crap roads in darkness and that was just dangerous. We were due to meet a truck tomorrow morning at three a.m. and the driver would take us to Varanasi. If we couldn't ride there, we'd just have to figure out another way of getting there. More long-term we had to think about what we were going to do about filming if it turned out that Mungo was going to be out of action. Russ had already been on the phone to London trying to find another shooter to join us further on. He could take over himself in the meantime if necessary; we'd made a documentary together called *Missing Face* where Russ filmed the whole thing.

Mungo had his MRI scan, which took thirty-five minutes and was interrupted by a power cut. Russ and I waited for him in a room full of bandaged people. We had to pay 3,500 rupees – about £38. Once it was done we had an hour or so to wait for the results and then it was back to Dr Kapoor so he could interpret them for us.

In the meantime we kicked around a few suggestions as to what we'd do if Mungo had to go home. We decided that if it was only bruising and he could get away with a few days' rest, we'd wait for him. If it was a torn cartilage we'd fly him home either to rest or have some kind of treatment. His brother-in-law had said a tear could be sorted very quickly with keyhole surgery and Mungo was convinced he could be up and around in as little as a few days. Personally I wasn't sure about that, but then I'm not a surgeon.

Russ and I talked about how we were going to get to Varanasi. We'd been on the phone to the office already and Robin, another member of the team, was flying out to meet us. There was a potential problem getting him a visa so quickly but Lucy was on to the embassy trying to pull out all the stops.

I wanted to spend a decent amount of time at Varanasi on the banks of the Ganges, where people bathe in the water to cleanse themselves of their past, present and future wrongdoings. Considered one of the most spiritual places on earth, it's a sacred city of Hinduism, and believers say it's where the physical world meets the spiritual.

Meanwhile we were doing our own bit of praying for Mungo. He was looking more and more disconsolate.

Russ suggested a bath chair: 'We could push you to Nepal,' he said. 'Or chuck you in a rickshaw.'

'Yeah, right,' Mungo said.

An hour later we had the magic envelope and got a taxi back to Dr Kapoor's office.

'*Should I stay or should I go?*' I was singing the old Clash song as we climbed the steps to the clinic, where the guard with the shotgun looked on impassively. '*Should I stay or should I go now?*' I was waving the envelope. '*Should I stay or should I go?*'

Mungo wasn't impressed.

'Two words,' Russ stated. 'Bruise or tear. Bruise he stays, tear he goes.'

For all the jokes the uncertainty was getting to us. Back in the office Dr Kapoor sat down, the only sound the hum of the air-conditioning. He took a moment, Russ seated opposite him, me at the door and Mungo perched on the examining table looking worried.

Dr Kapoor perused the document: 'Well,' he said slowly. 'There does seem to be a minor tear.'

'Tear?' I said.

'Yes.'

Mungo was almost in tears.

'You can't do anything about that here?' Russ asked the doctor. 'You can't fix that?'

He shook his head. 'Three weeks' rest would do it. Anything else – surgery, for example – would be up to the doctors back in Britain.' He looked sympathetically at Mungo. 'I'm sorry,' he said. 'I don't want to tell you that, you're on such a lovely mission. But I'd rather see you walking properly in Sydney.'

'A partial tear,' I repeated.

He nodded.

It was bad news, the worst. Russ was looking at Mungo. 'OK,' he said. 'The best thing to do is get Mungo home rather than jolly you along, mate.'

'We can meet up with you again in Hanoi,' I said. 'You can't walk, Mungo, and in Nepal that's pretty much all we'll be doing.' I was doing my best to let him down gently. 'We have to fly into China now anyway so you won't miss as much and . . .'

'What do you think?' Russ asked him.

Mungo was silent, the emotion etched in his face. 'There are two things,' he stuttered. 'I want it to heal properly otherwise it'll be an ongoing problem. The other issue is . . .' Suddenly he broke down, chin on his chest. 'I can bury my grandfather.'

It was all too much: he'd been keeping a lid on his emotions about his grandfather and now this.

Russ was on his feet. 'Oh, Mungo, man.' He threw an arm round Mungo's neck and Mungo held on to him. 'In that case you have to go back. When is the funeral?'

Mungo grabbed a breath. 'A week on Friday.'

'Then you can come back,' I said. 'Go to the funeral and get better. Then you can come out again.'

Tears were rolling down Mungo's face. 'I wanted to,' he said, 'since I found out, of course I did, but . . .'

'Do that,' Russ told him. 'That's the right thing to do anyway.'

'It makes sense,' I said. 'Go back, get better and then you can fly out and join up with us again later. Fate has brought us to this point, Mungo. I'm a great believer in that. Everything happens for a reason.'

'He's right,' Russ added. 'This injury means you can go to the funeral: it's a silver lining to that grey cloud. Go back and get fixed. We'll make ends meet and hook up with you again later in the trip.'

The doctor bandaged Mungo's knee and fitted his leg with a brace. Then we headed back to the hotel to regroup. 'See what your brother-in-law says,' I told him, 'then come back if you want to.'

'Want to?' Mungo had recovered a little now and looked long and hard at me. 'You'll have to cancel every flight to wherever you are to stop me. I hate doing this to you, guys, leaving you in the lurch like this.'

'Don't worry about us,' I said, patting his arm. 'You're a shit cameraman anyway.'

14
The Longest Day

We booked Mungo on to a business class flight back to London so he'd have some room to stretch his leg. He planned to see his brother-in-law as soon as he got home and he'd keep us posted.

We hadn't realised how much Mungo had been affected by his grandfather's death. We'd been sympathetic but he's not a demonstrably emotional guy and I don't think he really knew himself until that moment in the doctor's surgery. Russ and I would have happily camped up for a couple of days so he could go back for the funeral, but he probably felt he would be letting the team down. We told him that no matter what the prognosis was regarding his knee, he must not come back until after his granddad's funeral. As I said, I'm a great believer in fate – this was his opportunity to say goodbye and he had to take it.

Mungo's flight wasn't until two the next morning, and it was hard leaving him behind in Agra. I know how that feels – it's no fun when you're injured and the expedition is going on without you. We moved on to a small town about 170 miles further on and I finally fell into bed around eleven p.m. Four hours later I was awake again, just before the alarm went off. We were heading out to a truck stop where Rina reckoned we ought to be able to hitch a ride. We had a boat booked to get us across the

Ganges from Ramnagar at four this afternoon and I really wanted to make it.

Truck drivers are hard to track down in advance – I'd thought there was one waiting for us, but had misunderstood the situation. Instead we were just going to rock up and see what we could get – they tended to set off early in the morning, so this was the best time to catch someone.

The truck stop – a cluster of buildings by the road – was a little way out of town. A bunch of men were sitting on tables watching some old B movie on TV while others slept on makeshift beds lined up along the wall outside. It was still pitch-black, but there had been a huge storm last night and even now the odd bolt of lightning lit up the sky. Inside the cafe flies were buzzing round the drivers, the food, the urns of tea. No one seemed very communicative. Standing on the sandy ground pitted with dark puddles I started to think that a lift wasn't going to be very likely.

However, after a few negative responses, a young guy called Raj, wearing a vest and baseball cap, slapped away the flies and told us he could take us to a town close to Ramnagar. We could get a bus the rest of the way.

He pointed out his Tata truck, a big beast with a massive cab, and said we'd leave at four forty-five. When the time came the guy he shared the driving with was still asleep on one of the beds outside. Raj prodded him but he just rolled over. When Raj called his name he rolled over again. Taking a glass of water Raj tossed it over him and the poor guy sat up spluttering. This was Lallan, Raj's partner. Raj told him it was time to get going.

They covered very long distances, driving all over India, and took it in turns at the wheel. Today they were transporting vegetables, and there was a third guy called Kamar riding along with them. Kamar's dad owned the truck.

It was just what we'd been hoping for – ancient, flat-fronted, with the windscreen split in two sections with a partition between them. The cab was double sized with a bench seat in the back and a place between the driver and passenger where I would be able to squat with my back to the windscreen. We all piled in and Raj got the engine started. The steering wheel was worn from years of use and it had the old-style gear change on the column. After idling for a few minutes to get the engine warm we left the TV, the flies and the half-dozen sleeping drivers and headed off between the parked trucks.

It was strange and exhilarating taking off like that in the dead of night. The last few days had been pretty emotional but this was fun – it was exactly why we were here. I sat between Raj and Kamar with Russ and Rina in the back, Lallan on the far side, eyes closed, slumped against the window. I was tired but excited, riding along the clear roads in the dark, heading for the Ganges in an old vegetable truck. We'd watched so many of these trucks barrelling along on our side of the road, the drivers indifferent to the oncoming traffic, and now it was our turn to experience it first-hand.

The truck was personalised just as Asadollah's had been in Iran, a home away from home for the crew. Raj told me he made about £100 a month, which appeared to be a decent wage here: I'd spoken to cleaners in Agra who only made about £10. Raj had been driving for eight years or so and made enough money to buy a house with his family. His story echoed many others we'd heard here. India isn't a poor country, it's just that the money isn't evenly distributed. If you could get yourself a half-decent job in the city you could maybe pull enough money together to get a nice home and a pretty decent life.

The sun came up revealing a flat, dry landscape, with skinny trees and battered-looking buildings. The road was a narrow ribbon of tarmac in an otherwise sandy world; I wondered what it would look like when the rains came.

A little further on we stopped for tea, passing between lines of parked trucks before pulling off on to a patch of baked ground. These stops were spread out across the country, and drivers would stop, eat and sleep here, hooking up with old friends and generally shooting the breeze. Next door the cafe owner was making spicy naan bread in cast-iron frying pans and served us milky tea. I watched a couple of his helpers fetch water from a large metal tank; they used the water for the tea and for washing the pots and pans. I thought it might be the cover to some kind of well, but taking a wander over I found it was in fact just a tank, with a large catfish swimming in the bottom. As Russ said to me later, there isn't a minute in any day when there isn't something to see in this country.

With the sunrise came the traffic, and the cacophony of horns. India truly is an amazing and vibrant country; there was so much going on I spent most of my time staring in wonder. It felt very safe, too – the people were universally friendly and despite travelling so far and so wide, we had never once felt even vaguely threatened.

By nine-thirty it was forty degrees and we were roasting. We decided to ride on top of the load for a while and get some fresh air. It was quiet up on the roof, away from the engine. The breeze was a relief – it was very hot here, as hot as it had been in Sudan.

'Nice to get the wind in your face,' Russ said. 'It's a fantastic place, isn't it? And have you noticed that everywhere you look there are kids playing cricket?' He pointed to an open patch of waste ground where a bunch of barefoot young lads in rags were bashing a ball around. 'Anywhere else it would be football, but in India it's cricket. I was thinking only last night how you can really see the influence Britain has had on some of the places we've been through: good and bad.'

I noticed that I had been putting on weight: we'd eaten fantastic food throughout our journey and in the last few days I'd really porked out. And moving from one form of transport to another meant that I wasn't getting much exercise. I decided to eat less and do more exercise from now on, starting right then with some push-ups on top of Raj's cab.

Raj let us off at a crossroads on the edge of a small town where he told us we could get the bus to Ramnagar. We had all our bags and Mungo's camera pack and we were due to meet the boat at four p.m. I'd missed both the sunset and sunrise at the Taj Mahal and I did not want to arrive in Varanasi in darkness.

It was almost two p.m. now and having been up since three I was pretty tired. The truck had been great, just what we wanted, and we were on time. Now, however, things started to go wrong. Looking around for a means of getting to the bus station we couldn't find anything. We were too far out of town and the only vehicles passing were motorbikes or carts drawn by bullocks.

I was hot, sweating and frustrated, worrying that we'd never get the boat in time. At last a couple of tuk-tuks came by and we flagged them down. They took us into town and the traffic just backed up. It was bedlam again – narrow streets packed with people, carts, bikes, tuk-tuks and local buses weighted down with passengers. And all the time the incessant honking of horns.

I watched the buses lumbering along at a snail's pace, stopping every two minutes. 'We'll never make it to the boat in a bus,' I said. 'It's forty miles and they're too slow. What about a jeep?' I gestured as one clattered past. 'You can rent those. If this guy drops us at the bus station we can grab one. There are bound to be some hanging around.'

There weren't. The tuk-tuk dropped us inside a gated courtyard of baked earth surrounded by old, broken-down buildings. We got out, unloaded our gear and I stood there with my hands on my hips, the sweat pouring off me. There was not a single bus in sight and no jeeps, nothing but a couple of ancient tuk-tuks and the odd rickshaw. I was beginning to feel a bit stressed.

'Well,' Russ said. 'I've never seen a bus station with no buses in it before.'

'Come on, this is a waste of time.'

We took off into the streets, looking for someone who could take us to Ramnagar. We made our way through streets heaving with rickshaws; market stalls and darkened shops selling just about everything you can imagine. At last we found a line of jeeps, the type the US army used to use – a couple of seats in the front, benches on either side of the flatbed, and a canvas canopy.

'That'll do,' I said, pointing to a blue one that looked in reasonable condition. The driver assured us we could get to Ramnagar by four p.m., so we loaded up. The seats were incredibly hard and there was no suspension, but the major problem soon turned out to be that the jeep wouldn't actually start. Jesus, it was turning into that kind of day. The driver spent a good few minutes spinning the engine over with no sign of it firing before he got out.

'Here we go,' Russ said. 'The bonnet's coming up.'

I jumped down and was about to tell the driver we'd find

another jeep when the engine burbled into life. Russ hauled me back and we tore off through the crowds with the horn blaring all the way to a petrol station.

I sat back with a sigh. All that haste just to sit beside a petrol pump. Roll with it, I told myself: it's hot and you've got a headache. If Ewan was here he'd tell you to suck it up, Charley: it's just one of those days.

We bounced all the way to Ramnagar. Every time we hit a bump Russ and I would leave the seat and smack our heads off the metal bars that held the canvas hood in place. I already had a headache from the heat and lack of sleep, and this wasn't helping. Neither was the traffic: we were nose to tail, the only respite from the fumes and the heat the bit of breeze that drifted through the hood. Stopping at a level crossing we waited in a mass of other vehicles as a goods train thundered by, boxcar after boxcar. When the barrier finally lifted nobody moved. There was so much traffic bunched together on both sides of the railway line nobody was going anywhere.

Suck it up, Charley. Hands hooked in my armpits I took a breath, sat back and closed my eyes.

Somehow the drivers got it sorted. After lots of yelling and hooting of horns they got the traffic into a line that filtered across the tracks and on we went. The driver was as good as his word and despite all the hold-ups he got us to Ramnagar just after four. Hoping that our boat would still be there, I hefted the gear and looked around for the river.

The River Ganges is 1,500 miles long, and the epitome of atmospheric, spiritual India. We couldn't find it. After much hunting I suggested we head to the old fort. All the other forts we'd seen had been built close to rivers. Sure enough, the Ganges flowed on the other side. We met our skipper, Supla, outside a cafe, and he led us down a dirt road with derelict buildings on one side and some empty-looking shops on the other.

For some reason I'd been expecting some kind of power boat, but this was a skiff – a rowing boat with an oarsman in the front and a surly-looking guy with a moustache on the tiller. The travel company Explore had arranged this for us. There were lots of them all moored together with kids swimming alongside, laughing and joking, duck-diving and splashing each other. I could see Varanasi on the other side. Supla promised he'd have us there before the sun went down.

Climbing aboard I took a moment to stretch out under the canopy where some rugs were laid for us to sit on. After the sweating metal of the jeep it was bliss.

'What a way to end the day,' I said to nobody in particular. 'A trip up the Ganges.'

The guy at the back poled away from the shore. After a few minutes I sat down alongside the oarsman. Taking an oar each, we pulled into the middle of the river.

'2012,' I told him. 'The London Olympics. England and India rowing side by side.' It was just what I needed, a bit of therapeutic exercise after a hectic, stressful day. 'Hey, Russ,' I said. 'Isn't this great? Here we are on the Ganges rowing a boat to Varanasi, one of the holiest places on earth. I'm going to ask for all my past, present and future sins to be forgiven – hope it works.'

I'd say a prayer for my little family as well.

'I spoke to Mungo on the phone,' I added. 'He's on his way up to Newcastle and they've pencilled in an op for tomorrow. He told me he's desperate to get back.'

'He needs to be fully fit,' Russ said, 'for his sake. Did I tell you we tracked down another cameraman in the meantime? Indian guy called Wency – short for Wenceslas, apparently. He's pretty experienced. We're meeting him later for a beer. There's another guy coming down from Nepal as well, so we should be all right.'

We made it across just as the sun dipped behind the river temples. Varanasi – one of the oldest and most spiritual cities in the world. The perfect place to wash away the cares of the last few days.

The following morning I spoke again to Mungo who was already in hospital, about to have his operation. It was only a couple of days ago that he'd been in the back of that pickup when his knee gave out. Funny to think we'd been spending all this time escaping air travel, but I had to admit that it certainly came in handy in a crisis. Mungo said the operation would take about forty-five minutes and all being well he should be released later that afternoon. By then he ought to know how long the recovery time was likely to be and how soon he'd be back. It was great news – Mungo was very much part of the team and I missed not only his camerawork but his company. In the meantime, though, we had Wency and Deepak, the new shooter who'd come down from Nepal.

Varanasi felt different from anywhere else we'd visited in India. There were the same mad streets, of course, full of wonderfully ramshackle buildings, narrow alleys and backstreets, open doorways and lines and lines of washing. There were children playing, dogs sniffing around for scraps; but unlike Delhi or Mumbai the roads were not jam-packed with cars. The main mode of transport seemed to be rickshaw or tuk-tuk and there was a different atmosphere. Mumbai had been bonkers; wall-to-wall people full of bustle and industry. Delhi had been more open and there were more cars, people were more serious and it had the feel of a capital city. In Varanasi there was a mellow feel although it was still incredibly busy. Walking through its streets the morning after our arrival, I felt refreshed and very relaxed. I passed shops selling all kinds of food, silks, rugs and lots of brass objects. There was a strong, distinctive smell to the place: spices, incense, the river.

Russ and I each jumped in a rickshaw. I told my driver we wanted to go down to the river. He was a skinny guy of about forty with oily black hair, very quiet except for a really terrible cough. Halfway through town I felt so guilty I asked the poor guy to stop. He thought the fare was over and began working out what I owed him but I helped him down from the saddle. 'You ride in the back,' I said. 'I'll pedal.'

He looked puzzled, eyes wide: he didn't understand.

'You sit there,' I pointed to the multi-coloured seat. 'I'll pedal.'

Still he stared, not quite getting what I meant. He spoke a little English but I don't suppose anyone had ever offered to carry him before.

I needed some exercise and riding a rickshaw couldn't be that difficult. Ringing the little bell I joined the melee, the little guy sitting uncertainly in the back. The streets were thick with other rickshaws and tuk-tuks and I was part of society now, a rickshaw driver in Varanasi avoiding shopkeepers and stallholders, priests in red skirts and sashes. I was competing with tuk-tuks and motorbikes, scooters piling past me. Everyone was looking on and laughing: a traveller, a tourist, riding the rickshaw with the owner in the back. It was hard work and hot, and I had to avoid people who just sauntered out in front of me. I also had to avoid the cows.

The cow is sacred to Hindus. Rajiv, a local guy we had hooked up with, had explained that the cow represents the maternal force, because it gives milk and nurtures the young. There were lots of mothers here, wandering about all over the place; black ones, grey ones, they reminded me of the oxen we'd seen in Ethiopia. Oblivious to the traffic, they just stood there or lay down where they fancied with drivers having to go round them. I wondered what they ate, where did they sleep? Where did they go at night?

The answer was they didn't go anywhere – they just crashed out where they pleased. They are so revered, they can do whatever they want. They scavenged for vegetables, dropped food, samosas, bits of bread, anything they could find. The trouble was much of the food these days came wrapped in plastic and I saw one black cow trying to lick vegetables from a bag and ending up swallowing the whole thing. I'd seen it in Africa – the plastic bag, a blight on the animal kingdom.

Despite the traffic, the pedestrians and the cows, the rickshaw was just what I needed. I got the hang of its weight and weaved my way towards the river. I had thought it would be impossible to crash in a rickshaw, but I soon saw I was wrong. I got up a bit of speed but was bunched in behind a tuk-tuk when the driver braked and, taking evasive action, I almost slammed into two other rickshaws. My passenger was having kittens. I tried to placate the other drivers. 'Sorry, guys, my fault. Sorry,' I said.

They forgave me and we rode on but having almost lost his rickshaw the driver had had enough and demanded I give it back. It was hot and sweaty and by the time I got off I had the ubiquitous wet patch on my bum. I paid the driver and, leaving him still looking pretty bewildered, Russ and I found a roadside vendor and grabbed a cup of tea. There were tea sellers everywhere, stirring great pots of the stuff already mixed with milk, kept warm on stone-block burners fired by charcoal. The guy who served us dipped a saucepan then filtered the tea through a homemade sieve into a teapot. When the pot was full he grabbed a couple of glasses and poured from a great height like some Spanish wine waiter.

'Smells just like English tea,' Russ said.

'Which mostly comes from India,' I reminded him.

There was a really mellow feel to this city: it was chaotic, yes, but there was a method to the mayhem. I loved it, the lack of cars brought everything closer – the tiny shops, the market stalls. Rajiv told us that the market was the heart of Varanasi, and I could see what he meant.

As I sipped my tea, I watched grey monkeys climbing telephone poles. Apparently they were the cause of a lot of vandalism in the city. Like some raucous, unruly gang, they tear bits off rickshaws, chew shops' canopies and pick up food wherever they can find it. They even find their way into people's houses.

I could hear bells ringing everywhere – from rickshaws, and from the hand bells used by priests in their religious ceremonies. I could hear them even above the blaring of tuk-tuk horns. From streets and narrow passageways hundreds of half-naked kids ran down to the water and yet amidst the pandemonium there was a feeling of peacefulness, a real sense of spirituality and well being.

Varanasi is the melting pot of India, pilgrims come from all over the country to bathe in the river and cleanse themselves of their sins. There is a morning ceremony and an evening ceremony with each priest enacting the same ritual at the same time on the *ghats*, or steps, that lead from just about every major street down to the water.

Everywhere we walked people had red lips and teeth from chewing betel nut. I'd had some in the truck yesterday and it was foul: here, it seemed, everyone was into it. Maybe that's what kept them mellow.

I could smell the river now: it was filthy, full of pollution and yet people swam in it and bathed in it. Some of them even walked on it.

I did a double take. At the far end of the street I could see the water, muddy brown between the buildings and I swear people were walking on it. Two or three at least. As we got closer, though, I realised that it wasn't the river, it was mud: what I could see was the bank on the other side. I turned to Russ, shaking my head and laughing.

'I really thought people were walking on the water. What an idiot!'

Rajiv took us out on a boat rowed by his mate, who was full of smiles and laughter. He told me he'd been working on the river all his life. His father had done the same and his grandfather before that. He carried pilgrims and tourists, and in the monsoon months when there were no tourists, he transported cargo back and forth from Ramnagar.

We headed gently downstream. The water really was filthy: some workmen were fixing a sewage pipe jutting from the beach, and it looked as though the sewage was pumped straight into the river. The workmen told us it was filtered but I could see human turds lying among the stones. What really amazed us, though, was the water supply, a couple of pink stone towers that sucked up river water and fed the city. The problem was they were downstream from the sewage outlet. We pointed it out to Rajiv but he just shrugged.

They took us close to the temples and massive houses with their turrets and towers; imposing structures that spoke of the old days and provincial rulers. It was dusk now and kids were swimming, just their heads bobbing above the water. Women in brightly coloured saris stood waist deep, or poured water over their heads while squatting on the steps. I bought a flower candle and, saying a prayer for my family, I sent it on its way.

At night the city took on a whole new aspect as about forty priests gathered on the ghats, where they set up Hindu shrines and altars. They performed their ceremonies standing on strips of carpet at intervals along the paved stone promenade, and pilgrims gathered for songs and worship. Assisted by groups of young women blowing conch shells, each priest went through the same rituals at exactly the same time, so the whole city seemed to be singing. The sound echoed across the water, reaching our boat as we drifted by; an incredible experience, and very moving.

As we stared out across the water we could see funeral pyres burning, the bodies laid on piles of wood with no coffin, just their faces covered. It was believed that if they were cremated they would not be reborn, allowing their spirits to rise free. Rajiv told us that people brought the bodies of relatives from all over India, and even abroad, to burn on the banks of the Ganges. He pointed out a blue building with two stone tigers overlooking the water – the tax office where the families of the dead paid the cremation duty. The tax was high if you were wealthy and low if you were poor. No one was denied the right to send their loved one to heaven in the traditional way.

I really liked this place, it was so rich and diverse; the people so full of life and yet with an acute sense of death that was as much a part of their lives as making tea or driving a rickshaw. The houses along the front were beautiful and ancient, weathered by river winds and monsoon rains. We asked Rajiv if there was any way we could see inside one. He thought about that for a moment then said perhaps there was.

We tied up the boat and, leaving the commercial area, followed Rajiv through a labyrinth of passageways and alleys, before climbing some steps to a large house that was split between four families. He introduced us to a small, white-haired man, a former banker who was now a Hindu priest. He explained that he had worked in the bank all his life, but had taken early retirement. Now he devoted himself to worship and meditation. He showed us round the house, leading us to the balcony and its stunning view, taking in the curve of the river and the mud banks beyond. Our host explained that in the old days all these great houses had been owned by kings and queens, but when it was decreed they could no longer own property, their workers took possession. They'd been split into apartments and passed down from generation to generation. This had been his uncle's place and he lived here for fifty years before his nephew took it over. He loved books and art and spent most of his time meditating or portrait painting. The rest of the time he taught literature to schoolteachers so that they in turn could teach the children.

In a way, the priest personified Varanasi perfectly – calm, spiritual, but fully engaged in life. When we had soaked up the view, we thanked him for letting us into his home, and left him to his meditation.

15
The Cold Chain

Tomorrow we were leaving for Nepal. We had decided to buy a tuk-tuk in Varanasi and drive it to the station before taking a train to Gorakhpur. After that we would try to ship the tuk-tuk back to our office in London. We already had bikes stored there from Long Way Round and Race to Dakar and one of the trucks from Long Way Down, so it seemed fitting to have a suitable souvenir from By Any Means. I quite fancied pootling around in it in London, too.

When we told Rajiv our plan he looked at us a little strangely then shrugged his shoulders and said that anything was possible. An hour later a driver showed up with this really battered-looking tuk-tuk which he said he would sell us. It was almost midnight by now so we asked the driver to bring it back the next morning, where we could see it properly and give it the once-over.

Back in my room I called Mungo.

'Charles.'

'Mungo, how are you?'

'I'm OK. I'm at my sister Claire's house with my leg up on the sofa.'

'How did it go?'

'Really well, though the tear was more serious than they first thought: it's what they call a "bucket handle".'

Mungo explained that they had had to remove most of the cartilage, which did sound a lot more serious than we'd thought. He didn't think it would cause him any problems in the short term but he might suffer a bit of arthritis when he was older. He reckoned it would be ten to fourteen days before he was fit enough to come back out, but should have full mobility in as little as three or four days.

I couldn't believe it: literally a couple of days since it happened and there he was already recovering from an operation. His only problem was he'd rented out his house for the duration of the trip and so for the next few weeks he'd be kipping on people's floors.

In the morning Rajiv showed up with the guy and his tuk-tuk. In the daylight it looked pretty ropey, but, pulling the lever to the left of the driver's seat, the engine started first time. The only thing wrong with it was a broken plug lead, but it clearly still functioned. The exhaust was held on by a piece of wire and Russ reckoned one of the wheel bearings was shot, but the brakes were fine. Taking Rajiv to one side we told him how much we were prepared to part with and left it to him to negotiate a deal: if he beat the seller down far enough to make a profit for himself, that was fine by us.

Deal done, we had our very own tuk-tuk. Loading the bags, I drove Russ across Varanasi to the station. Halfway there the tuk-tuk conked out and rolled to a stop. I thought I knew what it was, though, and when I lifted the seat I could see that the plug lead was off. Wedging it in place, we were going again. By the time we made it to the station – a beautiful old building with a massive wheel on the top – we were both quite attached to our new vehicle, and were quite sorry to leave it behind. We wrote little dedications on the front – 'hope to see you in London'.

The train was half an hour late, so we sat on the platform and waited. It was the hottest day we'd had so far – sticky and humid – and we were very glad to get on board the air-conditioned train when it did finally arrive. I rode by the open door, the wind blowing in my face, watching the flat and thirsty scenery flash by – small villages and arid farmland. Later on we got a call from

Lucy confirming that as far as China was concerned a direct flight from Kathmandu to Guangzhou, north of Hong Kong, was our best bet.

On our last day in India I was woken by a thunderclap and rain rattling the window of my hotel room. It was just about dawn and the power was off, but I could see enough to pick out trees being buffeted by the rain and wind. Rain was seeping through the window frame and forming pools on the sill: it was a real old tempest and it looked set for the day.

We were heading for the border in an Ambassador, the iconic car of India: 1800 cc with five gears. Ours was creamy white and in lovely condition. We'd borrowed it and I'd hoped to drive but the owner was nervous so he supplied a driver. At that time of the morning in a raging storm there was little point in arguing so we set off through empty streets with just the odd bicycle out and about; one guy on the back of a motorbike holding an umbrella over the rider.

Out of town the rain got so bad that the road partially collapsed; we were heading deep into the country where everything was very green and very, very wet. Diverted off the road to avoid an obstruction, we ended up negotiating a stretch where the bank on our left had collapsed, massive hunks of rock strewn across our path. It was pretty hairy, the bank on our right looked as though it would go at any moment and two lanes of traffic were gingerly trying to pass each other. Now I was glad I wasn't driving.

The Indian side of the border had to be one of the weirder crossings we'd experienced. Sunauli was a border town situated on a dirt road, with a really busy and really narrow main street. Shops sold everything from saris to plumbing supplies, with immigration on one side and customs on the other. Beyond that was an arch which said 'Goodbye to India' and fifty metres further you were in Nepal. Immigration was a building with a table under an open porch where we did the paperwork. After that it was across the road to customs, another open-fronted place where a couple of guys in soldiers' uniforms were lounging around. They made it clear that they wanted money and when we wouldn't give them any they decided to inspect our equipment item by item. They hauled the gear out of the boot and spread it on the road in front of a sari shop. Russ sat in the car covertly filming while Rina and I tried to deal with the soldiers. Rina had vouched for our equipment when we arrived so she had a lot riding on us not having any problems. The trouble was when Mungo had gone home he'd taken some gear with him, so some stuff on the carnet wasn't actually there. The other thing was the carnet itself: when it was printed in London someone had duplicated a page so it looked like we had more equipment than we actually did. It took a while and a bribe would've done the trick but we're not into that. We let them poke through all the gear and pick holes in the carnet while we waited under a sign that indicated we should report anyone asking for a bribe. Finally they got the message and let us repack and cross into Nepal.

In an instant, everything changed: India was gone. Nepal looked cleaner, fresher; the buildings were part colonial and part oriental with balconies and pagoda-style roofs. The people looked different, too – it was clear we were getting closer to oriental Asia.

We were met by a Nepalese guy called Binot who would try to help us reach Kathmandu by tomorrow night. He introduced us to another Binot who drove his tractor to and from the border, and was heading our way.

We were now on possibly the slowest form of transport we'd encountered so far – with the possible exception of the elephant in Delhi. I sat under the canvas canopy while Binot, who was a bit of a cheeky chappie in his twenties, told me about his job, which he'd been doing for about two years. He let me drive; the first time I'd driven a tractor since I was about thirteen. It was straightforward enough, though a bit wobbly, and so slow a bicycle went by. I think I saw a mouse overtake us at one point.

Leaving Binot to deliver his load we jumped on a local bus, which we hoped would take us up the road to the banks of the River Rafti, the third largest river in Nepal. The Rafti bordered the Chitwan National Park, which was where we'd arranged to meet Robin. He was finally arriving from London to help with the filming: we still had Deepak but Wency had left us in India. Robin filmed part of the Race to Dakar and would stay with us until

Anne, the Danish camerawoman, flew out. It was all a bit complicated in the camera department but after Mungo's injury it had been a case of improvise, adapt and overcome.

The bus dropped us close to the river where we found a couple of guys waiting with dugout canoes. The last time I'd been in one I was seventeen and fearless. Now I was forty and fatter than I wanted to be and these looked very unstable. The river was wide and green and I wasn't fooled by how calm it seemed: I swear I could hear the roaring of rapids up ahead. But this was the most direct way of getting to the lodge. Fishermen and traders had been canoeing the river for thousands of years. I decided if it was good enough for them it was good enough for me.

Fortunately we had a guide, who sat on the back with his legs stretched out and a paddle in his hands. The canoe was very long and very narrow and felt really unstable. I went up front with Russ a few feet behind and the whole thing rocked so dangerously I thought Russ was doing it deliberately.

'Keep still, Russ, will you,' I said.

'Believe me, Charley – I'm not moving.'

Of course the river didn't remain calm: pretty soon it got choppy, then choppier still until there was quite a swell lifting. It would take us an hour to the lodge, and with the waves slapping the sides this was not going to be very relaxing. We bobbed along, rolling from side to side, all the time feeling as if the boat would tip over at any minute. We held on for grim death. It was some kind of welcome: a day of rain and paperwork, a striking difference in cultures and now the most unstable form of travel known to man. If that wasn't enough, in the morning we'd be riding elephants.

I called mine Betty. That wasn't her name but I couldn't pronounce the name the keeper told me, so Betty it was. We had a jeep waiting an hour up the road and this was the way we had decided to reach it – two elephants, both females. But first we had to take them down to the waterhole for a bath.

Betty didn't want to get down on her knees, and I didn't blame her. I waded in to offer some encouragement, wincing at the sharp stones underfoot. Meanwhile Russ's elephant wandered in and rolled over without any fuss, while the driver worked his way up her shoulder and onto her ribs – once perched there he began washing her down. Betty, seeing that it wasn't so bad, finally followed suit. The keeper told us that these two elephants got along well, as most of their elephants did. However, the ones that didn't like each other didn't like each other's driver either, which made life interesting. Elephants have long life spans and are famed for their ability to remember so much: if you mistreat one and you come across it again twenty years later, it certainly won't have forgotten you.

Betty had pink patches on her ears and a pinkish trunk that had once been bitten by another elephant. I climbed onto her back as she knelt down, using her tail as a rope and stepping on her foot. I sat with my legs spread on a canvas saddle behind the driver and waited while Russ hesitantly mounted his, telling me he just didn't feel right about stepping on her foot. Then we were off, lumbering across open pasture to the dirt road that drifted through the trees. It was a gentle, rolling and rocking motion – much easier and more comfortable than riding a horse. The view was superb; sitting so high we could see for miles and the country was spectacular. The villages were beautifully kept; the houses neat and the yards swept. Some were traditional thatch while others were made of whitewashed concrete blocks with tin roofs. The pace of life felt gentle: an old world and yet touched by the new. We passed one traditional home with ochre and stucco walls and a magnificent old thatch, chickens pecking for grubs in the yard while a barefoot woman chatted on a mobile phone. We wandered past a little school and the kids came chasing after us, yelling hello and asking for pens.

My driver had an umbrella and I perched underneath it for shade. Perfect, I thought. We'd been in Nepal for less than a day and already we'd canoed the Rafti, and now we were heading towards the capital on a couple of elephants.

Back on the ground we commandeered another Willys-type US army jeep: this one was grey with a grey hood and the driver had plastered the interior with pictures of famous Indian actresses. The weather was changing; we were climbing now and the sky had slipped from a brilliant blue to an ominous-looking purple. We had forty miles to the next town and another five hours after that to Kathmandu.

'You know, I love this place already,' Russ told me as we loaded the gear. 'There's an almost magical feel to it.'

There was a definite colonial feel to some of the houses now; balconies supported by pillars, surrounded by fenced-in gardens with the land beyond them tilled for farming. There was a gentleness to the atmosphere that made you want to stop off and chill out for a few weeks.

Halfway to town we were flagged down by a policeman who said there had been an accident up the road and he wanted a lift. We took him to where a bus was parked, a kid was sitting on a motorbike and there was glass all over the road. Thankfully, it didn't look as though anyone was hurt. The policeman thanked us for the ride and we motored on.

We left the jeep in Hetauda, two hours south of Kathmandu. It was a scruffy place, not like the well cared-for villages we'd passed through. Rubbish littered the streets, and it was crammed with rickshaws and tuk-tuks. The guy who owned the jeep told us it might cost a bit to get to Kathmandu because there was a fuel shortage: India supplied diesel and petrol and lately the bills hadn't been paid so they'd stopped delivering.

With that in mind we hunted down some kind of taxi: private hire cabs were supposed to be very common here. In the middle of town we found a bunch of drivers hanging round some fairly modern cars. We plumped for a Suzuki – the driver was a young guy with a bit of a swagger. There was a strange, twirly thing fixed on the roof, about the size of my hand – it looked like a miniature jet engine. Some kind of turbo, clearly.

We hadn't even made it out of town before we were caught up in a disturbance. The roads converged on a square where a bus was stopped. A swathe of kids was swarming all over it. It was a real ruckus; vehicles lined up with a couple of policemen trying to deal with them, crowds of children shouting and gesticulating. Winding down the window we tried to see what all the fuss was about.

A schoolboy came over and I asked him what was happening.

'It's a demonstration,' he said. 'We have no books and we've had enough.'

A demonstration by schoolchildren who weren't able to get a proper education: how cool was that? We told the boy we hoped they got the books and soon; they certainly deserved them.

In late afternoon we stopped at a place where a sign indicated 'The Beach, The Trail, The Bridge, The Village and the Banyan Tree'. The bridge was made of cable and wood and spanned the river to a jungle trail beyond. Downstream we could see the freshwater beach with a tented encampment on the banks. We didn't see any banyan trees but we took a look at the village, a gathering of stone houses built on cobbled lanes where streams trickled from the mountain. It reminded me of the kind of place they'd build in Disneyland: a mass of colours and overhanging gables, all steps and ladders leading to open balconies and upstairs walkways.

We met an English girl called Nikki who was staying there for a week. She told us she'd been watching a Nepali film on TV, waiting for the rain to subside, when she looked up and saw us. That's Charley Boorman, she said to herself. I wonder what he's doing here.

Nikki had been an outdoor pursuits instructor in England before training as a teacher. Now she lived in Bangkok where she taught in an international school. She wished us all the best for the rest of the journey and we moved on.

An hour or so later we stopped at an overlook 1,460 metres above sea level. From there we could see Kathmandu, a great scattering of buildings that sprawled across the basin.

'Not bad,' Russ said. 'Ten thousand miles by any means we could find and we're arriving the exact day we promised UNICEF.'

The next morning, 26 May, we met up with Wendy Zych – an old friend from UNICEF. Wendy took us across town to the health centre, from where we would take vaccines for TB, measles and diphtheria to remote villages in the mountains. We've worked with UNICEF for a long time now and, given the philosophy of the expedition, we thought it would be interesting to find out how the vaccines were transported. UNICEF calls it the 'cold chain', where vaccines manufactured in India are transported on dry ice to the different regional offices in Nepal. In total over three million children are being inoculated on an ongoing basis. The country is split into districts with as many as 600,000 children in each. Once the vaccines have reached the regional office, they are stored at a temperature of between two and eight degrees before being divided into the requisite quantities each area needs. Today we were going to accompany one district health officer on his journey into the mountains; by bus, van and finally on foot.

We had to take the frozen ice packs out of the freezer and leave them at room temperature for twenty minutes before we could pack the vaccine. When they were ready we lined a large metal box with the packs and placed the vials in the middle. With more ice packs covering them the box was ready. I grabbed one handle and the district health officer the other and together we set off, walking a couple of kilometres through the tight, twisty streets of the capital to a bus stop. We had an hour and a half on local transport because, like all UNICEF projects, the vaccination programme had to be sustainable and public transport was part of it. It was a normal rickety old bus where we paid our fare like everyone else, passengers stepping over the box of vaccine stowed on the floor.

'What these guys do is heroic,' I said to Russ as we hung on to the overhead rail.

'Life saving,' he agreed. 'The vaccinators walk for three or four days to get to people in the really remote areas.'

We jumped off in very green, very rugged country, where rice fields cut swirling patterns in terraces picked out by banks of red earth. The town itself clung to the hillside, the shops and houses built in tiers on the far side of a wooden-railed bridge that spanned the river below. It was stunning country with mind-boggling views and I took a moment to soak it up before we carried the box of vaccine to the health post, a tiny building with a tin roof, tucked away in a dusty street littered with landslip rubble. We decanted the contents into fridges powered by a rack of batteries that were fed by mains electricity, with solar panels as back-up.

Separating various bottles into a smaller cool box, we were due to hop in a van and drive as far as the road would take us before walking the rest of the way. But even before we got going, the road was blocked by three massive trucks.

We asked the district officer what was going on.

'The drivers are on strike,' he explained. 'The road is bad; it's just dirt cut from the mountain. Buses and trucks travel it all the time and when it rains it's very, very dangerous. The side slips away and the drop is straight down. Just the other day a truck fell over the edge and the driver was killed.'

'And that's the road we're taking?'

The district officer nodded.

At last we wormed our way out of town, climbing narrow, twisty, crumbling clay roads littered with fallen rocks. An hour or so later the driver pulled over and we continued on foot. The path was steep and gnarly, the world falling away below us. It was hard on the calves and very hot. We climbed through trees and deeper woodland before coming out once more to peaks that were just visible through the low-lying cloud.

We finally made it to a village; a few women were already at the health post with their babies, waiting for the next vaccination course for measles and TB or the diphtheria, tetanus and hepatitis B combination.

The community health worker told us that the take-up rate was just about a hundred per cent. Since the programme had begun, people had realised its importance very quickly, especially mothers. Now just about every child in the country was vaccinated free of charge. I watched while a couple of babies were inoculated: sweet little doe-eyed tots wearing checked coats and little caps; they just about bawled the place down.

It really helped to sum up why we're involved. On these expeditions we're lucky enough to see how the money people donate is being spent and we're able to highlight how important it is that the money keeps coming. It's easy to forget that UNICEF doesn't receive a penny from the United Nations; they have to generate all their income themselves. It is always a privilege to see the UNICEF teams in action, working in such harmony with local people.

Back in the van we had to climb through thick forest to get to the village of Chaubas where we would be spending the night. The pitted, boulder-strewn road was as bad as any I've ever ridden, a real teeth rattler. We were bounced so hard we were almost off the seats most of the time. To compound matters it started to rain heavily and the road turned to mush. It rained a lot here; the dirt was already deeply rutted and those ruts quickly filled with water. The van was only two-wheel drive and we slithered along with a truck and public bus backed up behind us.

Pretty soon the rain became torrential, an unbelievable downpour; the whole forest running with water. Ahead we could see a bend where great troughs were beginning to overflow. The driver clearly knew what the road was like in these conditions because he slowed to a stop and we sat there with the engine idling trying to work out if we could make it through the next section. I jumped down to check the depth of the water and see how loose the mud was. It was deep and loose. I could see how high the centre ridge was too, and looking at the van there was every possibility the thing would beach. The only chance we had was to lighten the load. The others piled out and we stood in the rain while the driver took the bend with the offside wheels in the rut and the near side on the ridge of earth in the middle. He almost made it; steaming round it looked as though he would but then the wheels spun and the thing slithered to a halt. We all got behind and pushed. The wheels churned but didn't grip, showering us in mud and puddle water before they finally got some purchase and the van inched forward. Soaked to the bone, we climbed in and shivered our way to where the trek would begin.

It was another uphill hike, carrying the precious vaccines along a boulder-battered path; stepping over fallen trees and old branches and constantly avoiding furrows filled with red clay and rainwater. The height of Nepal was staggering: all around us now there were the most wonderful views. We could hear birds and cicadas; we saw scattered rice paddies and single dwellings; larger settlements where tin-roofed stone houses seemed to gather together among the trees.

At Chaubas a couple of dozen women had gathered outside the children's club, a gorgeous stone building with a roof that was part tin and part earth, to wait for us. They'd been waiting a while because after the episode in the forest, we were later than we'd intended. The women were all wearing similar red saris and they welcomed us with handmade garlands of flowers and a dot of paint for our foreheads.

It was humbling. All we'd done was carry the drugs from the capital; these women ensured the well-being of every child in the region. They made sure young mothers were aware of the vaccination programme and kept tabs on who was being inoculated and when; they were totally in charge of their own programme. UNICEF always advocates community empowerment; their aim is to ensure that the health worker educates the people to take responsibility for the future of their own community.

We had about fifteen children to immunise in the morning and that night we were due to sleep on the floor in the health post. The women wouldn't hear of it and instead they took us into the homes of a couple of different villagers. Russ and I stayed with the young mother of ten-year-old Bheena Bandari and her younger brother Parvan Kurran whom Russ nicknamed 'Cheeky'. The kids gave up their rooms and went to sleep with an aunt while we laid our sleeping bags on the rough planks they used for beds.

I wasn't sleeping well. The miles we were covering, the constant changes in transport, the different bed every night . . . none of it was conducive to good sleep. Tonight, for some reason, my watch alarm kept going off. I hadn't set it, but it went off three times and on the third I flicked on a torch and saw it was set to go off another three times. I couldn't understand it. I hadn't touched the watch, it was really bizarre.

In the morning I woke up with a monumental headache. I think it was partly the altitude and partly dehydration. We were above the clouds here with savage peaks like sharks' teeth marking the horizon. I could smell breakfast cooking on an open fire in the kitchen. There was no power; last night our room had been lit by candles and the only light in the kitchen now was from the intermittent shafts of sunlight that breached the wooden walls.

At the clinic we helped inoculate the fifteen children. They greeted us with flowers and so many of them wanted to paint a red spot on my face that the colour ran down my cheeks. The inoculation programme had only been going for six years and the women told us that before then they had no forum for discussion, no common goal around which they could congregate. Immunising their children had not only given them hope for a healthier future but an opportunity to discuss issues that concerned them all. Now they had taken control of their children's health as well as their education. They kept a profile of the entire community: there was a record of how many men there were, how many women; how many children were in school; how many had been vaccinated with what and when, and it was updated almost every day.

It was really inspiring to see the 'cold chain' at work. It was tiring, though; we'd been full-on for ten thousand miles and I was looking forward to a little down time tomorrow.

That's if there'd be any.

We had no idea before we arrived, but 28 May was going to be an historic moment in Nepalese history. Deepak told us that tomorrow there was to be a meeting of what he called the 'constitutional assembly', which would decide whether to abolish the royal family. Deepak reckoned there was a 50/50 chance of trouble. Having ruled for two hundred and fifty years, he thought the monarchy wouldn't take kindly to being abolished.

He explained that ten years ago the Maoists set out to replace the royal family with a communist republic. In 2001 the King and Queen and most of their family were murdered, allegedly by their son Dipendra, who then shot himself. That was the official line but Deepak said there were all kinds of conspiracy theories. The new King, Gyanendra, was the murdered King's brother and his first act was to get rid of what had been a royal parliamentary political system; a sort of halfway house to try to placate the communists. The army was loyal to him but the Maoists had their army and the fighting was intense. Finally, in 2005, the Maoists agreed to a ceasefire if the King would reinstate parliament, which he did.

They of course immediately voted to cut the powers he'd given himself and tomorrow they were voting whether to get rid of the monarchy altogether.

It ought to be an interesting day.

16

Never Forget and Never Regret

Actually it turned out that the decision to remove the King had pretty much been taken already – but today it would be ratified. Watching BBC World in my hotel room I discovered that what the reporter called a 'hasty constitutional amendment' had been made five months ago, though there was talk that it hadn't been implemented democratically. It did seem certain the King would be told to go, however, and it was purely by chance that we were here to witness it.

We weren't quite sure what the implications would be but the meeting was happening at nine o'clock and I imagined the full significance would hit the streets later; sitting outside with a coffee, Russ and I discussed it.

'The Maoists killed a shopkeeper,' he said. 'And yesterday a couple of bombs went off. It's a good job we were in the mountains.'

'It's scary, but I'm glad we're here. It's kind of exciting to see history in the making.'

Russ sipped tea. 'Quite a country, isn't it? Until now, when I thought of Nepal I thought of Everest, and mountain farms. Not bombs and chronic fuel shortage. People have to queue for two days – have you seen the cars backed up along the road?'

There had been power cuts as well, for anything up to forty hours a week. Businesses and homes were plunged into darkness and the city's tram system had pretty much ground to a halt.

Meanwhile we had some political and technical pressures of our own to contend with. The night before I'd spoken to Mungo – his knee was healing and he thought he'd be fit enough to join us in Hanoi in roughly a week's time. But in the meantime, we had China to deal with. We had hoped that Robin would be able to help with the filming but there hadn't been time to arrange a visa in London. We'd been trying to get one here in Kathmandu but Robin's a Scot of Chinese origin and the Chinese were suspicious because he has what they called a Tibetan-sounding surname. He'd been down to their embassy this morning hoping that he would come away with a visa but unfortunately he didn't. They told him that foreign nationals should get visas in their own country. He'd obtained one once before in Hong Kong, though, so there was still a chance.

In the meantime Anne, our Danish camerawoman, was trying to get a visa in London so she could meet us in Guangzhou. Russ also had another shooter lined up – a mate of Mungo's called Matt, who lived in China. If Anne got her visa we didn't need Robin, but if she didn't . . . then we did. We had to make a decision on the spot, though, because if he was flying to Hong Kong he was flying right now. We had an agent on the phone asking if we wanted the ticket and reminding us that check-in for that flight was imminent. Russ decided that we couldn't risk Anne not being there and not having Robin either: that would leave us with just one cameraman we didn't know. Ten minutes later Robin was on his way to the airport.

At lunchtime we heard the news that the constitutional amendment had been ratified and King Gyanendra had fifteen days to vacate the palace. People were on the streets and the Maoist-led government declared a three-day holiday. Russ and I decided to head out in separate directions to see what was going on.

I went down to the Narayanhity Palace, the King's official residence. The surrounding roads were surprisingly empty: just some kids and a few people on motorbikes. The heavy police presence probably had something to do with it.

With nothing doing at the palace I wandered down to the assembly buildings where there were huge crowds out on the street. Looking round, I could see hundreds of pink umbrellas shading women from the sun. People were playing music, singing and dancing; one little toddler was be-bopping away like there was no tomorrow. A bunch of men wearing red sashes with the letters YCL were helping the police. Deepak told me they were from the Young Communist League. Further on, people were marching, flanked by policemen with long batons. A couple of the marchers were carrying a dummy, which I imagine symbolised the King. I asked one guy what they were chanting.

'Bye-bye to the King,' he said.

'Right: bye-bye to the King. Are you happy about it?'

'Very happy.'

We were staying in the Kathmandu Guesthouse, famous in Kathmandu among climbers, situated in an area full of little shops and bazaars. Russ was looking for a gong to take home as a souvenir. Whilst trying to hunt one down, he spoke to two guys sitting outside a shop.

'The Republic of Nepal starts today,' one of them told him.

'And what do you think about that?'

'I think it's very well.'

'What about you?' Russ asked his mate.

'I think it's OK.'

'Are you happy?'

'Very happy.'

'Do you think the King will go quietly?'

'Yes,' they said. 'We think so.'

Further on he came across a band of marchers yelling slogans into a microphone. Russ spoke to three young men looking on from an open doorway.

'They're saying the King is a thief,' one of them told him. His name was Sujan and he spoke English very well.

'Do you agree with the change to Maoism?' Russ asked him.

'I don't agree with anything.'

'What do you prefer?'

'I prefer peace.'

'You don't think you'll get peace with the Maoists?'

Sujan thought about that. 'These people don't have a clear motive,' he said. 'They're killing people and they're also looking for peace. You cannot kill for peace.'

It had been an historic day; the vote had been passed and Nepal had officially become a Republic. The following morning both the US and UN sent messages of congratulation to the government. A couple of bombs had gone off on 27 May, but apart from that the only sign of trouble had been at the palace where there had been a row about the King's flag flying when the flag of Nepal should be raised.

We didn't know what the Maoists would be like, but most people seemed to want them in. It wasn't a coup, there had been voting and the party wasn't Maoist in the true sense of the word: in fact, the Chinese had asked them to change the name because they didn't reflect the teachings of Chairman Mao.

China, of course, was the next leg of our expedition and so far just trying to get in had been fraught with difficulties. We were leaving tomorrow by plane. With a day left in Nepal we took a helicopter ride to the last village on the trail to Mount Everest.

I wasn't feeling great – I hadn't been sleeping well and I was missing my family much more than I had expected, probably because I had spent so long away from them last year as well. I don't think any of us had realised how much of an impact another long separation would have. I was pretty jaded, I had an upset tummy and as we were flying up to 3,800 metres, I'd had to take a tablet for altitude sickness.

The five-seater helicopter was piloted by a very cool guy who'd been operating in the Himalayas for fifteen years. I spotted the initials AD painted on the tail section: it turned out the helicopter had been owned previously by Alain Delon, the French actor who was really big in the sixties. That made us laugh; on Long Way Round there had been an ongoing joke that Russ looked like him.

I love helicopters, they're my favourite way of flying and we had a brilliant pilot. We lifted off from the flat, scrubby basin around the capital and struck out east towards the mountains. Close up the hills looked purple and blue, and seemed almost gentle, but as we headed further east they grew increasingly steep and white, their peaks sharp and jagged.

We flew through gorges thick with jungle, rivers and waterfalls. The further we went the tighter the gorges became until finally we were above the clouds and the big summits looked so clear and close you could almost reach out and touch them.

We had to carry extra fuel in jerricans because there wouldn't be enough in the tank to get us there and back. The pilot also explained that he would have to drop us in Lukla for a couple of hours. He'd had a call and had to make a detour to Everest to pick up an injured climber. Apparently he made lots of these rescue runs; so many people were climbing these days that there were cases of frostbite and altitude sickness all the time. He said some people only pretended to be injured though, so they could get a ride out rather than walking for ten days.

We didn't mind stopping, it gave us a break to acclimatise. Lukla was a pretty town perched on a plateau 2,834 metres up the mountain. Tengboche, the village from which we would be able to see Everest, was another thousand metres higher.

A couple of hours later the pilot was back and we made our way to the roof of the world. The surroundings were stunning now: with the sky crystal clear, we could see every contour, every tree and crag, the breaks in the river and ahead of us the crisp white peaks of Lhotse, Nuptse and Everest.

At Tengboche we hovered above a tiny apron made from cobbles with a crowd of people on the ground watching. There were a whole bunch of tents pitched in the meadows and beyond them clay-coloured trails led into woodlands where a yak train was waiting.

It's hard to put into words exactly how I felt: it was one of those 'pinch yourself' and 'yes, you're really here' moments. I was aware of the altitude, the Buddhist monastery that dominated the village. I was aware of the amount of people trekking in and out. There was even a marathon taking place; twenty-six miles with backpacks at 12,000 feet. We were introduced to a local Sherpa called Sharab who'd been guiding climbers all his adult life. He explained that today – 29 May – was the fifty-fifth anniversary of the first successful ascent of

Mount Everest, and Peter Hillary, Sir Edmund's son, was here in the village.

Russ was struck by the same sense of awe that took away any words. No superlatives would ever be enough. It was a beautiful day, and I had that feeling of serenity I'd experienced in Varanasi. For a while we just gazed the length of the valley, wondering at the way the hills enveloped each other, reaching out to the shoulders, the ridge and the white summit of Mount Everest.

'We've seen some sights, you and me,' Russ said. 'But nothing compares with this.'

The yak train was leaving and the dull echo of the bells seemed to set off this landscape as nothing could. Ancient, shaggy cattle, they headed out laden with everything from blankets to food and great barrels of fresh water, driven along by Sherpas who controlled them with sticks and whistles.

Edmund Hillary had died in January but Peter and his daughter Amelia had trekked to base camp as part of the fifty-five-year celebrations. Sharab told us there was to be a ceremony in the Buddhist Temple. It's a holy place, conceived in the sixteenth century by the Lama Sangwa Dorje, who flew here in his mind and chose it as a good place to meditate. The Buddhist monks believe that his spirit landed, his footprints marking the sacred rock where he touched down. He envisioned that one day there would be a monastery here and subsequently one was constructed. In 1890 it was destroyed by an earthquake. Rebuilt, it was destroyed again by a fire in 1989. With the help of Sir Edmund Hillary, the local people and an American foundation, it was rebuilt a second time.

Russ was worried about how the altitude might affect us. We were both a little breathless and we knew we couldn't stay long if we wanted to avoid getting sick. Looking after yourself in air this thin is absolutely vital.

'We were right to come though,' Russ said.

'Of course: how many opportunities do you get to see Mount Everest?'

We were sitting on the grass just taking it in; a little village perched on a narrow trail with the tallest mountains on earth gathered around us.

'This expedition has truly lived up to the ideal,' he went on. 'I know we're away from our families again but it's worth it. No regrets, eh, Charley? Never forget and never regret.'

I nodded.

'Did you hear they're expecting a major earthquake though, in the next thirty years? And not one building is prepared for it. If it happens it will be devastating. UNICEF has already made contingencies in terms of vaccines, water supplies and so on, and the people up here, the villagers, I reckon they might be all right. They would lose their houses but they'd rebuild quickly: they're used to subsistence living, aren't they? It's people like that who really know how to survive.'

We spoke to Peter Hillary, a tall New Zealander – slim and very fit. He was only a year old when his father conquered Everest, but he climbed it himself for the first time in 1990. Since then he's climbed it again as well as lots of other peaks. He's also raced the Ganges on a jet boat with his father.

Peter's daughter Amelia looked terrific in her traditional dress, though she'd hurt her foot coming out from base camp. She's not a climber, but when she'd seen the wind-burnt, weather-beaten mountaineers, she'd thought she might like some of that herself. Peter said he'd be happy for her to climb if she served her apprenticeship. Everest was a test of endurance: it's the lack of oxygen and the rapid change in weather that claims most lives. As we stood there he pointed out the aspects of the summit, explaining that Everest is part of a horseshoe with the summit rising eight or nine thousand feet above the Nuptse–Lhotse Ridge.

'Will you climb it again?' I asked him.

'Look,' he said, 'I've climbed it twice. I've been on the West Ridge, the South Pillar and the South Col Route. I know that mountain well, too well.'

He wasn't saying he wouldn't climb it and he wasn't saying he would. He was on his way to Alaska right then, however, to climb Mount McKinley – his seventh of the seven great mountains. We talked for a while about why people climb in the first place; why they undertake any great challenge – as I'd done to a small extent when I had a crack at the Dakar. Peter told us he'd spoken to an economics professor from New Delhi who suggested that people risked their lives simply because the old adage is true: the greater the risk the greater the reward.

We were able to stay long enough to see some of the ceremony and have a couple of Himalayan scarves we'd bought blessed by the monastery's lama. We hoped that would bring us some more of the kind of luck we'd had in our short time in this wonderful country. By chance we'd been here when Nepal became a Republic and amazingly, only twenty-four hours later, we'd met Sir Edmund Hillary's son with Everest in the background, fifty-five years after it was conquered.

Back in the chopper Russ asked the pilot if he could take us to the Friendship Bridge – a narrow gorge with tree-lined hills where we'd originally planned to make the crossing to Tibet. The pilot guided the chopper to a little town squashed between the hills. A string of dilapidated buildings marked the Nepalese side and harsh-looking concrete structures the Chinese. We hovered: drifting halfway across the river, the skill of the pilot just about keeping us in Nepalese territory. We were so low we were in the town and could see the number plates of the trucks backed up along the road. Russ had the door open so he could film the point where we'd planned to cross before China closed off Tibet. Chinese soldiers were gesticulating angrily. Watching through binoculars, we saw a couple get on the phone.

'Maybe we should go,' Russ yelled.

The pilot had no choice but to bring the chopper about in the hover – if we had gone any further forwards, we would be in Chinese airspace. It's a really hard manoeuvre and for a moment it was a bit hairy; then we were climbing so steeply and so close to the trees I could make out the veins in the leaves.

The flight back took much longer than it had on the way out because the clouds had drifted into the gorges and we had to avoid them. We skirted south in an arc to make sure we had plenty of visibility; no pilot flies in cloud in this area and they rarely fly beyond midday.

Back in Kathmandu we discovered that the Chinese had been on the phone to the Nepalese Aviation Authority demanding to know what the chopper had been doing and what we were filming. We were very grateful to the pilot, and hoped we hadn't accidentally got him into trouble and that, at most, he would only get his knuckles rapped. The NAA did want a report though, the Chinese were insisting on it. We asked them to hold off until we'd left if they possibly could: the last thing we wanted was to be accosted at the airport and have the rushes confiscated.

17
Tales of the River Bank

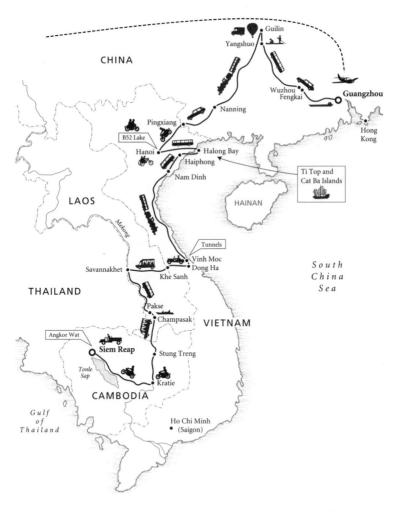

There is no question it had been one of the great days of my life. In fact the whole Nepalese experience had been amazing, and on top of everything else we'd been able to raise awareness for UNICEF: the vaccination programme being another example of how the money you donate is spent.

Mentally I was floating with happiness, but physically I was feeling pretty bleh. I had the poops and my stomach was churning; I also had the beginnings of a bothersome toothache. Once again I couldn't sleep, and in the brief moments when I did manage to drop off my dreams were so vivid I kept waking up. I was thinking about Olly and the kids and all of a sudden I felt incredibly lonely. I know that might sound stupid, even selfish given the day we'd had, but I had to admit it again – I missed my family. I've been away from them so much over the past couple of years – I just wish there was some way I could have them with me.

Tomorrow we were to take off for China, so with a little time to myself I jumped in a cab and paid a quick visit to Craig, a New Zealander I'd first met in London. It had been one of those chance encounters. I'd been about to get on my bike one morning when this guy walked round the corner. He was working on a house nearby, and he told me he was taking part in the 'Rickshaw Run', a tuk-tuk race from Kathmandu to southern India. He wanted some advice on getting sponsorship so that he could raise money for a prostate cancer charity – his father had been diagnosed with the disease.

It was purely by chance that we were in Kathmandu at the same time. I found him working on his tuk-tuk in a yard alongside a whole bunch of other racers. It was dark blue with a line of polished air horns on the roof and a map of India painted on the front. They'd rigged up a canopy to keep the sun off while they were working and the tuk-tuk was almost ready to race. I loved the idea, a sort of Gumball Rally on three wheels. We chatted for a while and compared tuk-tuks – Craig's was two-stroke like ours, but in much better nick. I wished him luck and headed back to the hotel.

Next stop China.

We flew overnight to the city of Guangzhou, north of Hong Kong. It was a new city, built when Hong Kong became too overcrowded. We were acutely aware that we had vowed not to take a regular airline flight, but the Tibetan border remained closed and Burma was, of course, out of the question. It was disappointing, but we really had no other option.

The airport was very state-of-the-art and westernised. With its McDonald's and Starbucks, it was like landing in America. We had expected customs to be a nightmare, but in fact it couldn't have been easier. Walking through laden with camera equipment, the officials just stamped our passports and waved us on: they didn't ask us what we were doing, what we were filming or anything. Outside it was hot, humid and raining. Hailing a cab, we were soon whizzing down a modern motorway in a very modern city, all high-rise offices and apartment blocks. There was a lot of industry here, in particular a large cement works; we'd arranged to cadge a ride on a cement barge downriver to Wuzhou.

When we arrived in Guangzhou we met up with Shiyi and Taotao, a couple of Chinese girls who would interpret for us. We also caught up with Matt, Mungo's mate, who would be filming at least as far as Vietnam. Everything seemed to be going swimmingly, everything, that was, except my toothache. A pressurised cabin was the last thing I'd needed and what had been the odd twinge had turned into a sharp, jagged stab. I had only managed about an hour's sleep before the intense pain woke me up.

There's nothing more debilitating than toothache and I knew I had to find a dentist. Fortunately it hadn't been this bad when we were in Kathmandu because I'm not sure I'd have gone to the dentist there.

Shiyi took me to an ultra-modern clinic where they spoke English. It was fantastic – as far as any visit to the dentist can be fantastic – everything spotlessly clean and white. They had all the latest technology, and after three injections and a lot of drilling, I'd had some work done on a root-canal. It wasn't a permanent fix, we weren't going to be there long enough for that, but the dentist told me it was good for a couple of months. At that moment I didn't care how long it was good for – walking out I felt like a new man.

Shiyi told us that over the last ten years things had really taken off in China: the country had embraced capitalism and the economy was booming. We took a walk through narrow streets with vibrant, colourful shops selling just about everything, and apart from the signs you could be in any modern European city. On our travels we bumped into a skinny guy called Mah, who was riding a tricycle with a large storage box on the back. He told us he was in the recycling business. He'd ride through the streets buying rubbish from shopkeepers: paper, cardboard boxes, Styrofoam, aluminium cans . . . pretty much anything that could be recycled. The shopkeepers stored it until he came round then they'd barter for a price, Mah working everything out on his homemade set of scales.

It was fun to watch; lots of hand waving and finger gestures. He paid twenty yuan for a six-kilo parcel, which he then sold on to the recycling plant for thirty. It was an interesting concept, and I wondered if it would work in Britain.

Mah had a second bike so I jumped on that and followed him on his rounds. The streets were narrow and there were lots of cars, but everything seemed very calm – people just ambling along, without the great cacophony of horns we'd become used to in India. But I got the same reaction cycling as I had when I rode the rickshaw – people stopped and stared, kids pointed and laughed. I had a go at bartering for some cardboard boxes and discovered that the shopkeepers, mostly hard-case women, happily fleeced me. They said five yuan and I said two; they said five and I said three, they said five and I said four. I was useless. I did fill the cart, though, and I paid for some of the stuff with my own money, so at least Mah's profits went up.

That evening I took a call from Mungo, who told me that his knee was getting there but it was not as good as he'd hoped. He was actually booked to see the physio on the day he was due to fly out to Hanoi and realistically he thought he might need another week. I told him there was no point in coming out until his knee was fully operational; the last thing any of us wanted was for him to break down and have to fly home again. He sounded pretty down. He'd been to his grandfather's funeral the day before. I told him to keep his chin up and reminded him that if he hadn't done his knee in, he wouldn't have made the decision to go to the funeral. That was fate and when fate strikes you just have to roll with it.

Not all of Guangzhou was high-rise. Close to the hotel there was a suburb of smaller, tightly packed buildings with red tile roofs that looked much more traditional, and the following morning we went exploring there to buy food. We found a cool indoor market selling not only a vast array of fruit and vegetables, but live shrimp and fish. There were live chickens, too: you pointed out the one you wanted and they killed it, plucked it and you took it home for dinner.

The revised route was taking us south-west towards Hanoi, and somehow Lucy had managed to locate a family that operated a cement barge. They lived on it permanently, working their way up and down the Xun Jiang River with five hundred tonnes of cement dust in the hold. We were due to meet at midday after they'd unloaded their cargo and were preparing for the weekly run west to collect another load. Shiyi knew roughly where the barge would be and we found it nestled up against a bunch of other barges in one of the older and more tumbledown river districts. To get there we had to make our way through some pretty dodgy backstreets, little alleys between old brick buildings, most of which looked as though they were about to fall apart. I had my suitcase on my head and was making my way between the houses when behind me this dog leapt from a doorway. Barking and snarling it lunged at Russ. For an awful moment he thought he was going to get bitten. Thankfully the dog backed off, more bark than bite. We had all been concerned about rabies, but it was only protecting its territory.

When we arrived at the mooring we clambered from deck to deck until we reached our barge. Black-hulled with blunt bows, it was basically a cargo hold with a wheelhouse and living quarters at the back. Taotao told us that the southern provinces (where we were heading) had had the most horrendous weather recently: massive thunder storms, torrential rain and gale force winds. She said that though it was naturally wet in that part of China, this year had been exceptional and as many as a hundred thousand people had been displaced. In the last couple of months ninety-three had died in the storms and because of the swollen river; only yesterday someone had drowned and another person was missing. It was disturbing how so many countries we'd been travelling through had been struck by natural disasters, and the thought of a grotesquely swollen river was hardly comforting, especially when we realised there was no rail around the deck on our barge. There was just the wheelhouse and then flat, open deck, nothing to hold onto in bad weather. I had visions of getting up for a pee in the night, missing my footing and splash – *hasta la vista*, Charley.

Leaving the mooring we steamed down-river. It was busy here, the water thick with cement carriers and barges transporting household goods, or loaded to the gunwales with lengths of bamboo. Chi-Chi, the eldest son, was driving; he looked about twenty-two. Wearing shorts and a singlet, he sat in a cane chair, constantly adjusting the wheel. We couldn't speak each other's language, but he had a broad smile and so did I and I guess that was all we needed.

Seven-eighths of the barge was devoted to the cargo hold, whereas the living area and wheelhouse seemed to have been an afterthought. The bridge was no more than a rudimentary console with a couple of garden chairs, a fridge and an old TV. The living quarters consisted of a couple of cabins and a rough kitchen. Not that it mattered: there was a really nice atmosphere, just Mum and Dad and their two boys. This was home; their space, their work place.

Mum was called Ayi; a small, smiling woman who ran the 'house' while her husband and sons ran the business. I chatted to her as she washed vegetables using a hose that pumped river water. Later I discovered that when you squatted over the knee-trembler toilet, whatever you deposited was dropped directly into the water.

Ayi's husband was called Liang-Su. He told me the round trip was a two-week cycle of steaming west to pick up cement dust to unload in Guangzhou. The only time anyone got a break was every three or four months or so when Ayi went to visit her mother. Sometimes their younger son would go with her so he could hook up with his old school-friends for a few days. Liang-Su stayed on the boat: he'd been on this river all his life and he'd never had a mishap; no collisions, no running aground, and in thirty years we were his only passengers.

Ayi had lunch ready and we sat down to fish and vegetables with garlic and ginger: I could taste menthol though, which was weird.

'What is that?' I asked nobody in particular. 'That taste in the food is like menthol.' I studied my bowl trying to figure out where the flavour was coming from then . . . shit, I could feel the filling in my mouth. I spat it out. The menthol I could taste was the clove oil the dentist had used on my tooth.

Russ was outside on deck. Feeling really pissed off again, I told him what had happened.

'That's bad,' he said. 'We've got five days before we make it to Hanoi which is probably where the next decent dentist will be. If your tooth gets infected we'll be in real trouble.'

'It's a fuck up.' I wagged my head. 'He obviously didn't put it in properly.'

'Spinach,' Russ suggested. 'Spinach and chewing gum, that'll fix it. Or there's always Claudio's old remedy: him and Jim Foster, remember? Whenever they cut themselves they'd sew the wound with a line of superglue. You could use it to fill the hole in your tooth, Charley. What do you think?'

'Superglue in my mouth. I don't think that's a good idea. Mind you,' I added, 'I did have my lips superglued together once.'

'Really?' Russ said. 'Now that's an idea.'

Luckily, because the dentist had removed the nerve the tooth didn't hurt. We were landing in a town tomorrow where there was bound to be someone who could refill it. Talking of town, we'd been on the barge a few hours already and it looked as though we'd never left Guangzhou. Buildings dominated the concrete levee; industrial complexes, apartment blocks and one old brick house that looked like something from a film set. It was half on the bank and half on stilts: an incredibly ancient place that looked as if it would collapse any moment.

There was still a lot of traffic – barges, smaller boats and some traditional Chinese junks with oval black panels and canopies. They looked like water beetles skating across the surface.

Passing beneath a bridge we found ourselves side by side with another barge, which had the boom of a crane sticking out the front like the sword on a marlin. With two more coming the other way we passed four abreast on a stretch of river no wider than the Thames at Westminster.

Five hours after we'd boarded we were still among buildings, at least on the starboard side. The other bank was low and lush, the landscape flat and grey with buffalo cropping the grass close to the water. Liang-Su told me that as little as fifteen years ago there had been nothing here; even ten years ago Guangzhou had been pretty much the clutch of buildings we'd seen near the hotel – now the industrial sprawl seemed to go on for ever.

It had been raining hard, but later in the afternoon the sun came out, warming up so much I changed into flip-flops and shorts. Then it started raining again, so I went to help Ayi in the tiny kitchen. Somehow she managed to do all her cooking on one single-ring electric stove.

Regardless of how basic their lifestyle might be, there was a wonderfully chilled and friendly feel to this family. I took a moment sitting with Liang-Su as he steered close to the concrete levee. We could only communicate if Shiyi translated but we didn't really need to talk: I've learned that you can often get a good idea of someone's life just by hanging out with them and saying very little.

It was dusk before we left the last of the buildings, the banks hazy and the water a rich terracotta as the sun went down.

Although the boat was about a hundred and fifty feet long, it was impossible to get away from the noise of the engine. I tried sleeping in the wheelhouse, but lying on the steel floor with the noise and the vibration, there was no way I was going to get any sleep. At around five-thirty I took a chair outside and slumped back with my feet on the rail and a blanket over me. When it started to rain again, I got up, bleary-eyed, and sought shelter under the bamboo canopy, where I found an empty hammock. Lying back and closing my eyes I dozed for an hour or so.

Despite another restless night, I loved being on the barge: the method of travel and the pace were a terrific antidote to the disappointment I'd felt at having to take that plane. The way the family lived and worked together really touched me and I kept thinking how cool it would be to have Olly, Doone and Kinvara along with me. Ayi was the hub of the whole thing, while Liang-Su and the two boys worked the boat. Chi-Chi had been on one barge or another for fifteen years and told me it was good fun: they made decent money and he enjoyed life on the river. He knew every landmark, each industrial area or cement works; he knew where the ferries crossed. He pointed out a pagoda-style tower and the spots where buffalo liked to wallow. The further west we were moving the more the countryside changed: it was mountainous now, the hillsides thick with vegetation, sloping right to the water.

I felt really privileged; few people get to see China like this. Liang-Su said that ten years ago there had been lots of passenger boats on this river, but then the economy went into overdrive and the roads were built: now everyone travelled by bus or car.

The two brothers seemed to get on really well, always messing about, laughing and joking. Lorau (or 'younger brother') was eighteen, and had been on the barge for a year. Prior to that he had been at school in his mother's village, living with his grandmother.

We were due to get off in Wuzhou around midday, but because the river was so swollen we'd slowed to nothing last night and Liang-Su told us we were five hours behind schedule.

'Five hours!' Russ said when I informed him. 'How can we be five hours behind schedule?'

I explained about the river and that the barge was only doing three miles an hour, but regardless of the reasons the fact was we wouldn't be in Wuzhou when we'd planned, which threw us right out. If we carried on at this pace it would be five or six in the evening before we made it and we'd miss the bus to Yangshuo. There was another leaving at one a.m. but that would mean an overnighter when already we were suffering from lack of sleep.

'We have another option,' Russ said.

'What's that?'

'We get Liang-Su to drop us at one of the ferry crossings. Shiyi thinks that Taotao could meet us on the road and get us to Wuzhou in time to catch the bus.'

'Why don't we get off at the next town instead?' I suggested. 'It might take a bit longer to get there but at least it's a town. That makes more sense than hopping off any old place.'

Liang-Su told us the next town was Fengkai, still a couple of hours away. We should get there at around three o'clock. If Taotao met us, we would still have two hours to make the bus station at Wuzhou.

All decided, we kept to the shade of the bamboo now that the sun was high, watching water buffalo swimming off the starboard bank. We spent the rest of the trip watching fishermen trying to scrape a living either with rods from the bank or rowing flat-bottomed skiffs.

An hour and a half later Liang-Su cut the engine and steered the barge to the banks on the southern side. Chi-Chi tied off and we unloaded the gear. It was blisteringly hot and with my clothes sticking to me and my old suitcase on my head, I waded up through the undergrowth to the road.

It was sad to say goodbye, we'd been with this family a day and a half and it had been one of the most enriching experiences of the expedition so far. We'd eaten with them and slept with them, we'd seen a way of life we'd no idea existed. But we were on the move again now and the next few hundred miles we'd cover by bus and train before taking Russian motorbikes on to Hanoi.

As promised Taotao picked us up and took us to Wuzhou. We made the bus, riding seven bumpy hours through open country on rubbish roads littered with roadworks. By the time we arrived in Yangshuo it was late and, pretty knackered, we rode pillion on a couple of motorcycle taxis to a small hotel in the oldest part of town.

All of a sudden it hit me: we were in China. The plane from Nepal was forgotten. Rolling into bed I fell asleep thinking of the river family, my dad in Ireland, and how far we'd come.

18
Pigs on Bikes

We'd been on the road a long time now so we decided to relax for a bit when we got to Yangshuo. It's an old town, and a lot of its streets are closed to all but pedestrians. There are very few cars, and loads of motorbikes. There were more tourists here, too. The buildings were older than many we'd seen, with flaking paint and scrolled iron balconies overlooking the streets. The town is built on the banks of the Little Li river amid a valley of rice paddies dominated by the most incredible mountains – gigantic green domes thrusting skywards from an otherwise flat landscape, the result of tectonic plate movement two hundred million years ago.

Today was our fifty-third on the road, and jumping aboard a raft we crossed to where the summits sloped into sheer cliffs that disappeared beneath the surface of the river. 'It's amazing here, isn't it?' Russ said. 'The perfect place to chill for a while, and recover from being on the road.'

I couldn't agree more. It was stunning – mountainous but tropical, with rice paddies and bean fields on one side, and a clutch of fishermen's huts built on bamboo stilts on the other. Our pilot explained that it was a holiday destination for many Chinese people, but he didn't encounter that many westerners.

Our raft was made from lengths of plastic pipe tied together. In the past it would have been made of bamboo, but the driver explained that bamboo wasn't strong enough to carry more than two or three passengers whereas ours could cope with as many as eight. It was powered by an outboard, with the propeller on the end of a long metal shaft. I felt a bit like Martin Sheen sailing down the river in *Apocalypse Now*, the mountains and lush green landscape rolling by.

The area was much more geared towards tourism than we had been used to on this trip, which was a bit of a culture shock after our day on the barge. Rafting further downriver we did find a traditional village, which from the water looked like a Buddhist temple. In fact it was home to farmers and fishermen. There were no cars, just handcarts and animals; the buildings, bean fields and paddies interlinked by stone walkways. It was a little contrived, perhaps, a 'minority village' maintained specifically for tourism. Even so, it was a tranquil place, with buffalo wallowing in a pool of water, women in straw hats picking the rice crop and young men squatting on bamboo rafts with fishing rods and catch nets.

Returning to Yangshuo, we visited some water caves close to the town and took a mud bath three hundred metres underground. The locals claimed the mud had healing qualities but I have to admit I didn't find the experience very therapeutic. Wearing hard hats, swimming trunks and flip-flops, we made a nervous descent into the caves. There were no guides and no lights – we had to carry torches to find our way.

We had to squeeze through some very narrow gaps – potholes in the walls and floors leading into tight, spiralling chimneys. In one section there was only a heavy chain to grip on to as we edged down the rough steps. It was hard work and I felt quite anxious as we picked our way down.

'They call this "spelunking" in the States, you know,' Russ called out.

'Spelunking?' I spluttered. 'That can't be right, can it? I mean, it sounds a bit like—'

'Charley!' Russ cut me off. 'Don't go there.'

In the torchlight the mud looked like butterscotch Angel

Delight, but with a thin, slimy consistency. I kept thinking of all the bodies that had been slopping around in that same bath of mud. It was so cold it took your breath away. I lay there for just a few minutes then quickly rinsed off. Coming back in semi-darkness, I stopped to sort out my flip-flop and the others went ahead. Moving on again I stepped down to what I thought was the tunnel. Instead I found myself in a recess in the rock, with a pool of water below. It was a little unnerving: I was sure we'd come that way, but I couldn't hear the others any more. Shining my torch over the walls, I realised I had indeed taken the wrong turning. As I headed back up, I squinted at all the passages, fissures and clefts in the rock. It would be very easy to get lost down here. There had been flash floods in the area and earth tremors: given what was going on in other parts of the country it was probably not a good idea to be underground at all. I was relieved when I finally made it back into the open.

Later that afternoon we were lucky enough to take a hot air balloon up to see the mountains – a stunning view of conical peaks stretching away while the glittering river bisected the valley below. Unfortunately there wasn't much wind, which meant we couldn't travel very far. When the pilot opened the burner it was so hot it felt as though the top of my head was on fire.

After about an hour we descended. At first I thought we were going to land smack in the middle of a farmer's crop: but then the pilot threw out a line which was picked up by three men on the ground. They steered us over the fields until we could set down on the road.

That evening we watched the sun going down in shafts of gold that grazed the sides of the mountain. It was spectacular and reminded me of some of the sunsets we'd seen in Sudan. That started me thinking about motorbikes. All of a sudden I was itching to get to Vietnam, where we would be riding bikes and then driving an old US army jeep.

Back in town we took a walk along the quay and came across a few bamboo rafts where the owners were fishing with cormorants. I'd read about this but had never seen it. I wasn't sure how it worked but we were keen to find out. With half a dozen birds perched on the front of the boat, the fishermen took us out to where the river was flowing swiftly. The birds were in the water now, swimming ahead while the men lit the surface with lamps held on poles. The fish were attracted to the light and as they appeared the birds dived after them.

The Chinese have been using cormorants for about three hundred years, though these days it was more of a tourist attraction. The Japanese have been using them even longer than that, since at least the fifteenth century, but the oldest records came from Peru a thousand years before that. They say necessity is the mother of invention, and I imagined some old guy watching these birds and realising their talents could be harnessed. How the first one was tamed I have no idea, but the fishermen tied a snare at the base of the cormorant's throat so it couldn't swallow its catch completely. It dived for a fish, swallowed it as far as it could and then back on the raft a fisherman made the bird spit out the fish.

Heading back into town, Russ and I decided to go for the whole tourist experience and had a massage and reflexology session before dinner. Then we decided to get drunk and stay out till two in the morning.

Early the next day, and feeling a little fragile, we headed off to the train station. As usual our platform was as far away from the entrance and up and down as many steps as it possibly could be. I seemed to be carrying most of the luggage; not only my suitcase, but a laptop and the tripod as well as a camera bag. There were at least six flights of steps to negotiate and because I couldn't carry it all at once I had to do it in stages, back and forth, up and down. By the time I finally got everything to the platform the train was in and I was sweating buckets.

The double-decker train was very crowded and ringing with the high-pitched chatter of children. My head was pounding; we had very upright seats and a five-hour journey to Nanning ahead of us. At least we had some food – there had been no time for breakfast at the hotel, but we had managed to pick up some tea and a few hard-boiled eggs marinated in soy sauce. I felt a lot better with something in my stomach, and as we passed through various stations the crowds of passengers gradually thinned. After a couple of hours I got a double seat to myself, and was able to lie down, albeit with my legs tucked in and my bum sticking out. Fixed in that rather inelegant position, I tried to get some sleep.

This was the first of two trains we were supposed to be taking to the border, but when we arrived at Nanning we found there wasn't a train to Pingxiang that day. Packing the gear, we jumped into a couple of taxis and headed for the bus station, hoping to catch a ride on from there.

Heading into the city, I stared out of the window, thinking how nice it was to be in the back of a cab. The driver was separated from us by a grille of metal bars that completely surrounded his seat, presumably designed to stop anyone robbing him. Still, it was a comfortable ride, and – sitting in nose-to-tail traffic – I had to admit that my heart sank at the thought of another bus ride. The buses here were pretty gnarly and the drive to Yangshuo really hadn't been much fun. The seat backs kept collapsing without warning and I reckon we must have almost crashed twenty times. Still, I was resigned to the fact that with no train it would have to be a bus. That was until Russ phoned me; he was in the other cab and they were already at the bus station.

'Listen, mate,' he said. 'We've just missed a bus to Pingxiang.'

'Have we? That's handy.'

'Why don't we ask these cab drivers if they'll take us all the way?'

A splendid idea, and in fact it turned out to be a pretty reasonable option for five people. And on top of that we could leave immediately. Fantastic, I had the buzz again. The last throes of my hangover were receding, I wasn't on a bus and tomorrow I'd be back on a motorbike. Yee-hah! It was turning out to be a good day after all.

You get good and bad days when you're travelling and no matter the circumstances you just have to suck it up. The up side is that when you do get the buzz, boy, do you really get it. The down side is that travelling with someone other than your wife or girlfriend can be potentially awkward. If you're not careful you can fall out with your best mate – even Ewan and I came close to that for a couple of days on Long Way Down. It's almost inevitable – nothing tests a friendship like travelling together for a long time, especially when you're separated from your family.

Russ and I have been working side by side for the last four years but this was the first time we'd done anything like this. When I'm with Ewan on motorbikes I might not see Russ for a couple of days, but this time we were travelling in the same vehicle almost all the time. Because he's a great organiser, he likes to do things his own way, and now and again you have to fight your corner to make sure that you get what *you* want. There's no question that when we find ourselves in trouble he's the first person to step forward without thinking about himself, but I still get irritated by some of the things he does. Then again, I imagine he feels the same way about me – it's the norm in situations like this. It would probably be a bit weird if we didn't fall out occasionally. Generally, though, we were getting on really well, and as we made our way to Pingxiang I realised how glad I was to be sharing this amazing experience with him.

By the time we pulled up outside the hotel I was pretty jaded and looking forward to a good dinner and bed. We paid the drivers, unloaded the gear and wandered into the lobby. It was as if we'd walked into an Austin Powers movie: the furniture pure sixties, leather sofas with polka dot cushions; garish abstract paintings on the walls; glass tables with sway-backed chairs covered in striped suede or flowers. *Yeah baby!* The restaurant tables were separated by lengths of purple gauze and pink nylon, like an opium den in old Shanghai. All we needed now was 'Mini-Me' and a couple of bongs and we could sit and smoke and devise a plot to hold the world to ransom.

Of course the day we were due to ride motorbikes it was pouring with rain. I thought I heard the patter when I woke up and looking out of the window I could barely believe it. My one hundred per cent record was intact: it had rained in Ireland, then again in

Georgia when we picked up the Urals, it had been pelting down the day we rode the Enfields out of Delhi, and now it was raining here. What is it about me and motorbikes and the rain? Oh well, I thought, at least it wouldn't be cold.

We'd had four days to cross China – and while we had only seen a tiny fraction of this huge and diverse country, I didn't think we'd done too badly, considering the problems we'd had getting here. Perhaps I'd get the chance to explore the country more on a future trip. Before we'd set off, Russ and I had agreed that if we made it just as far as Nepal on this trip we'd be happy. As it turned out we'd not only made Nepal but we'd seen a flash of China too. Now we were on our way to Vietnam, then Laos and Cambodia, and I was really excited. Despite the rain and the clouds hanging grey and drab over the mountains, I couldn't wait to get back on a motorbike.

We had a bit of hassle at the border: because of the situation with Mungo's knee we'd flown Anne in but we also needed Matt, Mungo's friend, as back-up. He only had a faxed visa for Vietnam, and we thought that might be a problem. It turned out we were right.

Arriving at the border we transferred from the cab to a government tuk-tuk which took us on to customs. The Chinese inspected the paperwork and stamped our passports, but when we showed them Matt's visa they wouldn't let him out of the country. They were looking out for his interests: he was living in Beijing and his Chinese visa was up for renewal. They told him if they stamped him out of China he couldn't come back. If the Vietnamese wouldn't accept the faxed copy – which they thought was quite likely – he'd be stuck in no-man's-land. It was a very good point. Once Russ's paperwork was in order, he went across to the Vietnamese side to ask the question. The Chinese had been right – Vietnamese immigration would not accept a faxed visa.

Luckily we had people waiting on the Vietnamese side who might be able to help – not only our interpreter Chi, but a government attaché the authorities had insisted should travel with us. We'd had the same type of 'guide' in Libya on Long Way Down, and though being watched all the time is a pain in the arse, it might just work to our advantage now. I crossed into Vietnam, found the interpreter and explained the situation. I'm not sure exactly what happened but she spoke to the attaché and after a bit of to-ing and fro-ing the Vietnamese immigration officials located Russ, who was back on the Chinese side of the border with Matt. They told him that they'd spoken to their 'leader' and a special dispensation would be granted. If Russ filled in the form they would issue Matt with a visa there at the border.

At last we were all standing on Vietnamese soil. And we had motorbikes waiting. I'd already spotted them: two military-green Minsk motorbikes that had been brought to the border by an Australian called Digby, who runs a tour company in Hanoi. They looked like a couple of World War Two scramblers with knobbly tyres and chunky frames, the serial numbers painted on their petrol tanks. The bikes were named after the city of Minsk in Belarus where they were made. First produced in 1951, the factory had been manufacturing bicycles since 1945 and decided to expand their market with a motorcycle. They were simple and reliable and ended up being exported all over the world.

Digby told us there was a freeway that linked the border crossing here at Dong Dang with the capital, but the last thing we wanted was to sit on some manic motorway. He suggested a route through the northern hills instead.

It was great to be riding again, back in control of my own destiny after a succession of other people's vehicles. The bikes, which had been built in the 1950s, were 125 cc and being two-strokes there was no engine braking: in fact there didn't seem to be much braking of any description. They had the old drum system that people like Geoff Duke used to use and when I tried them they didn't offer much. But then they didn't go very fast either and we were both experienced riders. The gearing was one down and three up; there was no battery, but the most important part was the horn. Everyone in Vietnam rode on the horn – you were expected to hoot and be hooted at; that's the way it was. If for any reason the horn stopped working we'd have to pull over and fix it. Digby told us to watch out for the driving, which apparently was as bad as anywhere we'd been, though after avoiding articulated trucks hurtling down our side of the road, I wasn't overly bothered. What could Vietnam throw at us that India or Georgia hadn't?

Even so, Digby warned us that no one looked when they pulled out from a side road or backed out of a driveway, so we needed to be ready to take evasive action. The only other rules of engagement were the usual ones; namely give way to anyone bigger than you.

After getting a feel for how the bikes handled we took off, weaving our way between a line of trucks and a 4×4 that was backing, unsighted, across the road. We headed down the freeway for a couple of miles before turning on to a minor road and climbing into the hills. This was more like it: riding a bike on bumpy roads in the middle of nowhere. I loved it.

It had stopped raining, but it was almost as hot as India and even more humid. We were in jeans and T-shirts, open-faced helmets and no gloves, and even with the bit of breeze we were creating, my clothes were sticking to me. At least we were riding though, and not just any old bikes either; these had been here since the Viet Minh fought the French.

We climbed slowly into the hills on fairly empty roads. The countryside had a similar feel to what we had seen of China: thick, tropical vegetation, the same green-domed mountains and lush damp valleys. It had a different atmosphere though; it was less ordered, the people seemed less well off and their world a bit more chaotic. We rode through little towns where kids waved and Mediterranean-style villas sat alongside old shops with tin roofs and thatched stucco houses.

The road was sweeping rather than switchback; the mountainside kept at bay by stone walls, many of which had partially collapsed, rocks littering the tarmac. We passed a few trucks and the odd bus, but most people were on motorbikes. Spotting a kid who was struggling with a bike that wouldn't start, we pulled over to help. His bike was so overloaded it was ridiculous; he had four enormous – and I mean huge – sacks strapped onto this tiny little two-stroke. Covering the seat and scraping the road on either side, the sacks weighed the bike down so much that not only would it not start, there was no clearance on the suspension either.

I gave him a hand, keeping it upright while he got enough purchase to try and kick it over. He tried and I tried and he tried again before eventually it started. Then he swung a leg across the tank while I stopped the bike from falling over. He took off with his toes trailing the ground and the load wobbling precariously. I steadied the back end and gave him a bit of a shove and he waddled off up the hill with the engine straining so hard we took bets on how far he'd get.

An hour or so later we were cutting through hills filled with grazing cattle, a few of them wallowing in pools of mud alongside the road. They had black faces and massive curving horns. They'd been shitting everywhere and I remembered how good an explosion of dung or mud looks from behind, so coming up on a huge pile I steamed right through it.

I got it badly wrong; I hadn't realised how high and short the mudguard was and instead of fanning a great wave either side of my bike the pile erupted like a geyser. Immediately I was covered in evil, stinking cow shit – all over my shirt and jeans, in my eyes, my beard, in my mouth. There was so much of it I couldn't see properly. I had to get off the bike and hunt down a bottle of water to wash it all off. I wouldn't be trying that again in a hurry.

It was incredibly hot now; the clouds low and the humidity almost total. We stopped for lunch and sat on a wall gazing across paddy fields to the distant hills marking the horizon. It was great to be riding again, but it was also very draining in this heat – the air was so moist it sucked your breath away.

On the move again, we made our way down towards the main road that would take us into Hanoi. There were lots of scooters and mopeds around, and small-bore motorbikes like the ones we were riding. We'd seen plenty in India, of course, but there they only carried people: here they seemed to carry everything from piles of bamboo, to hessian sacks and pigs. I'm not kidding; I was taking a bend when this guy came by on a bike no bigger than mine with three live pigs strapped to it. They were tied on their backs one on each side and one crosswise like a top box. The guy gave me a nod and a wave, chugging along to market as if it was the most natural thing in the world, which I guess for him it was.

We took the old road into Hanoi, crossing the Red River and following a tree-lined avenue where villas stood in gardens surrounded by ornately crafted wrought-iron fences. They had been built by the French in the nineteenth century and while some were as sumptuous now as they'd been then, others looked run down and dilapidated. We passed an open stretch of parkland overlooked by Ho Chi Minh's mausoleum: a massive flat-roofed building with marble pillars. It reminded me of the Lincoln Memorial in Washington. Ho Chi Minh's embalmed body is on display in a glass casket just as Lenin is in Moscow. His face is still on every bank note even though the communist government abandoned his policies back in the 1980s. Some people revere him, some hate him; the Vietnamese who fled to the US after 1975 will tell you he was nothing more than a murderer.

Hanoi blew me away with the high-pitched whine of strokers, the constant honking . . . the energy and buzz were intoxicating. The motorbike was clearly the main mode of transportation here; I reckon they outnumbered any other vehicle by about 70–1. Taking a slip road towards the heart of the city, all we could see as we approached the junction were motorbikes flashing past in front of us. The humidity was even worse than in the mountains – the walls of the buildings were stained and even the trees seemed to drip with sweat.

We'd phoned ahead from China and found a dentist who could fix my tooth (hopefully once and for all), so I had that to look forward to. Meanwhile Anne had jabs she had to get through; the poor soul had so little notice in London she'd flown out here without being fully inoculated. Tomorrow we could compare needle marks.

At the hotel I took a shower and dried off, though I don't know why I bothered because by the time I made it down to reception I was soaking again. We were going to eat dinner in a place Digby had recommended: the Delicious Restaurant. Not a bad name for a restaurant. The food was apparently a combination of the best flavours from all over the country.

It was dark outside now. I watched a woman ride by on a bicycle loaded up with empty plastic bottles; hundreds of them tied in two enormous bundles one on top of the other. I don't know how she managed to get them tied on, never mind ride the thing – the load was at least a dozen feet off the ground. She waited at the lights: when they're red they count down 10, 9, 8 . . . which is kind of cool. When they went green she tottered off looking slightly less stable than the guy we'd seen with the hessian sacks.

What an amazing place. Welcome to Vietnam, Charley. Or should I say, Welcome to Bike Country.

19
Dead in the Water

The following morning I went to the dentist on the back of a *Xeom* or motorbike taxi – last night over dinner at the Delicious Restaurant, a piece of what was left of my tooth had broken off. Not so delicious.

The driver gave me a black plastic helmet to wear. With its short peak, it offered about as much protection as a baseball cap. At first glance the driver seemed to be wearing a steel helmet rather like the GIs used in the Vietnam War, but when I looked closer I saw it was also plastic – like a toy helmet. Up until a year ago there had been no helmet law in Vietnam, but so many kids had died from head injuries the government introduced legislation. Apparently since then there had been an explosion of shops selling these useless plastic crash hats.

The ride across town was slow: one of a million bikes, we criss-crossed the main roads into smaller side streets where the buildings kept the heat so compressed the tarmac was sweating.

When I got to the clinic the dentist said all she could do was stuff the hole with a block of composite. I'd need the tooth crowned when I got back to London. Fine, I didn't care, really, just as long as she could do something that would last that long.

That afternoon we would be taking the bus to Halong and then tomorrow we would be crossing to Cat Ba Island on a junk. But before we left Hanoi we were due to meet up with a Vietnam Vet, an ex-soldier who'd fought against the Americans. Chi explained that he had been disabled in the war and made his living on a tricycle taxi provided by the government.

I was looking forward to meeting him – this expedition was all about taking local transport and it would be interesting to speak to a man who'd fought on the Vietnamese side. Jumping on to a couple of motorbike taxis Russ and I were ferried across the city. It was wonderfully chaotic, with a similar feel to India, though perhaps with a little more western influence. We left the streets for a labyrinth of alleys, and a different world altogether. We were among the poorer houses here, where dogs were yapping, kids were playing and washing hung from windows. Now and again the lines were strung across the alleys themselves. The warren opened into a large square surrounded by buildings with a lake in the middle. Sticking out of the slack, green water was the mashed-up wing of an American bomber.

At 23:05 on 27 December 1972 a B52 was shot down and part of the wreckage crashed into Huu Tiep Lake. There was a plaque on the wall commemorating the event in both Vietnamese and English: it stated that the downing of this plane galvanised the people and helped bring about eventual victory against the American forces. Standing there, gazing at the wing, I had a very strange sensation – an incredibly strong feeling of déjà vu. I swear it felt as if I'd been there before and yet this was my first time in Vietnam.

The guy we wanted to speak to was waiting for us on his motorised trike on the far side of the lake. The trike had a motorbike's front end, though the gear changing was done by hand and the seat came from a car. Behind it there was a luggage/passenger compartment with two benches. The whole thing was covered with a canvas canopy. The driver only had one leg and I assumed he must have lost the other during the war. It was thirty-odd years since the Americans withdrew, though, and this guy looked no more than forty. He had a calm, thoughtful face and wore a green pith helmet. I asked him how he'd lost a leg.

'In a traffic accident,' he said.

I looked quizzically at Chi, but she didn't comment.

'Right,' I said, nodding. 'And the government provided you with the trike, is that right?'

'No,' he said. 'I bought it.'

Clearly there had been a communication breakdown somewhere. Never mind – he was a lovely bloke. Hopping in the back we asked him if he could take us to the hotel so we could pick up our luggage, then on to the bus station. He explained there wouldn't be enough room for us and the gear, so one of his friends, another disabled driver, followed us with a second trike.

I was sorry not to have seen more of Hanoi – my trip to the 'Veteran' had taken up most of the morning. However we'd seen enough to know that in two years the city would celebrate its one thousandth birthday. In that time it had been ruled by the Chinese and the French, from 1940–1945 it was occupied by the Japanese, and from 1946 to 1954 it was the battleground between the French and the Viet Minh. We could have spent a month here and barely scratched the surface.

The trikes dropped us at the station where we boarded an old coach. It was small and crowded but we'd been on a few buses now and this wasn't too bad. The humidity was killing me, though, my face felt as if it was glowing and there wasn't a single part of my body that wasn't soaked in sweat. We knew the heat was going to be the major challenge here – and almost certainly in Laos and Cambodia too. Just sitting on a bus was arduous enough, never mind driving in the jungle and riding a couple of dirt bikes later on.

It took for ever to get out of the city: at least a four-hour journey and the driver went all around the houses trying to fill the bus. Fill it he did, though, and with so many people on board the atmosphere was even more oppressive. We headed south on open road with flat, green fields on either side. Matt had a window open and his arm dangling which, unbeknown to us, was illegal. Halfway to Halong the police stopped the bus and boarded it, then spent half an hour reading us the riot act about windows and arms and the laws of the road in Vietnam.

The next morning – 7 June – we were at the harbour by

seven-fifty to pick up the junk that would take us to Cat Ba. Vietnam was the eighteenth country we'd crossed through since we left Dad's house. Even this early it was baking, the air still, the sun hidden in dense clouds. It was sticky and breathless and felt as though the monsoon rains would unleash any moment. The harbour was heaving; a real bun fight with hundreds of junks tied up and people clamouring to get on board.

The junk we were taking had two storeys. It was beautifully built with a polished wooden deck and carved rail, and a staircase leading to the upper deck. Inside there were four or five really nice cabins. I decided I could quite happily live on it; the main deck was decorated with potted plants and little shrubs like someone's courtyard garden.

There was no order, each vessel just cast off and steamed out hoping for the best. We did likewise, picking a path between other junks and flat little skiffs. It was as chaotic as the streets of Mumbai; there were boats shunting each other, people shouting, horns blaring. I looked around for a harbour master, or pilot maybe, to take charge, but couldn't see anyone. It was only when we were steaming away that I glimpsed a uniformed guy arriving finally in a speedboat.

'Too late, mate,' I muttered, 'they've all gone already.'

Finally we were away, and having escaped without damage we headed across an emerald green sea in the direction of islands that rose steep and sharp in the distance. It was very close now – one of the stickiest days I can remember – the water flat as a mill pond and what little wind there was was so incredibly hot and clammy that you could barely even stand in it.

It was stunningly beautiful, though, an island paradise that reminded me of the mountains around Yangshuo, the way the land climbed almost vertically out of the sea. It was a little touristy, I suppose, though most of the boats were heading in the opposite direction from us. The skipper, Hang, told us they were going to a group of islands where they'd moor up with a police guard in case they were attacked by pirates who rode small, fast boats that came down from China. I could imagine pirates in these waters. Apparently the area was notorious, and they preyed particularly on tourists.

There are more than three thousand islands off the coast at Halong, which means 'Where the dragon descends into the sea'. Legend has it the islands were formed by a huge dragon that spewed out precious stones and thrashed its tail, raking up the seabed as it swam out to defend the area. Even today fishermen claim to have seen a giant sea creature they call Tarasque. I don't know about sea monsters but as far as the precious stones go, we'd been told there was a fishing village among the limestone cliffs where the people cultivated pearls. Hang had never been there before but he knew roughly where it was and said he'd try to show us before heading to Cat Ba.

Leaving the other boats behind, we motored between enormous hunks of rock. With their short beaches and towering cliffs it wasn't hard to see how the dragon legend came about. They all seemed to look much the same though, and I imagine navigating this area would not be easy. We toured bay after bay and rounding one island we'd come across another ten just like it and ten more beyond that. Finally we crossed a wider stretch of water and on the far side I glimpsed a patch of blue. It was the roof of a hut: I could see a line of them built at the base of the cliffs. Strung across the water in front were hundreds of floating buoys, markers for oyster nets.

The huts – spread across the beaches of a number of neighbouring islands – had concrete walls and tin roofs and most had a yard area covered by a canvas canopy. Pushing off from the shore, one of the boats came out to meet us.

It was rowed by a teenage girl wearing a straw coolie hat, her young brother sitting next to her. Russ and I climbed down and they took us to the home of an oyster fisherman who cultivated pearls by seeding the host oyster with a tiny slice of another. The 'fertilised' shell was then soaked in the sea for two years while the pearl grew. The oysterman was a young guy with smiley eyes and a shock of black hair. He said he had a million shells that generated twenty kilos of pearls.

Sitting there looking at an open shell I suddenly felt incredibly lucky. Here I was in a rowing boat off the coast of Vietnam with an oysterman. I was swept away not just by where I was, but the enormous distance we'd covered. I bought some pearls for Olly and my children and a few for the girls back in the office.

There was a whole community here; an unnamed village with its own way of life, a school that the kids rowed to every day, their parents making a living from pearls sold to wholesalers or people like us who just showed up. The oysterman separated the pearls we'd bought into various different bags and, shaking hands, we headed back to the boat.

In late afternoon we docked at a concrete quay. We tied up and, having collected our luggage, said goodbye to Hang and the junk.

Cat Ba is the largest island in the Halong archipelago and a fairly popular tourist destination: there are lots of fishing villages dotted along the beaches and one main town with a bunch of hotels. We took a van from the harbour, driving inland through roadside farming villages that backed on to rice paddies.

At the hotel we took a moment to check the map, tracing the line we'd taken from Yangshuo to here and all the way back to Ireland. As Russ put it, we'd come two hand-spans and had another hand-span to go before we reached Sydney. Amazing. But first we had a night in Cat Ba before we took a boat to the mainland and a train south. After dinner we wandered through town and came across a competition where people were making mummies out of toilet paper.

Maybe I should have taken that as an omen. The next morning we arrived at the quay, and as soon as I clapped eyes on our boat I knew it was too small.

'That's not very big,' I said, staring unconvinced at the tiny vessel flopping about in the water. I looked out to where some of the smaller islands formed a natural barrier that kept the water here pretty calm. It wouldn't be so calm on the other side and the same ominous-looking clouds that had dogged us since we arrived were still threatening to unleash the rain.

They say you should always go with your first instincts and over the years I've learned to trust mine. Only not today, apparently. I knew this was wrong but I kept my mouth shut and like stupid sheep we all clambered aboard. There were quite a few of us on this part of the trip as well as myself and Russ – Anne and Matt were filming, Robin was with us again taking still photos, and then there was our translator, Chi, the government attaché and Seb and Brighade, two of Chi's friends who were hitching a ride.

ailing down the Xi Jiang river on a cement barge.

Vith Liang-Su and his two sons Lorau and Chi-Chi. The family all lived together on the boat and rarely
pent time on land.

Yangshuo is set against stunning scenery.

Irresistible, eh girls?

In Vietnam. Those little piggies went to market!

On the Minsk motorbike – 125cc, two stroke engine. I rode from the Vietnamese border through the mountains to Hanoi. It rained, of course.

Rowing to the house of an oyster fisherman near Cat Ba.

Our one-legged taxi driver near Huu Tiep Lake. The heat and humidity here were really extreme.

The Willys jeep – left over from the war.

A boat fashioned from a dumped B52 fuel tank.

Taking the rocket boat from Voen Kham in Cambodia.

I rode this Honda 250 dirt bike 250 kms through Cambodia.

Possibly the slowest form of transport I tried.

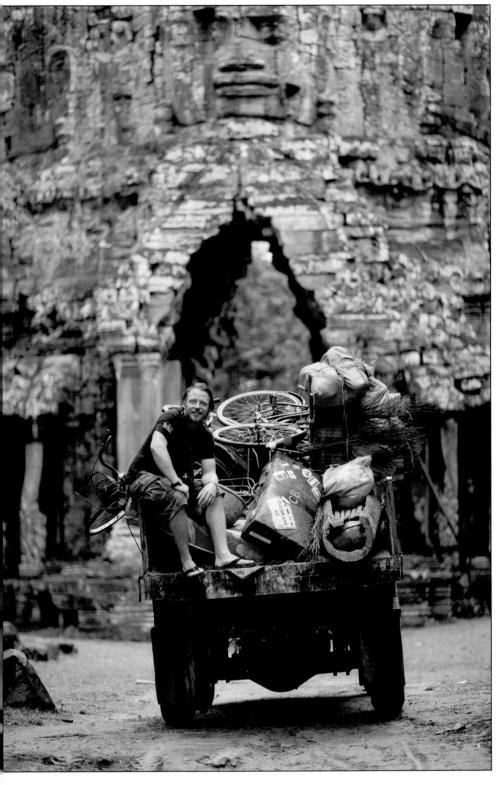

Angkor Wat, Cambodia.

The last bamboo train in Cambodia.

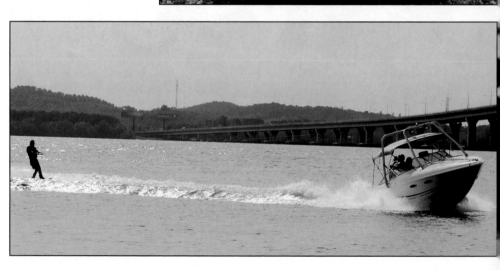

Wakeboarding across the border from Danga Bay to Raffles Marina, Singapore.

On top of that there was the luggage. By the time we'd piled in we were sitting on bags with three people hunched precariously in the bows. The pilot was young and looked inexperienced: I should've known better, I really should. But he got the boat going and we pulled away from the harbour and turned into the swell.

As soon as we hit the bigger waves the boat rocked awkwardly and I knew we were overloaded. We were also making our way straight for a narrow channel between the small islands instead of going around them. Glancing across, I saw that the pilot looked nervous. I looked at the grey, swollen sea and the high, choppy waves breaking through the channel and just knew this was a mistake. We were low in the water and the closer we got to the channel the higher the waves became. By the time we got to the first of the rocks they were slapping the bows and soaking us with spray.

This was no good: we were weighed down as it was and this guy was taking us on some crazy short cut that didn't look at all safe. I should've said something, asked him to turn back and go around the islands, but it was too late and we were in the channel with massive black rocks on both sides and the choppy open sea directly ahead. It was no longer a swell – it was rough, the waves tightly compressed and coming at us one after the other.

'Fucking hell,' Russ said, as a wave hit the bows with a sound like a pistol shot.

I could feel a sudden dip in the revs and the bows went down. I shook my head. This felt wrong, stupid: we'd been taught how to pilot a speedboat in Southampton and when the waves are rough you don't suddenly close the throttle.

'He's got to keep the power on,' I shouted to Russ, pointing at the pilot. 'The bows are far too low.' We were in a dangerous place, the waves coming thick and fast. Sitting there, helpless, I was sure now that the guy didn't really know what he was doing. But surely he knew these waters?

Matt turned the big camera, the Z7, to face the oncoming waves. As he did so a huge breaker reared up right in front of the boat.

'Fuck!' I saw Matt duck away and turn towards us, trying to save the camera. The wave hit and he was almost knocked off his feet. Up front the others were hanging on to the gunwales. Russ and I were in the stern and we were saturated by the spray; the boat was yawing badly now. Then the engine conked out.

This was serious: what might have been a bit of a concern thirty seconds ago had suddenly become a deadly situation. We were without power in a rough channel and there was every chance we'd be pushed onto the rocks.

I could feel my heart thumping. I thought of Olly and the kids and for a nanosecond everyone was silent.

Then we all started talking at once.

The pilot was trying to start the boat but it wouldn't go: it coughed and spluttered for a few moments then nothing; not even the whirr of electrics. He'd lost his confidence, I could see it. He had brought us in here then bottled it and cut the power. That last wave must have got into the electrics. Now we had no protection against *any* waves, we couldn't steer, the boat was spinning and there was nothing but rough water between us and those rocks.

'This is really serious, guys,' I said. Looking at their faces, I knew I was only saying what everyone else was thinking. We were dead in the fucking water. Shunted around at the mercy of the sea, we were shifting ever closer to walls of rock and there was nothing we could do about it.

Behind me, Russ was clinging on to the flimsy struts that held the canopy in place. The boat was rolling badly, turning in the swell and see-sawing so the waves were coming from behind us now. The government attaché was looking grim; Anne was silent behind the camera that (God bless her) was still rolling. The pilot was on his cellphone. He told Chi that he was trying to get another boat to come out and help us. Looking at how close the rocks were I wasn't sure there would be time.

'If we do go down make sure you've got your life jackets on,' Russ said. 'Best to try and swim back through that channel because it gets smoother on the other side.'

For a moment nobody said anything then, almost surreptitiously, Anne reached for her life jacket.

This was really grim. I'm not good in small boats, I never have been. We all had families and we were in real danger of never seeing them again. Yes, we might be able to swim, but the channel was so tight and the waves so unpredictable, there was every chance we'd be slammed into the rocks. One good whack on the head and if you weren't killed outright you'd be knocked unconscious and drown.

'This is not good at all.' I was staring at the pilot. 'What has this guy done?'

I had my passport in my pocket together with the pearls I'd bought from the oysterman; they were the last things I'd packed when we left this morning. Instinctively now I slipped them into the waterproof pouch I was carrying. If we went over I promised myself that somehow I'd swim ashore. I would make it. I'd have my passport and the pearls and I'd take them home to my family.

Suddenly, from nowhere, a long, blue fishing boat appeared at the lip of the channel; a traditional open boat with furled sail. We could see two men on board and started yelling to them. Seeing us, without hesitation they turned into the channel.

The swell was getting worse and minute by minute we were being pressed ever closer to the islands: we were pitching and yawing, rolling with each new wall of water that was forced through the channel. I looked at those jagged grey rocks and shook my head. I should have trusted my instincts right from the start.

The fishing boat had either answered a summons generated by the phone call or they had just happened to see us: either way they were coming, thank God. Much longer and we'd be on the rocks and would have no choice but to bail out.

They were close now and the waves were so rough I thought they were going to crash right into us. That would be a disaster; if their boat hit ours it would force us onto the rocks. The guy at the front, who was barefoot and wearing a coolie hat, was calling out and gesturing for us to throw him a line. The pilot slammed their boat into reverse and they kept steady long enough for us to get a rope to them. It was short, though, and their boat was beginning to turn. We were turning also, pitching badly, the boats too close with massive waves rearing at the edge of the channel. We gripped the sides, the struts to the canopy, anything we could find to brace ourselves. The fishing boat was still turning and I realised they were tying our line to a longer one so they could pay us out some distance.

A big wave hit side on and the boat almost capsized: another like that and we'd be over.

Just then a second fishing boat appeared on the island side of the channel. It was bigger than the first, with a wheelhouse, and sat higher in the water. Yelling and whistling, we tried to attract their attention but whether they saw us or not, they just kept going.

'This is fucking crazy, man,' I muttered.

'The worst thing is the waves coming behind us,' Russ stated, almost matter-of-factly. 'When you're learning to sail they teach you to steer into the waves, waves coming over the back will fill up the boat, that's why it sinks.'

'All right, all right.' I looked round angrily at him. 'Thank you very much.'

Mercifully, the guys in the fishing boat seemed to be winning. They had worked the line around and turned their craft. Suddenly there was hope and I watched as they took up the slack and we straightened up behind them. They didn't mess about; as soon as that line was secure they hauled ass out of there.

At last we were moving, no longer at the mercy of the waves. Realising we'd make it I took a long look at the rocks, ragged and sharp; if we'd hit one of those it would've been curtains.

My heart rate slowed a little as we made it safely out of the channel into calmer water. We were heading back to Cat Ba and right now all I wanted was to feel land under my feet and phone my wife.

'That was lucky,' Russ said.

'We should've gone round that headland like everybody else,' I said. 'What the fuck did he think he was doing taking us through there when we're seriously overloaded to begin with?' I was no longer scared, I was bloody angry. The pilot had no right doing what he'd done: and then to lose confidence in the middle of the channel – that was unforgivable. He kept his face forward, steering the boat under the tow and not looking at any of us. The fishermen left us at the nearest pontoon and we thanked them; a couple of guys who'd risked their lives to make sure we didn't lose ours.

Fifteen minutes later a larger cruiser came out and threw us a line, towing us to the harbour wall. As I spotted the steps leading up to land I felt an immense sense of relief. The main camera – the

Z7 Matt had been using – was broken. Matt had tried to keep it dry but after that wave it had worked for a while before completely giving up the ghost. But thank God that was all we'd lost.

'He doesn't expect to get paid, does he?' I said, pointing to the pilot as we unloaded the last of the gear.

Back on dry land with our lives and most of the equipment intact, we had to decide what to do next. There was a car ferry across to the mainland but we were too late for that so after a coffee and a phone call to Olly, we headed for the other side of the island and the passenger ferry. Russ and I decided that once we were on the mainland again we'd try to rent a van and scoot down to Nam Dinh as fast as we could.

I was pretty shaken, kicking myself for ignoring my first instincts. Jesus, just thinking about it put a few grey hairs on me.

The last thing I wanted to do was get on any other kind of boat: someone had suggested we get another private boat for the sake of speed, but forget that. The passenger ferry was about as small as I'd go: a decent size with two massive Caterpillar diesels to power it over the waves. Forty minutes after we boarded we were back on the mainland.

It was nearly five o'clock now and we had maybe four hours on the road to Nam Dinh. We climbed into a minibus we'd managed to organise from the island. Settling back, I realised I was actually looking forward to the train.

We were all a little quiet – not surprising after the events of the day. Everyone reacts in different ways in that kind of life-or-death situation; I'd worn my heart on my sleeve, swearing and probably stating the obvious, whereas Russ had been sitting there calmly talking up the worst-case scenario. Brighade had a cut on her arm, which I cleaned and dressed; it was just a scratch but in this climate you have to be careful of infection. It was the only injury, thankfully. All in all, not a good moment and the closest we'd come to disaster since we'd left home.

It was dark when we got to Nam Dinh and the train that would take us south. The roads had been decent and we made it with some time to spare, but we couldn't see much of Nam Dinh because it was dark and the street lighting wasn't good. Physically tired and emotionally drained, we found a family-run cafe with a gathering of small tables and chairs set up outside. We ordered noodle soup and while we were waiting I called Mungo to see how his knee was. He wasn't there so I left a message: no doubt we'd speak tomorrow.

A young student and his sister were sitting at a nearby table. We chatted about our trip and what they were doing: we talked about Vietnam and London. The lad was an earnest soul, very committed, telling me about his country and how it had always been misunderstood and in many ways still was. He was very passionate and I liked that: it was good to hear such a solid opinion and I'd noticed the Chinese too had the same kind of passion for their country. The two of them were travelling on the same train we were taking and had bought a parcel of food from the cafe to take with them. There were also three or four little kids running around – they'd rush up to us and yell: 'hello' before tearing off again. There was a warmth to the place, and it was good to be in the open air even if it was still ridiculously humid.

The soup arrived, steaming hot and very welcome. I worked out that it was the children's mother who was serving and their father doing the cooking: three generations with an old woman, probably the grandmother, hovering in the background.

They brew their own beer in this part of Vietnam; it is light and tastes very fresh, though it only lasts for a day and I imagine if you have too much it will give you a thumping headache. They call it 'Beer Hoy' and it was served in glasses that were half beer and half froth, European style. It was good stuff.

As we drank together, I realized we'd become a real team now. I'd felt it before, of course, but there are moments on any expedition when things suddenly click. Today was one of those days. Despite that bloody boat and those rocks, nobody had panicked – we held our nerve and got through it together. All for one and one for all. We raised our glasses and drank a toast to being alive.

20
Rainy Season

I woke early on another train going God knows where. Peering blearily out of the window I could see green fields and scattered trees, and mountains in the distance. I'm not sure how much I slept: I found I always drifted in and out of half-dreams sleeping on a train. Every time the train lurches you're thrown awake, and this one was a right old bone rattler.

We were following a river not far from the coast and, standing at the window after the obligatory visit to the knee trembler, I watched people already working in the fields. It's not easy squatting over the hole first thing in the morning with the movement of the train and the knowledge that your bowels are looser than they should be. But I've got good thighs and – touch wood – so far there hadn't been any accidents.

We'd been on a few trains now, and while they had their down sides, I'd decided it was much better than a boat: at least the kind of boat we were on yesterday. I still couldn't get over that guy trying to take us through that little channel. I can't believe I allowed myself to get on the boat in the first place, but I suppose by any means is by any means and an abortive trip was bound to be part of the expedition.

None of us were very sure what time the train was arriving at Dong Ha, but we'd spoken to the guy who came round selling noodles and he told us we'd be in at seven. Sure enough seven came around and we pulled into the station. I rushed about telling everyone we were here and in a hurry because the trains didn't hang around long when they stopped. We grabbed our gear and piled into the corridor, had the doors open even, only to discover it wasn't Dong Ha. The signs said something else altogether: we still had an hour to go before we got to Dong Ha. So it was back to the cabins, four bunks in each and so close you could feel the breath of the person lying opposite.

An hour later we were definitely in Dong Ha this time and I could feel the excitement bubbling. We were picking up a Willys jeep left behind by the Americans after the war, and the thought of driving it through Vietnam of all places would be an extraordinary experience, I was sure.

The station was more of an open-air platform, and there didn't seem to be much of Dong Ha but dust and sun. We spotted the jeep parked outside a little cafe. It was everything I'd hoped it would be: newly repainted in a dark military green with a cargo net stretched across the bonnet and another wrapping the spare wheel. It was in really good nick and the owner had obviously done a lot of work keeping it together. It dated back to 1971 and still carried everything the US army would have carried: picks and shovels, an axe, and there was even a deep-water fording kit – a lever on the dash that you pressed when crossing a ford and pulled out again when you were through. It was four-wheel drive, of course; twin gear sticks that looked freshly cleaned and oiled. The seats were comfortable, two up front and two in the back, the windscreen was the type that folded flat and was fitted with a couple of straps that doubled as a handhold when you were getting in and out. God was I looking forward to driving it.

My excitement was dashed almost immediately. When I mentioned driving I was told I wasn't allowed to. No one had said anything before, but foreigners aren't allowed to drive in Vietnam unless they take a test and get a special licence issued by the government.

Shit. We had a six-hour ride ahead and I wouldn't be able to drive. Oh well, at least we'd get to ride in it. Gear loaded, we jumped in. The driver was a nice guy who didn't say much; he was wearing a smart green pith helmet just like the one the disabled cabbie had worn in Hanoi. We were heading for the coast and a place called Vinh Moc that had been just outside the demilitarised zone in the Vietnam War – the demarcation line between North Vietnam and South that had been drawn after the first war back in the fifties. Vinh Moc had been part of the Ho Chi Minh trail, the supply route for arms and supplies. After being bombed incessantly by the US air force the villagers had dug several kilometres of tunnels and hidden in them.

Our driver took us through small towns on dirt roads baked hard by the sun. Flat and smooth, they were really good quality and the jeep rattled along at a fair old pace. It was very comfortable and a great way to see this part of the country especially given our destination and its significance. Weaving through dense, smoky jungle I could begin to imagine what it must have been like to be a GI en route to wherever, never seeing the enemy and never knowing when a couple of bullets might hit you.

Halfway to Vinh Moc the driver decided to hell with the law – he'd let me drive anyway. I wasn't expecting it, but he knew I was itching to and when the roads were clear he pulled over and we swapped places.

It was fantastic; the gears were smooth, the brakes good, and the whole thing felt really well maintained. The steering wheel had the kind of delicious play you expect in old vehicles. We were in the open air on tightening bends and the deep growl of the engine was immensely satisfying. It wasn't long before we reached Vinh Moc.

I'd been reading a little of the history before we arrived. The French had colonised Vietnam largely from the south, and they were fighting Ho Chi Minh long before the Americans. When that war ended the Geneva Accords proposed elections for the whole country but the South Vietnamese and the Americans refused to sign. The emperor – who was in exile – appointed a prime minister who then rigged a referendum that got rid of the emperor. Civil war broke out. What we know as the Vietnam War began in 1959, though the Americans didn't send troops until much later. During the war 58,000 US personnel and close to 350,000 Vietnamese soldiers were killed. It also left over 3,000,000 civilians dead or wounded.

It was very interesting to be here because everything we knew about the country had been from a western perspective, and, as we'd already found out, the Vietnamese are a fiercely proud and independent people. That trait was personified in the guide who showed us the tunnels.

The entrance was hidden in elephant grass and thick vegetation that covered the area all the way to the Gulf of Tongkin. There's a heritage centre there now, a museum where the village of Vinh Moc had been, and we saw photos of how it looked before the Americans bombed the place: a symmetrical landscape of bamboo and thatch.

Our guide showed us the alarm bell the villagers used to warn of incoming air raids, shrapnel from an old bomb they'd put to some use. The tunnels ran for five kilometres to the sea.

We walked up a narrow, dusty trail into deep jungle before the trail opened and a stone wall indicated the entrance to the underground network. It was hot and narrow, the passage reinforced with wooden bulwarks. We could walk without bending, but as we went deeper the passages became narrower and lower and the walls were polished stone. The tunnels were created over an eighteen-month period between 1966 and late 1967 and the Americans had no idea they were under construction. The villagers dug in the day time and at night they'd ferry the earth and soil off shore, leaving no sign that anything was going on.

Three hundred of them lived underground for six years; each family allotted a tiny living space, a little room carved off one of the tunnels. It was a labyrinth, very close and tight: the tunnels never running straight for very long so that if the enemy found them the people wouldn't be mown down. There were bends and clefts, security posts where villagers could return fire if they were attacked. We saw rooms where eighty or more people gathered to plan what they were going to do; there were hospitals with operating theatres, schools, communal kitchens and freshwater wells. This place was not only a refuge, though, it became an important staging post: food and arms were carried through the tunnels to an outlet on the beach that doubled as a ventilation shaft. The supplies were then transported to a small island off shore and shipped south to the Viet Cong.

It was hot and dark inside, and I found it hard to imagine whole families living in tiny caves like this cut into the rock. Seventeen children had been born underground and the larger your family the bigger the space you were allotted. We saw rusty pitons fixed in the walls where washing lines had been hung, and carved nooks where petrol lamps were lit. Every tunnel we went down there were tiny rooms left and right, the village partially recreated underground.

'This is amazing,' Russ said as we stood at the lip of the tunnel overlooking the sea. 'Most of it was to protect the villagers. It's horrific to think what it must have been like, your village obliterated by bombs and having to move underground and live like that, survive for six years.'

'The Americans had very modern weapons,' our guide told us, as passionate as the student we had met the night before. 'But Vietnamese people are very brave: we struggle for our freedom, our independence. We have a real purpose.'

Seven miles from the Laos border we stopped at a site commemorating the battle of Khe Sanh: a seventy-seven-day struggle between US marines and the North Vietnamese. Khe Sanh was one of the largest bases in the country and had been established in 1962 as an airfield by US Special Forces. It became an outpost from which they watched the PAVN (People's Army of Vietnam), many of whom were ensconced in villages along the Laos border.

The battle raged from 21 January to 8 April 1968 with the base under constant attacks from artillery and rockets. Over 200 US marines were killed, and we saw some of them in a series of grim photographs adorning the walls of the museum. There were other reminders too: battered helmets, tunics, boots, artillery belts and webbing . . . outside we could see the twisted remains of rockets, shells and massive bombs. It was impossible to imagine the devastation. There were helicopters, the old Huey you see in the movies and the bigger troop carriers with the twin rotors. In all 197 helicopters were brought down and I remember reading how for a long time the pilots weren't provided with body armour, even though they were the number one target for snipers. It's crazy how politicians justify war and this had been a particularly stupid one.

I couldn't get over the bombs, how thick the metal was, how many there were: in the Vinh Moc area alone there had been forty dropped for every villager. 'Living hell' is what people had called it.

It was sobering: a first-hand glimpse of what so many people had so tragically been forced to go through. Not just the Vietnamese but young drafted Americans, many of whom must have wondered what on earth they were fighting for. Officially there are still 1,500 US personnel missing in Vietnam.

Seven miles west we crossed the border at a tiny place called Lao Bao. Standing in the immigration hut Russ and I dripped sweat on the entry forms. Apart from the heat it was a breeze of a crossing and there we were in this little town where the streets were wide and the buildings made of wood, many of them with rusting tin roofs and walls that were steadily rotting.

The people of Laos were poorer than their neighbours, that was obvious, but we were greeted with smiles and laughter. The name is pronounced 'Lao' with a silent 's', but when we spoke to the older people they did sound the 's'. It was only after the war in Vietnam that the pronunciation was changed. We were looking for our next means of transport, a pickup truck where the bed is fitted with a framework canopy and benches to sit on. It was also the local bus service, called a *songthaew*. Unfortunately, there were only two and one had a flat tyre.

We would eventually be heading for Pakse, but tonight we'd only get as far as a place called Keng Tueb, and leaving Mae, our translator, to negotiate a price with the *songthaew* driver, Russ and I took a good look at it.

It was basically an old flat-fronted Toyota pickup. It looked OK. It was what the locals used and that was what we wanted. Mae did the deal and we piled in. The buses operate just like a *dolmus* with the driver stopping off to pick up and drop off passengers. Our first stop was the petrol station: a wooden shack with two oil drums standing outside. On top of each was a clear plastic measuring container marked in litres. The fuel was pumped by hand from the drums into the containers so they could mark the amount before it was drained into the fuel tank. We were filling plastic jerricans fixed on to the side of the flatbed, but first the son of the driver siphoned what was left in them by sucking on a plastic pipe and shoving it into the fuel tank. After that the jerricans were refilled with diesel from the drums.

In the back of the *songthaew* it was bumpy, but we were in the open air and the roads weren't busy. We passed through wonderful little villages of wattle and daub houses with straw thatched roofs perched on precarious-looking stilts. Kids in shorts and not much else came running out to wave. Everyone seemed to be smiling and my first impression was of laughter.

I took in the smells, the feel of the new country, the different atmosphere. None of it was even vaguely threatening and in fact we'd felt more than safe all the way through India, Nepal, China and Vietnam. The air was thick and humid, the road hard-packed and cutting through farmland or deep jungle. During the Vietnam War Laos had been bombed over and over again – many of Ho Chi Minh's top brass were thought to be based there. We'd seen a lot of bombs today and we stopped at Keng Tueb to see what the regular people had made of them, and in this case I mean *literally* what they made.

It was a pretty village surrounded by massive bomb craters, some of which had become ponds or muddy lakes. The houses were nicely spread out and linked by clay paths; the stilts allowed air to circulate and kept the people dry if the area flooded. The livestock sheltered in the space underneath – pigs, goats, chickens, and even cows with massive bells made from bits of shrapnel.

Remnants of the war were everywhere; many of the stilts had been made from the casings of cluster bombs dropped by the US air force. Some of them contained as many as seven hundred little bombs which scattered on impact, scything people down indiscriminately. B52s had dumped their long-range fuel tanks in this area: when they finished their mission they'd fly back and just unload the empty tank. Taking a wander down to the river we could see what had become of some of them.

The river was the focal point for the village – people were down there washing clothes and washing themselves, kids splashing about in the muddy water. Lots of people were paddling canoes. They'd taken the old fuel tanks the planes had dumped, cut them in half and made canoes out of them.

An older guy came wandering up the hill, his hair wet from washing. I asked him if he was old enough to remember the war. Nodding vigorously he pointed to where a woman was paddling seven children across the river in a fuel tank canoe.

'We thought those were bombs,' he said. 'They'd come raining down every day and we waited for them to explode like the cluster bombs, but they didn't.'

'They dropped bombs every day?'

'Every day.'

'What did you do?'

He pointed across the river to where the woman had beached the canoe now and was leading her children up the hill into thick, damp jungle. 'We hid.'

Another guy told Russ that his father had made the canoe he used today from one of the old tanks: he'd had to patch it up a little but it was still a good boat.

'It would be great to show this to some of those B52 pilots now,' I said. 'See what they thought of what had become of their fuel tanks.' We headed back towards the village. 'I'm glad something's of some use at least. All war is a waste of time but this one was really pointless.'

We spent the night close to the village, and the next morning – 11 June – we were away early with over 250 kilometres to cover to Champasak. Tomorrow we planned to take a boat down the Mekong River before crossing into Cambodia.

We travelled the first section on a *songthaew* owned by a guy called Somsanig who had his wife and baby with him in the cab. He'd rigged up a water barrel in the back for his passengers. He was a cool guy, tall and thin-faced with black hair and a typical Laos kind of smile. He made lots of stops, letting people on and off. I asked him if there was any chance I could drive. He said sure, no problem, he'd be happy to let me.

I'm not so sure about his wife, though. We were on pretty good roads and not going very fast but she had her baby with her and this vehicle was their livelihood. She didn't say much but then she didn't smile much either so I've no idea how nervous she really was. Russ told me the passengers were pretty nervous. They weren't sure what was going on but suddenly the driver was standing on a home-made footplate at the back and I was behind the wheel trying to find first gear. The stick was pretty wayward and wrapped in an old towel. I tried to pull away, but first gear kept grinding: Russ told me that back where he was there had been a collective look of extreme consternation.

We had a young schoolteacher on board who said her name was Vilaivon. She chatted about how the kids were good but with the summer they had three months off. The old guy next to Russ had been really nervous about me driving but Russ placated him by sharing a loaf of bread. I got the hang of the gears eventually and it was only really taking off that was the problem: Somsanig told me to give it more gas in first gear and I'd be fine. The horn was great and in faithful *dolmus* tradition I used it to great effect; it had a kind of echo and I decided I wanted one for when I got back to London.

Having such a full load of passengers was a big responsibility, but the roads were pretty empty. It was very rural here with flat cultivated land that opened up the jungle. Now and again hills reared up; stark, grey cliffs bare of vegetation. I think most people were subsistence farmers, living pretty much on what they were able to grow.

We stopped for lunch in a colourful little market town with broken-down trailers lying by the side of the road and darkened, lock-up shops with tin roofs. A bunch of street vendors came up with bags of bugs on sticks; crispy cockroaches marinated in something sticky before being impaled on a skewer like a kebab. The old guy had a stick, peeling the beetles like prawns before sucking out the flesh. Not very appetising – they reminded me of the grilled rats the Malawi people had tried to sell us when we were riding to Cape Town, those and the fly paste they made on the shores of the lake.

I drove for about an hour and really enjoyed it, but I think Somsanig's wife was relieved when her husband took over the wheel again. He dropped us in a small town where we boarded a coach, what the locals call a *lod mei*, that would get us into Pakse. It was ancient with narrow seats and an internal framework of bars like scaffolding poles to strengthen the structure. There were holes in the walls and the ceiling and passengers appeared to be entirely secondary to the cargo. The aisle and the overhead luggage racks were stuffed with brand-new school books. We had to climb over more books to get to a seat, the conductor making his way over them to collect our money. It wasn't just books either; there were sacks of rice and vegetables, and bags stuffed with cloves of garlic.

We endured five and a half crazy hours, the driver stopping for the odd passenger now and then, but mainly just to make deliveries. Gradually the rice dwindled, the garlic was dished out to customers and by the time we got to Pakse only the books were left.

The next morning we took a slow boat down the Mekong. It was long and narrow, with a cane roof, the engine and steering wheel taken from an old car. It appeared that people did that a lot here, lifting the engines from cars and converting them to fit the kind of direct-drive propellers we'd seen at Yangshuo. At over 2,700 miles, the Mekong is the twelfth-longest river in the world. We ambled along for a while, trying to avoid the fishing nets and disembarked in Champasak.

When we got off the boat we flagged down another butt-breaking *songthaew*, and headed for Voen Kham where we were due to cross to Cambodia. Just a few miles from there, however, are the waterfalls at Khon Phapeng and we couldn't leave Laos without stopping to see them.

The largest waterfalls in Asia, they were truly incredible. They didn't drop a long way but they were very wide; a series of boiling rapids that formed a massive natural hazard right across the river. We could hear the roar from a hundred yards away. Making our way through scrub and trees it got louder and louder until finally we could see black boulders, ragged at the edges like lava rock, splitting the river in a hundred different places. Water cascaded around them, tumbling a few metres before being forced over single trees and between bushes and flatter plateaus spewing a torrent of spray.

There was an official overlook and a visitor centre but, spotting a couple of fishermen working traps from what looked like a ruined boat, Russ and I picked our way across a section of slippery rock that stretched into the river. It was a little dodgy, slip and we'd be right in the midst of that tempest with no chance of escape. The noise was incredible, we had to shout to be heard. The rapids were at eye-level now and from that angle you really got a sense of their power. I've always found waterfalls to be therapeutic places; nature at its most awesome, and I took a moment just to sit on a rock with my elbows on my knees and take it all in. This was the Mekong, one of the great rivers of the world. Half its length is in China and the rest splits Laos, Cambodia and Thailand. I shook my head. I'd seen the Victoria Falls and now this – it was hard to believe I was really here.

Crossing into Cambodia at Voen Kham we met Nick, an Englishman who has lived there for nine years. He runs a tour company, speaks the language and would act as our guide and translator. I'm a petrol-head at heart: power and speed, it's my bag, and Nick had rocket boats waiting on the Cambodian side of the Mekong. I decided I liked Nick a lot.

The town hugged the banks, a clutch of buildings that looked even poorer than those we'd seen in Laos. With Nick leading the way we wandered through an empty market, the stalls no more than wooden poles supporting aged green tarpaulin. A lumpy track led down to the water between weathered houses. The path ended in a headland between thick palms and below we could see a jetty accessed by a plank of wood. Tied up to the jetty were two wooden boats with bows that curved upwards like a scimitar. They sat low in the water, narrow and sleek. Fixed to the back of each was a sixteen-valve, 1600 cc Toyota car engine. They were absolutely huge, with shaft propellers and massive open-piped exhausts. I could only imagine the horsepower.

'Oh my God,' Russ said. 'Like a drag racer on water.'

Climbing aboard I had the biggest grin on my face; boy oh boy was I looking forward to this. Late afternoon with the sun going down, we were soaked in the most spectacular scenery. I asked Nick if there were any rapids downstream.

He just smiled at me. 'Charley,' he said, 'the only thing that's rapid is the boat.'

The river was really high: it had overflowed its banks and flooded the paddies. We could see solitary trees, strands of vegetation and bits of debris swirling in the currents. It was a beautiful evening, though, the sun was low and it cast the surface in deep shadows. The mountains hung with mist, trees covered the banks and the Mekong, a thick-bodied serpent, uncoiled as far as the eye could see.

With everyone loaded I turned to the driver and asked him to fire up the engine. The pilot gave the engine some revs and we were off. I was in my element – the power, the petrol and the speed. The prow slapped the chop like someone rapping a table and I was bouncing around like crazy. With a roar we tore downstream, sweeping between the trees with the wind dragging my hair. We were flying along now – a complete contrast to the slow boat we'd taken this morning. Standing in the bows I could feel spray stinging my face. It was brilliant; by any means imaginable the best piece of transport we'd been on.

I was gutted when the pilot killed the engine and slid the bows up the bank. It was almost completely dark now, so we made our way to the hotel and sat down with a beer and a map. Nick showed us a couple of options for tomorrow: we were riding a pair of Honda 250 dirt bikes, which I was really looking forward to. I knew the bike well, having owned a 600 that used to pop the greatest wheelies.

Nick not only spoke the language, he knew the country like the back of his hand. He had planned a particular jungle route, but the monsoon had come early and most of that trail was either flooded or the roads were so messy they were impassable. It was a shame because he would have taken us to the hut where Pol Pot had died of malaria. His body had been burnt on a pile of tyres. One of the world's most notorious despots, he was supported by the West when opposing communist Vietnam. Nick has written about Cambodia for Lonely Planet and knows his stuff. He explained that these days there was a nominal democracy, although it's still pretty feudal. The people support the politician chosen by the village chief.

He also explained that the Chinese have an interest in the country and are building most of the roads; and now that gas and oil have been discovered the Americans are cuddly too, as are the

French. For years the country was ruled alternately by the Vietnamese and the Thai, but in 1863 the Cambodians sought protection from French Indochina and became a colony. Caught up in the Vietnam War, they were invaded briefly by the Americans. In 1975 the Khmer Rouge, Maoists from the ancient Khmer Kingdom, seized power. Under Pol Pot's rule the country was renamed Kampuchea. Their attitude to the civilian population was 'To keep you is no benefit. To destroy you is no loss.' Between 1976 and 1979, 26 per cent of the population were killed. The Khmer Rouge used to raid their Vietnamese neighbours and in the end Vietnam invaded and Pol Pot was forced to flee, though the Khmer Rouge maintained their seat at the UN right up until 1990. Their record on human rights was as bad as it gets and they were officially a party in exile, but a blind eye was turned to all that because people thought they were preferable to communist Vietnam. Ironically, the Khmer Rouge used the UN seat to secretly get arms back into the country and fight a civil war that didn't end until Pol Pot's death in 1998.

Now a little wiser about our surroundings, we were back on motorbikes. It was 12 June and with less than five weeks of the expedition left, we would be travelling 250 kilometres today on both tarmac and dirt. I'd slept really well, was feeling good and couldn't wait to get going. Little did I know it would turn into a marathon, a ride of epic proportions.

We left early and it was pleasantly cool. My bike was the perfect wheelie machine and I was wearing just a T-shirt, jeans and gloves. My helmet was a tad small though: it pressed my forehead and I knew that by the end of the day I'd have a bit of a headache. I didn't care – it was just great to be riding again.

We were on tarmac to begin with, a smooth road through open country with the clouds hugging the summits of distant hills. Close to the road the homes were made of bamboo and thatch built on stilts, with lengths of uneven planking for the walls. It looked a lot like Laos and for once a border crossing hadn't altered everything.

After an hour or so we hit dirt, the road narrowing into a track we shared with cattle and the farmers driving them. I was in my element now, part earth, part mud and puddles, and part gravel. I could slide the back end and really have some fun. We didn't pass many cars. We saw a few trucks but mostly people got around on mopeds and small motorbikes. Some drove carts pulled by oxen.

The towns seemed more chaotic than in Laos, with animals wandering the streets and gangs of kids skipping across in front of us. Music blared from shop fronts and stallholders tried to sell us stuff even though we were passing on the bikes. We stopped for breakfast and Russ admitted he was completely noodled and riced out: what he longed for now were two slices of buttered bread with English sausages cut in half and covered with brown sauce.

The roads seemed to be lined with huts and houses like one vast village stretching the length of the country. When they did finally peter out we were either in damp jungle or tracts of farmland, farmers ploughing the fields with teams of oxen. Mud-streaked kids splashed about in orange-coloured ponds created by the flood waters. Cattle grazed by the side of the road, skinny animals with bells made from more American munitions. They hunted for food between coconut palms that climbed above the houses.

It rained a little as it always seemed to do when we were riding bikes. I began to wonder if it wasn't my sister Telsche forcing us to slow down.

We had to cross the Mekong by ferry and to get there we rode through the backstreets – little paths between tiny homes with straggly washing lines and pigs grubbing for scraps. We wove our way between the houses, avoiding people and livestock until we descended through shoulder-height vegetation to the muddy banks of the Mekong.

There were plenty of people waiting for the ferry. This was a proper boat with a flat deck and solid metal sides. We were glad it was nothing like the one we'd seen from the deck of the slow boat, which had been three boats lashed together with ropes and carrying a couple of pickups. We'd watched, gobsmacked, as it inched sideways across the river, looking as secure as a house of cards.

This one was still powered by a truck's engine, though. A young guy called Saporo was piloting, sitting up high and overlooking his cargo of one car, a bunch of motorbikes and a whole stack of people. The steering wheel was from the same truck as the engine and he operated it like a truck driver, sitting with it flat before him. He told me he'd only been driving the boat for a year and before that he had indeed been a truck driver.

On the eastern shore we tore up the clay hill. I had the back end spinning and was catching air on the bumps. This was brilliant – my own private Dakar. Stopping for fuel we found the same drum and canister system as in Laos, only here it was complemented by Pepsi bottles filled with petrol which the attendants upended into our tanks.

We were a little behind schedule now. Tonight we'd be camping close to the ruins of the temple at Beng Mealea, and it would be good to get there before dark. We rode on, crossing ravines and tributaries of the Mekong. One bridge had been completely washed away and some villagers had built a temporary one which they allowed us to use at a cost of one US dollar. Beyond the village we climbed into the hills, the delta lying green and flooded, the village half hidden between clusters of palms, the road as red as the clay I'd seen in the slums of Mumbai. It was breathtaking scenery and the ride was turning into one of the great days of the expedition.

And then it rained. It rained and it rained. It rained so hard the roads turned to mush and we were sliding around corners, losing the back and bogging the front in ruts and divots. I've never experienced rain like it, falling as hard and fast as hailstones, slamming into the tank, the handlebars, our hands; it pebbledashed our faces and all the time the clouds got lower and lower. It was a total transformation. A couple of hours earlier we'd crossed a bridge in brilliant sunshine, stopping to watch a bunch of guys fishing from two bamboo barges.

At around five o'clock we hit a town and sheltered in the lee of a cafe where TVs blared and a whole bunch of men were betting on something. This rain was unbelievable: it fell in a single grey curtain, the drops so big they bounced. Within minutes the street was a river.

We watched a guy struggling to get his umbrella up, though there was little point – he was already soaking wet.

'I'm absolutely knackered,' I said. 'Even with the rain, the heat here is killing me.'

'Me, too,' Russ said. 'It's been like this ever since China: not just the heat but the roads, the rough country . . . And how many times have we switched vehicle? *Songthaew*, buses, jeeps, boats, more buses, motorbikes into Hanoi . . . that was an experience just in itself. It seems much harder to cross through the countries here. And I've never experienced humidity like this.'

'It drags you down, physically, doesn't it,' I agreed, suddenly weary. Talking to Russ, it dawned on me how much effort we'd been putting into the trip since Nepal. 'Travelling is tiring at the best of times,' I said. 'Especially when you've been on the road as long as we have. You're right, these last few countries have been amazing, but they've also been really tough going.'

We stood there quietly for a moment, watching the rain fall. It didn't seem to have any effect on the temperature, although by this point we couldn't tell if we were just wet from the rain instead of sweat. But having acknowledged all we'd been through, we were on a bit of a mission now, and we got going again, despite the rain.

It was getting later and later and the rain showed no sign of letting up but we had to carry on. We were riding on dirt and I was taking the bends supermotard-style with one foot forward, sliding round on my heel. The sky was plagued by a really big black cloud and we were doing our best to skirt it. In the end, though, a jungle road took us right through the middle and now the heavens opened like never before. We were riding in a monsoon. Nothing I'd experienced in Africa came anywhere close. It rained so hard we could barely see and as it got darker all we could do was follow the lights of whoever was up ahead. I rode standing on the foot pegs with rain running inside my helmet, down my face and into my beard. Russ was ahead of me and Nick ahead of him.

It felt crazy – dangerous, even. We were on a narrow fissure of road that was steadily being washed away. Every so often a cow would step out of the jungle right in front of us. As Russ put it later, if it was a white cow you could see it, but these were mostly brown and it was all we could do to avoid them.

Daylight faded completely and still the rain refused to ease, but far from worrying I was actually enjoying the ride. We'd been on the road for thirteen hours, and it was exciting. One section was a bit ugly, mind you, really dark and narrow, the road heavily rutted and pitching left and right. We hit puddles like ponds and the road surface was so loose it just seemed to be part of the flood plain. Oncoming vehicles were a real hazard; with the headlights in our eyes we couldn't see anything.

I decided it was getting just a little hairy, particularly for a tribe of frogs that decided to cross the road just as we were passing. A little further on we hit tarmac again briefly and found a proper petrol station with pumps and mechanics, the works. Russ pulled up, put the side stand down and got off. Behind him the bike toppled over: the stand wasn't down properly, the bike crashed on its side and snapped the clutch lever off. Luckily, Nick had a spare and the garage guys fitted it for us.

'Can you believe this rain?' Russ asked as the pair of us took shelter while they were fixing it. 'It's a fucking monsoon, Charley.'

'It's Telsche,' I told him. 'She's looking out for us.'

He stared at the wall of falling water. 'Looking out for us?'

I nodded. 'Making sure we keep the speed down and the bike shiny side up.' I knew I was right, I could feel her. 'It's rained every time we've ridden a bike on this expedition. It's my sister, Russ, she's looking out for us.'

21
The Last Train

I suppose it's typical that the night the monsoon hit we were not only on bikes but planning to camp as well. Nick had organised a site a kilometre from the ruins of Beng Mealea, a temple the size of Angkor Wat, in the heart of the jungle. We arrived very wet and very tired, but the tents had already been set up, there was a fire crackling and hot food cooking.

It had been a monumental ride, covering close to three quarters of the country in thirteen and a half hours, the last stretch during an unimaginable deluge. I thought there was a good chance we'd get washed away in the night so I took a camera to bed just in case: no point in disaster striking if we weren't able to capture it on film.

Fortunately the tents stayed put overnight, but in the morning my bike wouldn't start. I put it down to the rain, but when a mechanic from the company who supplied the bikes met us at the campsite, he said it was because I was too tough on it. 'You're a good rider, maybe,' he told me, 'but you broke it.'

Leaving him to his toolkit and his muttering I grabbed a cup of the rocket-fuel coffee we'd brewed and followed Russ and Nick to the ruins in the jungle.

This area had been mined during the civil war and a sign indicated it had been cleared by a German company. I was reminded of Tesfu, the Ethiopian lad Ewan and I had met at the border town of Zelambassa, who had lost his leg to an Eritrean mine. I'd learned then that the people who lay them rarely take responsibility for clearing them, and it was no different here in Cambodia.

We took a path between the trees, passing a massive fan-shaped piece of stone lying in the undergrowth. A short while later we reached a pile of slabs in a clearing and then, beyond it, the remnants of the ruined temple, as if growing up from the bush. There are a few temples that have returned to the jungle but none the size of Beng Mealea. The whole area felt serene and spiritual – and there was a special quietness amidst the carved stones. This was exactly the kind of thing I'd been hoping for on my travels – ancient ruins hidden in deep jungle. With the expedition in its final 'hand-span', I wanted to soak up every minute.

The temple is an amazing structure, with floors built on pillars and the remains of an ancient causeway winding through it. Nick told us that the builders had brought stones on rafts from nearby quarries then levered them into place with bamboo. We could still see the holes left by the poles in the ground. Many people thought the Khmer Rouge might desecrate the old temples as they had done with the newer ones – a few had even been turned into things like pig sties. But Beng Mealea and Angkor Wat had been left alone.

After an hour or so drinking in the atmosphere, we drove to the River of 1000 Lingas, at Kbal Spean, and the site of another temple high on a hill overlooking dense jungle. The lingas, or stylised penises, are carved from the rock of the river bed, an offering to the fertility gods in the hope that the rice crop in the valley below will always be a good one. Of course we had to touch the stones for luck. On the way down we found a different kind of snake. This one was black, and so slick and shiny that it looked like a trickle of oil moving across the ground. It was the weirdest-looking thing, with a hammer head like the shark. The locals claimed they'd never seen it before. Deciding it was a new species, Russ named it after Anne, who'd spotted it through the lens of her camera.

By the time we got back to camp my bike was fixed and we were soon on our way again. Our route took us into the mountains on some fantastic, tight and twisty dirt roads, bordered on one side by thick jungle and on the other by sandstone boulders the size of houses. The surface felt oiled, almost like a speedway track, and I had a fabulous time popping the front wheel and sliding the back of that poor little Honda.

At lunchtime we stopped for a breather. Finding a fold in the trees we gazed across paddies and marshland, sunken fields interspersed with tracts of higher ground where the houses were built. After that we rode the bikes as far as Siem Reap and found a hotel. We'd had no real break since Dubai, so we decided to take the next day off to recharge our batteries, get some sleep and speak to our families.

On the 15 June I left the hotel in a *coyonne* or elephant truck, a basic working vehicle with an open cab, bull-nosed and brutal.

This one ran a 25 hp Isuzu engine and had been loaned to me by a nice kid called Samuel. He had a pile of mattresses in the back, old bikes, all sorts of stuff. It was easy to drive, about half as big as a good-sized lorry, and chugged along merrily. I did a few miles with Samuel alongside me then said goodbye, hooked up with the others and headed for Angkor Wat.

This colossal temple was started in the twelfth century but never completed. Over a period of thirty-five years, 300,000 slaves and 6,000 elephants worked on it, but King Suryavarman, who commissioned it, died before it could be finished. Originally a Hindu temple, it became Buddhist when the religion of the country changed in the fourteenth century. It's a ruin now; the stone black with age and the humidity of the jungle. The towers are built in layers of stone that look almost like pancakes, and the steps are so steep that you have to climb backwards when you come back down, using your hands for balance.

I felt very calm here, just as I had at Beng Mealea. Angkor Wat is so huge that even with lots of other visitors it's easy to climb a tower, gaze across the gardens and steal a moment to meditate. I did notice the breasts, however. There are lots of statues of bare-breasted women and the breasts are all shiny. People rub them, for luck or fertility, I suppose. I rubbed them. God, I've been away from home too long.

A couple of hours later we were on the move again. The Thai border was beckoning, as borders always do when you get close, but we still had a way to go. And before the border we came to a village that in winter wouldn't have been there.

There's a huge area of very marshy land near Angkor Wat called Tonle Sap. Each spring, when the snows melt, the Mekong floods the whole area, forming a gigantic lake. And each year the whole town has to be moved. The place had been described to me as a village, and I had been expecting a few houseboats. But as I made my way through the 'streets' in a small fishing boat, I realised it was more like a city, with strange echoes of Mad Max or Kevin Costner's *Waterworld*. Like Venice, it was all hustle and bustle, with masses of boat traffic. I passed a school, shops, cafes – even a hospital. The houses floated on plinths, boats, anything that would keep them above the water, and seemed pretty well made.

They all had nets for catching fish set up underneath, and, although anchored for now, could be moved on when the time came.

I've never seen anything like it, so many boats, so many people, water taxis, bus-boats. Everyone did a double take when they saw the English guy buzzing along in a wooden skiff with a lawn mower engine on the back. There were no gears, not even neutral; it was either on or off, the rudder fixed to a stick that acted as the tiller. The throttle was a little lever close to the exhaust which was blisteringly hot and situated right under my nuts, which was a shade uncomfortable. Trundling along what I thought was probably Main Street I ran out of fuel. The engine note dribbled to nothing and there I was, stranded, with only the pole I'd used to propel myself away from the jetty.

A girl on a veranda of what looked like a cafe began yelling and beckoning at me. At last I realised it wasn't a cafe but a petrol station. I'd been confused by the large bottle of Pepsi in her hand; not cola but diesel. With the tank full I got going and motored back to the jetty.

We left Siem Reap the next morning and headed a little reluctantly towards the border. I was really sorry to be leaving because this country was up there with India and Nepal in my affections; something about the people, their warmth, smiles, just the whole crazy atmosphere of the place. It felt like a forgotten jewel that had finally been noticed and was beginning to sparkle. After years of war and oppression, tourism was growing and roads were being built; the only problem being that this spelled the end of some traditional ways of getting around.

Like the bamboo train for instance. We'd heard about these home-made affairs that people used on the railways, but as yet we hadn't seen one. We'd been told there was one in Sisophon, and of all the towns we'd been through this had to be the poorest. It was filthy, the houses little more than shanties. The railway line ran through here, though, or rather what was left of it did – a single line of warped tracks that had been laid by the French in the 1920s. The tracks were so overgrown and so knackered I doubted

244   By Any Means

any kind of train could run on them now. In the 1960s a train from Phnom Penh to Bangkok would take just eight hours, but in the 1970s the Khmer Rouge tore up the tracks between Sisophon and the border. A journey from Phnom Penh just as far as Battambang – about three quarters of the way – now takes sixteen hours.

It really was grim; the walls of the houses flimsier than plywood, the roofs made of rusty tin and straw. The station looked derelict, a tired old building with a minute platform and cows grazing on the line. Russ and I walked past people crouched under umbrellas selling bits of food, bottles of cloudy water: this was as poor as anything I'd seen and it was really sobering.

On the far side of the platform we found the elusive bamboo train, one of the simplest modes of transport we'd come across. Basically it was a platform made of wooden boards attached to a metal chassis. The chassis perched on a set of wheels that had been gauged to fit the tracks. The engine came from a lawn mower with a fan belt that fitted to the wheels, the whole thing mounted on a greased runner. To engage the wheels you pulled the engine back and to slow down you eased it forward again. It was ingeniously simple. Lori, the guy who drove it, told us that when two bamboo trains met, the heaviest one had right of way. Only there weren't two any more, this was the last one in use, chugging up and down between Sisophon and Battambang carrying bamboo, rice, cement . . . anything the people wanted. With so many roads being built the trains were pretty much obsolete, the wheels were no longer made and when this set wore out, that would be that. Lori had been working the line for twenty-five years and had no idea what he would do then.

He let me drive and together we trundled through thick jungle and paddy fields and people's back gardens. We passed little market stalls where kids yelled out trying to make us buy things. We slowed for other kids wandering up and down the line, for cattle and goats, we had to stop and move an old pushchair, and we had to slow down where the line crossed dirt roads because there were no barriers and the cars were reluctant to stop. Crossing an iron bridge that spanned the river I realised how privileged I was to have driven the last bamboo train in the country.

We went as far as the main road and an hour later crossed into Thailand. It was a sad parting, the saddest yet, and the excitement of entering another country was a little tempered. The rain didn't help; it was bucketing down now and the world seemed very grey. Russ and I had fallen in love with Cambodia. Nick had shown us a stunning place and we were very grateful to him. The people are very poor, many living only off what they can grow, but everywhere we went we were treated with smiles and kindness.

Having hopped in the back of a *songthaew* at the Thai border, we met up with the bus that would take us to Bangkok. We were pretty jaded: Russ had been feeling off-colour, which we put down to constant dehydration and the wearing nature of travelling. Sleeping in a different bed every night takes it out of you – you sleep less and less and eventually it all catches up.

It was still chucking it down when we arrived on the outskirts of Bangkok. Nothing could have prepared me for the contrast. I don't know what I'd been expecting but it was only four hours from where I'd been navigating palms and paddies and filthy backyards on a motorised platform made of wood. Now I was in a concrete jungle with overpasses, a sky train, office blocks and hotels, and the kind of traffic that made London look empty. We had a couple of days here to regroup and hook up with Mungo. After that we would be spending forty-eight hours travelling by train and coach to Singapore.

I wasn't happy about this. It was bad enough racing through Thailand and Malaysia to get to Singapore, without doing so on a fucking night train. But in reality we didn't have much choice: I wanted to sail from Singapore to Borneo, where we had a date to keep with UNICEF, and this was the only way of ensuring we'd get there in time.

At least we had Mungo back. We'd really missed him, although Matt had been brilliant, stepping into the breach at short notice, and we were sorry to say goodbye to him. Mungo had been gone a month: he looked well and said he felt fine, though he still had difficulty kneeling for any length of time. We didn't envisage him doing that any time soon. The only signs that anything had happened were a couple of marks from the keyhole surgery. Taking up the camera again he was ready and raring to go.

Ironically, as Mungo returned, Russ went home. Before we left England he'd promised his daughter Emily that he would not miss her thirteenth birthday. He'd missed her twelfth birthday on Long Way Down and this time he was flying back for her party, but he would rejoin us in Bali.

Perhaps it was a good job we were going to be sitting on a train for so long after all, though I wasn't looking forward to it. Before we left I went to see a guy called 'M'. Nothing to do with James Bond, he was a Thai businessman with a classic-car collection. I'd not been that keen to begin with because it was a detour, but I had an hour or so before the train and I suppose we'd taken the odd other detour along the way before now. Besides, M had a DeLorean and I wanted to go back to the future – just the three months, mind, so I could say a quick hello to Olly and the kids.

M lived in a massive, and I mean humungous, house behind a high wall and steel gates in the suburbs of Bangkok. He made his money from coffee and real estate and had got his passion for cars from his father. Even though he had a wife and four kids, M's dad always bought a two-door and tried to cram them into that, rather than a sensible family saloon. M himself was a really nice guy. He'd got his nickname from his mother when he was a boy – when his father was away he was the only 'man' in the house, so his mother called him 'Man' or 'M' for short.

Built over three storeys, the house was mind-blowing, with manicured gardens, wooden walkways and little bridges between the lawns and palms. There was even a lake with its own canoe. The whole of the ground floor was one gigantic showroom, the cars kept behind glass at room temperature, a bit like fine wine, because of the humidity. M had a whole stack of Mercs, a TR3, an American Bonnie-and-Clyde-mobile with stools in the back, a classic Daimler limo just like the Queen uses and a 1972 Ferrari 246 GTS Dino, the first mass-production car Ferrari made. It was named after Enzo Ferrari's son Alfredino, who died from muscular dystrophy at the age of twenty-four. Alfredino – or Dino as he was nicknamed – had begun work on a 1.5 litre V6 engine, though he never lived to see it built. His father fitted it in the car named in Dino's honour, along with an alternative V8.

M had one of only 8000 DeLoreans ever manufactured, and I

was really keen to see it. A classic gull-wing design, the car was made of stainless steel, which meant you had to be really careful. One dent and the whole body was ruined. M's DeLorean was immaculate. Lifting the door I hunched behind the wheel, looking for the knob that would take me back to the future.

From M's amazing house I headed to the station, and spent the next twenty-four hours on a train. What can I tell you? I'd had it with overnight trains and the best thing about the trip was the air-conditioned station. The carriages were compact and intimate, the food OK but the pull-out bunks pretty cramped, and after seven minutes I was bored. Twenty-three hours and fifty-three minutes later we got to Butterworth on the Malaysian Peninsula where we connected with a bus for the next leg of the journey, and a full thirty-one hours after leaving Bangkok we rolled into Kuala Lumpur. It was late evening on 19 June and it was raining. The clouds had been gathering all day and finally they let go.

The Petronas Towers helped to lift my mood, rising above an already tall city like a pair of rockets waiting for take-off. They stand 452 metres high and had been the tallest buildings in the world before being overtaken by the Taipei 101, which itself is due to be overtaken by the Burj Dubai. Architects: they're as competitive as bike racers.

I wandered around like a zombie, the victim of another sleepless night. My bunk had been far too narrow and I think I snatched only twenty minutes' sleep. I'd had enough, and having already cancelled a second train journey in favour of a bus tomorrow, I couldn't even face that. The first thing I did when we got to the hotel was hire a car instead. I'd drive us to the marina where we'd cross to Singapore. After sorting out some issues with the ongoing journey I headed to my room, and collapsed into bed. A real bed.

22
Abandon Ship

We left Kuala Lumpur with the sun in the east and a full moon still visible in the west. Driving instead of taking the bus south was definitely one of my better ideas. I was enjoying myself, and as we left the city we passed pristine white mosques and the grassy steps of an ancient burial ground.

But before I could get too comfortable, there was the small matter of a wakeboard challenge. I hadn't surfed for twenty years, but that was all about to change – in fact, I was about to wakeboard right over the border. At Danga Bay we met Brandon, a Malaysian surf dude with black shades, muscles and a ponytail. He'd been recommended by a friend of mine and Olly's called Catherine, whose sons Tico and Max are regular wakeboard customers. Catherine and Olly have known each other since college – years ago they travelled round Italy together trying to learn the language but mostly getting their bottoms pinched. Catherine lives in Singapore with her husband Rembrandt, and when she heard I was coming she suggested the idea.

'So, Charley,' Brandon asked. 'Can you wakeboard?'

'Yes – and I can mono-ski, too, though it's been a while. But it's like sex, right? You never forget how to do it.'

Brandon's business partner Ryan arrived, thirty-five, maybe, with dreadlocks and a bandanna, a couple of Asian-style tattoos and a Native American bracelet on his ankle. He was living the dream: staying on a boat at the marina with his little dog, spending his days in the sun teaching people to waterski. He took us to customs, which was about fifteen minutes down the road. It was so simple; we just took our passports into the office, got them stamped, then went back to the marina for lunch.

The old nerves were kicking in now, though. When Catherine had first suggested the idea I thought it was a great way to arrive in a new country, but now I realised I'd not planned it properly at all. I was about twenty the last time I'd been on a board. Imagine how stupid I'd look flummoxing around on my belly amongst these cool dudes. I told myself to keep the faith, think positive thoughts and everything would be fine. But my palms were clammy and my mouth was dry.

After I'd put on a black lifejacket Brandon sat me down on the dock and reminded me of the basics. 'Just sit in the water, keeping your knees bent and the inside of your elbows around your knees,' he said. 'When you feel the rope, don't pull against it. Just go with it and let the boat bring you up.'

Christ, I thought. At this rate I won't even be able to stand up, never mind wakeboard all the way to Malaysia.

'Just relax,' Brandon went on. 'The more relaxed you are the easier it will be.'

'Has anyone done this before? Crossed from Malaysia to Singapore on a wakeboard?'

'Not that I know of. Hey, Ryan – did you ever hear of it?'

Ryan shook his head.

A first, then – that inspired me. Right, I thought: nicely chilled. If I can do *dolmus* I can do chilled for sure.

Before any more doubts could surface I was in the water, adrenalin pumping, the boat ticking over making a fantastic burbling sound. Ryan pulled away and I could feel the slack taken up, the waves washing over me. I kept my knees bent, the insides of my elbows pressed against them and the board edge-up. Then I was on my feet; a bit of a wobble but I didn't lose it and we were off, the wind in my face and spray lifting from the wake.

We weren't going straight across; Ryan was taking us to Raffles Marina, beyond the causeway where you would normally cross from one country to the other. We turned into the channel and now everything on my right was Malaysia and everything on my left Singapore. I'd fastened the boots a little tightly and was aware of a bit of cramping, but ignoring it I looked ahead and concentrated on staying upright. The engine was revving hard, the boat was kicking up surf and I thought, Jesus – I've come all the way from Annamoe and here I am, possibly the first person ever to wakeboard into Singapore.

I was terrified of falling because I was sure I wouldn't be able to get up again, but after ten minutes I knew I'd have to loosen that boot, and reluctantly I let go of the grips and slid under the waves.

Ryan turned the boat and came alongside. 'First time in twenty years, Charley,' he said. 'Spectacular.'

I got up again and now I was holding on with one hand, then the crook of my elbow, giving it the full works, shifting a little to the left and a little to the right instead of cruising along in the nice smooth path created by the wake. Deciding to switch feet, I half turned the board. The next thing I knew, I'd face-planted.

The wake must have caught the edge of the board and dragged it under: before I knew what was happening it was smack, face-down into water that felt like concrete. God, it hurt – not just my face but my neck and chest as well. It knocked the wind right out of me.

'Nice face plant,' Ryan said as he pulled the boat round again.

I was spluttering. 'Jesus, I never knew water could hurt so much.'

'When you're trying to turn just relax: keep your knees bent and your back straight. Don't hunch – just work your hips and the board will come around.'

I took another big fall and another, but I got upright again and we passed under the causeway. Ryan made a left at the next headland and we cruised beyond a light-house. I could see Catherine waiting on the dock wearing a white dress and straw hat, with Rem and Tico at her side. Letting go of the handle I glided across the water and sank right in front of them.

We stayed with them for the next two days. It was wonderful to be around old friends again and have some home-cooked food. Rem and Catherine have lived in Singapore for the past four years but would be leaving for the States soon. They said they'd enjoyed their time but Singapore was a transient society for expats, and it took a couple of years to make good friends. It's a little strait-laced and of course it's ultramodern; very clean and very safe. They never locked the house and could leave wallets, computers, cellphones in the car without fear of losing anything. If you don't break the law I imagine it's a pretty cool place to live. If you do break the law you get beaten, thirty lashes with a cane. They have a doctor present, and if your back is too bad after ten they let you have a week or so to heal up before they dish out the rest. Every Friday morning at six a.m. the drug runners are hanged at Changi Prison.

On 22 June we took a look round the street circuit where Formula One was going to be holding a night race in September. It was still being built but turn one was complete, quite a tight left-hander. It would be a fantastic place to watch. The start and finish straight and the pit garages were just about finished, too; it was actually pretty exciting to see.

Close by is a stretch of beautiful parkland, where couples go to have their wedding photos taken. It's also the old expat area where the famous black and white houses (the official residences from colonial days) are located. When Singapore gained independence the government took them back and now if you want to live in one you have to bid the amount of rent you're prepared to pay, at auction. While we were there we saw a young couple all dressed up in their wedding clothes having their photos taken. They weren't married yet: in fact they weren't getting married until September. Rem explained that everyone has their pictures taken in advance. Three months, though . . . I shook my head. Anything could happen. You could travel halfway round the world in that time . . .

On 23 June we headed for Nikoi, a privately owned island where the boat we'd organised to take us to Borneo was supposed to be picking us up. Saying goodbye to Rem and Catherine, we jumped the ferry to Bintan, the largest of the three thousand-odd islands that make up the Riau Archipelago. Forty kilometres from

Singapore, it's where the Sultan fled after the Portuguese took Malacca in 1511. It's had a chequered history and the whole area is notorious for pirates, but for us it was a staging post on the Indonesian leg of our journey.

Once we reached the Bintan ferry terminal we picked up a 1971 Holden Kingswood, an iconic Australian vehicle noted for its V8 engine. Ours had been transplanted with a Nissan diesel, mind you, and had BMW wheels, but it didn't matter. It was gorgeous: turquoise paint with a five-speed column gear lever. It had been a taxi originally, but now belonged to a guy called Mark who very kindly let us drive it across the island.

I had a few problems finding fourth and fifth but finally got the hang of it and an hour later we stopped at a little beach where a pretty ancient-looking cargo boat was moored. We were due to meet the speedboat from Nikoi, but standing there, I had a horrible feeling that the old boat in front of us was our transport to Borneo. Peter and Andrew, the guys who owned Nikoi, had told us they could organise something traditional and this looked nothing if not traditional.

'Pretty wild, Mungo,' I said. 'It looks a bit scary.'

He nodded.

'Oh well. If we're going to spend thirty-six hours on something like that, then we deserve a night in paradise first, don't you think?'

Paradise is exactly how I'd describe Nikoi. The guests are picked up in a speedboat and ferried across the bay. A small island surrounded by black coral and massive boulders – some sixty metres high – it is part rain forest and part beach and only a tiny portion has been developed. Four years ago Peter and Andrew bought the place and set about building what they call a 'boutique hotel' out of driftwood. They gathered all they could find on Nikoi and the surrounding area and when that ran out they cut some, soaked it in the sea for a month then dried it so it had the appearance of driftwood. The result is outstanding; the guest quarters are pavilions built on stilts like the tree house in *Swiss Family Robinson*. There are no doors, no glass windows, and in the stifling heat the design creates a natural airflow that is so effective some guests have asked for extra blankets.

The whole complex is linked by beautiful wooden pathways

and there's an open-air kitchen, one long dining table and two pools with the most incredible views out across the reefs. We'd rushed through Thailand and Malaysia. Now we had a night in paradise before that boat and the voyage to Borneo.

I woke to a perfect sunrise and the grey hulk of the cargo boat we'd seen yesterday moored just off shore. I reminded myself that the old tub was exactly what this expedition was about, but I had a bad feeling. It was nothing I could put my finger on and maybe after what happened at Halong bay I was more wary than I normally would be.

We had to be in Pontianak in Borneo no later than Wednesday night because on Thursday we were off into the jungle with UNICEF. This gave us thirty-six hours to cross the Karimata Strait. I had no idea what the weather would be like; right now it was clear and fine but we were in the rainy season and things could change very quickly.

The guys from Nikoi took us out to the boat, the *Yeremia*. It had a grey wheelhouse built on two levels while the hull was a mixture of white and black paint as well as stained wooden planks that were rotten in places. I could see where it seemed to bulge here and there; the wood broken and splintered. It was definitely the stuff of adventure, but I had a few butterflies and I'm not sure they were all caused by excitement.

I kept telling myself this was what we wanted, and thinking back to Iran it was exactly the kind of vessel we'd hoped would get us to Dubai. We climbed aboard, the deck made from uneven slats like duckboard, bisected by a hold covered with numbered lengths of what looked like railway sleepers with a rope in each end to lift them off. Two of the sleepers were missing – I took a peek into the darkness where I could see the skeleton of the hull. It was wooden, of course, and looked solid enough. There was no water anywhere either, which is always a good sign. The anchor was winched by hand and there was a lifeboat of sorts, a dinghy hanging upside down at the bow end of the hold.

The owner – a nice guy called Ahong, wearing a grubby singlet and a baseball cap – was coming with us. He employed seven crewmen including the captain, the cook and a couple of mechanics, including a heavy-set guy in an orange T-shirt. They were very friendly and when we unrolled a chart and plotted the route I started to get really excited. The wheelhouse was spare, the controls pretty aged and basic, there was a bunk laid with an old quilt, and below the wheelhouse some crude sleeping quarters and the galley.

It took most of the crew to winch the anchor on board and with the engine running we all gathered on deck. Ahong formally introduced us to everyone and then he put his hands together: 'Before we go we pray,' he said.

I didn't think that was a bad idea at all; not when we were about to cross waters notorious for pirates in a boat that just didn't feel that seaworthy.

'We ask Jesus to come along on this trip,' Ahong said, then closing his eyes he launched into a prayer in Indonesian that we couldn't understand. I did notice he was clasping his hands pretty tightly, though.

As we headed out to sea I sat down with him on the lip of the cargo hold and he told me that their normal load was cigarettes, which they transported from Singapore to Malaysia.

'Have you ever been to Pontianak?' I asked him.

'Never.'

'Is it the longest trip you'll have made on this boat?'

'Yes,' he said.

I nodded slowly. 'Right,' I said. 'Right.'

'The captain's been to Pontianak,' he assured me.

Half an hour out, I was in the wheelhouse. It was a bit choppier now – there was quite a swell. A wave hit the bows with a real crack, sending spray flying across the deck. A few minutes later the chubby mechanic came rushing up the steps, looking very concerned. Taking Ahong to one side, he spoke in his ear for a moment then the two of them disappeared below. I glanced at Mungo and with a shrug beckoned him to follow.

Ahong was on his hands and knees bending over the hold, the mechanic squatting next to him chattering away and gesticulating.

'What's up?' I asked Ahong.

Then I saw water rushing into the hold. When we'd left Nikoi it had been dry.

'I'm sorry, Charley, something's broken,' Ahong said. 'When we hit that big wave just now something broke. The sea is coming in and we have to turn back.'

I was stunned. The sea water wasn't just slopping around, it was gushing in at a rate of knots. In fact, we were sinking.

Thankfully we could still see the island, and with the bilge pumps working full tilt we could turn around and make it back long before the boat went down. Thank God this had happened now and not when we were twenty hours out in the middle of the strait.

Now we had to find an alternative way of getting to Borneo, and I doubted we'd figure that out before the morning. In the meantime we needed somewhere to stay tonight, so taking my phone I punched in Andrew's number.

'Charley,' Mungo asked. 'What's going on?'

'I'm ringing Andrew. We're going nowhere on this boat, old bean. You'll have to make do with another night in paradise.'

'Yeah, baby!' He punched the air so hard he almost dropped the camera.

We went below and took a good look at the hold. The water was ankle deep and rising and I could see a tear in the bows where it was coming in. The seriousness of it really hit me then, down here under the roll of the ocean with the smell of seasoned wood and sea water rushing around my legs. If this had happened further out we would have been in real trouble: there was only that one little dinghy and there were ten of us. A cold chill worked from my hair to my toes. Climbing back on deck, I cannot tell you how glad I was to still be able to see Nikoi Island: the place was paradise now in more ways than one.

Gradually, relief was replaced by disappointment. This voyage across the strait should have been one of the highlights of the trip and now it wasn't going to happen.

Ahong couldn't have been more apologetic. 'I have another boat, Charley,' he said. 'It's bigger than this one and I can get it here by about seven tonight.'

I shook my head. Seven o'clock out here really meant nine or ten, and we'd never be in Borneo in time. It wasn't what we wanted – in fact it was the last thing we wanted – but if we were to meet UNICEF in time then we had no choice but to take another plane.

Back at the island the crew tried to launch the little dinghy to take us off the sinking *Yeremia*. It was a heavy old beast and they manhandled it to the side and hoisted it over the gunwales on lengths of flimsy rope. It was rolling badly and sure enough it tipped over and plummeted upside down into the water. I had to smile: there was a massive hole in the stern where I assumed the engine would fit and it looked about as seaworthy as a sieve.

I told Ahong we'd wait an hour for the Nikoi speedboat to come for us; we had a lot of expensive gear and I could see it ending up at the bottom of the bay. He was still apologising – he told me he'd only had the *Yeremia* for a year and that she was only four years old. The poor old girl looked more like forty; there was a charm about her but the romance of the voyage had been replaced by the reality of our 'lifeboat' and once again I was just grateful we were still alive.

23
There and Back Again

On Wednesday morning we returned to Bintan and caught another ferry to the island of Batam, where we took a short flight to Pontianak. I kept telling myself that at least we weren't using the plane to move from one country to another. We were still in Indonesia and the only part of Borneo we would be travelling through was the Indonesian part of the island, what the locals call Kalimantan. It's the largest part, the rest being split between Malaysia and Brunei.

When we got to the hotel Wendy from UNICEF was waiting for us with her colleague, Libby, and Anton, their local 'man on the ground'. Anton – a young, well-educated man who spoke English with a slight American accent – would be translating for us. They'd already been in touch to explain that the plane we'd arranged to take us to Ketapang had been commandeered. There had been a new district government elected and with a stack of official functions coming up, every bit of air transport had been taken. So instead of a short hop in a small plane we'd be up at three and travelling by car, boat, car, boat, motorbike and finally boat again to get to the village. It sounded like a seriously long day.

I felt surprisingly good when I woke in the wee small hours and met the others outside. It was pitch black but still very humid. We piled into a taxi to take us down to the Kapuas River, the longest in Indonesia. With so few good roads, it is the lifeblood of the whole area. All I knew about the town of Pontianak was that the place was smack on the equator and the local restaurants served turtle soup and fried python. Anton told me that a couple of hundred years back the town had been the capital of its own little sultanate, a major trading area strategically placed at the mouth of the river.

It really was incredibly dark still, and the air was full of smoke. They'd been burning the fields and the smog added a man-made mistiness to the atmosphere that gave the river an eerie feel. I was excited about the day ahead – an adventure within an adventure, really – and as we left on our three-hour voyage I felt a rush of adrenaline.

The boat – the *Hutan Express* – was sleek and powerful with plenty of seating, and it carried all of us and our gear pretty easily. It was powered by a 200 hp V6 Yamaha and we were soon cruising at about thirty-five or forty knots. It was a smooth ride, the river lit by a powerful headlight to avoid obstacles, though the driver told me he'd done this trip hundreds of times and could navigate just about blindfold. It was a good job because the surface was littered with bits of wood, rocky outcrops and fallen trees. Sitting back in the dark with the wind in my hair and the sound of the engine I had to pinch myself that this was Borneo and we were actually here.

They say the coldest part of the night is just before dawn and as the sun began to rise I huddled in my jacket under the canopy as the first rays of sunlight scattered gold across the black of the water.

We pulled into Teluk Melano just before eight. The town was a sprawl of wooden buildings built on deep pilings, the largest an imposing pagoda right on the water. A group of men watched with interest as we unloaded the gear then picked our way through an alley made of wooden planks. Kids crowded around us – youngsters in bare feet and no shirts, teenagers on mopeds – smiling and laughing and wanting to say hello. There were lots of people on bicycles – I helped one poor woman who'd fallen off and scraped her leg. It was all reminiscent of Nepal – the tightness of the streets maybe, and a kind of dustiness now to the humidity.

While we were waiting for the car that would take us to Ketapang I got a call from Lucy, explaining that we could no longer get the plane to Bali. We'd planned to spend tonight with the villagers, carry out the vaccinations tomorrow and be on our way after that. Now we would have to spend a night in Ketapang and another in Pontianak on the way back. I wasn't going to worry about it now: this was turning out to be the best day in the whole expedition.

When Anton mentioned the sultanate I asked him to give me a little history lesson. He explained that Indonesia is made up of seventeen thousand islands, though only six thousand are inhabited. The population is around two hundred million. Up until 1998 they were governed by a military dictatorship and since they became a democracy, centralised government has been replaced with four hundred and fifty district offices. It was one of those who'd elected a new leader. I'd heard that a couple of days ago there had been demonstrations outside parliament in Jakarta, thousands of students protesting at the hikes in the cost of fuel.

Ten years ago the police would have cracked down on any kind of public disturbance, but Anton told me these days debate was more easily tolerated.

Arriving in Ketapang we made our way to the UNICEF District Health Office, which serves twenty-three outposts and some seventy thousand women and children, and met up with Adi, the health officer for the village upriver. A trained nurse, he'd been working in this field for seventeen years. It struck me then that we were back on the 'Cold Chain', doing here what we'd done in Nepal, only this time we were inoculating against tetanus. That is if someone could find the key to the room where the vaccine was refrigerated. It had gone missing and everyone was hunting high and low.

It's amazing to think that UNICEF supplies more than 40 per cent of the world's vaccines, but it's a fact; and if you go online you can sponsor the activities of one of these outposts. You can choose to fund a cool box or the vaccine itself or the cost of transporting it. Lots of people I've spoken to do it that way because then they know exactly what their donation is being spent on and it makes their involvement so much more personal.

The purpose of our visits was to highlight the type of transport needed to get UNICEF and their medicines to remote areas – and you couldn't get much more remote than the village we were heading to. The key found, we crossed town in a truck for the Pawan River. Borneo is a land of rivers – they act as the highways, not the roads, which can present their own set of problems.

Once on the Pawan we headed inland in another large speedboat. I couldn't get the grin off my face – and we had another three hours ahead of us before we reached our destination. The engines fired up, the driver spun the wheel, hauling us away from the wharf. We were off. The buildings soon disappeared behind us and we were in thick jungle with villages built along tall banks where people climbed down ladders to get to their boats. Sitting back in daylight now I was able to take in the real span of this river, the narrower tributaries, the flotsam and jetsam floating on the top. We could see sprays of palm trees and thicker, deeper jungle behind. Every now and then we'd pass areas where the trees had been cleared altogether to make way for rice or coffee.

By four p.m. we were on the second leg, another town built on stilts where there seemed to be a lot of building work going on. The air rang with the sound of machine tools. The streets were skinny, pitted with potholes and lined with men in shorts and flip-flops squatting down to watch us. With the cool box over my shoulder, I jumped on a moped and made my way out of town, Anton on another moped beside me. Every corner I turned people were pointing and laughing. It had been the same in India and China: as soon as I followed some local worker onto his normal mode of transport I was the subject of much laughter and finger-pointing.

We rode along roads dug with gouges so deep that lengths of wood had been laid to try and flatten them. Of course we gathered another convoy. No matter where we seemed to ride bikes, the people came out to ride with us. Here it was a load of young guys and one older man with his three kids tucked in behind him. There are no laws in Indonesia about wearing a helmet and there were no helmets available so I rode very carefully. But we weren't doing any kind of speed and there was plenty of lush vegetation to fall off into.

Half an hour from town we passed through a few run-down villages where the houses were mostly hidden by trees. Beyond them the road narrowed even further. I could feel the box of vaccine bouncing around behind me. I hoped to God I wasn't ruining the stuff, the bottles were well packed but I was conscious of the temperature and how far we had to travel. The bottles are marked with heat-sensitive paper carrying a light grey circle on a darker square. If the temperature changes so does the colour of the circle, and if it becomes darker than the square the vaccine is useless.

Leaving the villages, we crossed a river on an old iron bridge and rode into thicker, denser jungle. The heat was absolutely stifling here and the roads about as bad as roads can get. We were riding street bikes but this was crappy dirt with cavernous potholes, and piles of earth and bits of stone littering the way. We did manage to find a little tarmac, but we soon had to leave it for a track that became no more than a footpath. This took us through a couple more villages then up a hill. I caught the smell of the river and sure enough, as we crested the rise, I could see it snaking between the trees far below.

I was pretty tired now. We had been travelling for fifteen hours and this was the fifth form of transport we'd been on. The sixth was waiting below, more speedboats bobbing about on the water. These were much smaller and open-topped with outboard motors. The river was narrower here, the banks not quite so high with trees overhanging so steeply their branches were almost scratching the surface. Mungo and I jumped in one boat, the UNICEF team jumped in another, and Anne took a third boat so she could film. As we set off a great gaggle of kids looked on, shouting and waving from the jetty. Glancing at them I realised this was my ninth UNICEF visit and by far the most remote outpost we'd been to. Talk about by any means – we were on our sixth transport change and I was having a ball.

Our pilot was a young kid with shaggy hair and a baseball cap worn backwards. He took us from one side of the river to the other, skipping shallow rapids, dancing around black rocks and branches that had been ripped from the trees when the river flooded. We raced on and on, rocking wildly on the wake of the boat in front of us, twisting the bows to avoid yet more debris. I loved the smell of the two-stroke engine and the backdrop was just incredible. As with other remote places I'd tried to imagine what Borneo would be like but I'd never come up with anything like this: the trees, the black surface of the water, the rocks and rapids, the sweaty smell of the jungle and these boats. I'd been thinking canoes, dugouts maybe, but nothing like this.

The four boats were not all keeping pace with each other, though. Our guy was taking us into the flatter sections by the shore so we could avoid gravel bars, and sometimes we were so close we could reach out and touch the bank. He rarely slowed, just avoided whatever hazard was ahead and kept going. Only when the sun was gone did he ease back on the throttle. By then Anne's boat was nowhere to be seen behind us. It got darker and darker, the gloom descending so quickly and so completely it was almost spooky. I kept looking back to see if the others were all right. I could see two boats but there was no sign of Anne.

Finally the darkness was so total we had no choice but to stop and pull the boat onto a bank of rocks where a group of men were camping. I spoke to them, thinking that this was actually a pretty good place to camp, and they told me they were going inland from Ketapang. The trip to their village took four full days. I was amazed; four days to take your goods to market and another four to get back again.

A few minutes later we heard the others approaching. I tried to see what was happening but by now the whole jungle was pitch black. A boat came in, the engine died and thankfully I heard Anne's voice. 'Are you all right, Anne?' I called.

'I'm fine, I'm glad to see you guys again, though.'

'Wasn't it fantastic? Or were you a bit nervous?'

'I was having a great time,' she said, 'until it began to get dark. There was no one on the boat I could speak to and I had no idea where you were. Then I was a little nervous maybe . . .'

After some discussion with the pilots we decided to carry on. We were just a few miles from the village of Riam Dadap and if we were careful we could make it without disaster. To be honest I would have been quite happy to crash out on the rocks with the night air on my face, nodding off to the sound of the river. We'd had our moments on boats on this expedition and the last thing we needed was someone to wind up in the water. But on we went and ten minutes upriver we could see lights glowing like fireflies along the bank, and a little after that we docked at a jetty where the villagers were waiting.

They gave us the most amazing welcome: flowers had been laid before a symbolic bamboo archway and they blessed us as we walked through. Women were beating the earth with long poles, a wonderful drumming sound backed with a kind of high-pitched chatter.

It was hard to work out the layout of the village at night – there were lights in the houses but none on the street and with people crowding everywhere it was difficult to get any sense of where we were. The chief – a man in his forties – came out to greet us and invited us into his house. We sat down in a long room with a TV, tiles on the floor and a coffee table surrounded by wooden chairs. He blessed me with flowers dipped in water, and wished me luck on my journey. Then one of the elders wrapped a leaf bracelet around my wrist and told me that when it rained it would not rain on me and when it was hot the heat would not wither me. I was incredibly touched to be so honoured, and after the most brilliant day's travelling. Not since I'd left my dad's house had I had such a wobble in the old chin: the villagers' generosity and kindness was very humbling.

Before we ate, the chief apologised for the food, which he said was all they had managed to prepare in time. It was palm-based, with local vegetables and coconut oil, served on plates like half shells. It was the best food we'd had in ages.

I woke up to rain, and Mungo looking out the window. We'd been sleeping on our mats at the chief's house.

'How did you sleep?' he asked me.

'Like a log, except I had to prod you a few times. You sounded like the foghorn on the *Titanic*.'

'And that was just my arse.'

'What are you looking at?' I wandered over to the window.

'That pig.' Mungo pointed to a slender-looking saddleback snuffling around in its sty. 'I love pigs, but they really piss me off.'

'Mungo, how can you love pigs if they really piss you off?'

He scratched his stubble. 'I never thought about that. Good question.'

It really was hammering down, but it was only six and there was plenty of time for the sun to come out and scorch us. Out on the porch I watched the rain bending the palms and rattling tin roofs all along a little street of baked earth that meandered away from the river. Now it was light I could see that the houses were beautiful – wooden homes snug among the trees, many sectioned off by white picket fences. The people clearly took pride in their village; they took pride in their culture, their way of life, themselves. We'd seen that last night – after dinner they had put on a performance of traditional dancing and singing then passed the local grog. They were so pleased to welcome us, so open and generous; just like people all around the world. Sitting there on that porch watching a tropical storm I thought again how privileged I am to travel so much and meet all these different people. So many countries' reputations are misconstrued by news or gossip. The reality is most places in the world are safe and most people will go out of their way to help a stranger. I've learned that if you travel with an open mind and a good heart, and remain respectful of the country you're in, then you should be fine.

After the dancing and the grog, I'd checked our day's route against the map, and realised that what I had thought were lakes was actually the sea. Pontianak is on the western coast and we'd come out of the mouth of the Kapuas then headed south-east through the delta before joining the Pawan River at Ketapang. When you think about that kind of distance and the amount of changes in transportation, you really begin to understand the obstacles UNICEF has to overcome. Although they account for such a high percentage of the world's vaccines, they also provide other important everyday stuff like soap, toothpaste and toothbrushes for the kids. On top of that there are the staff, the training and the transport costs themselves: with the price of oil going up and up it's getting more and more expensive to get the vaccines to these outlying villages. It took all yesterday to get here and without UNICEF or organisations like them, these places would be forgotten and people would die.

Anton told me that tetanus is a major problem in Borneo. 'In the developed world we don't even think about it,' he said. 'You cut yourself and get a jab, that's how it is. But here if you cut yourself, you can't just run to the doctor.'

'And it kills people?'

'Seventy per cent of people who contract tetanus die if they've not had the inoculation. And it's a horrible death that takes time – your whole body spasms. Imagine cramp in your leg, how much that hurts: then imagine that feeling compounded through your whole body for twenty-four hours before you lose consciousness. I've seen babies completely rigid before they finally died. Out here it's very, very serious. That's why we're having such a big push.'

We immunised the children in the community hall not just for tetanus, but also diphtheria, polio and measles. There was a problem, though, because up until three months ago they didn't have the budget to produce record cards for everyone so it was up to the mothers to remember what their babies had had and when.

The doctor, who visited about once a month, was there, and a nurse. The staff separated the hall into different areas: one where the stuff like soap and toothpaste was distributed; one for the doctor, one for the nurse; and then the area where the children and their mothers were vaccinated. This was UNICEF in action, coping with all the logistical problems and making sure children in the remotest, most inaccessible places still had access to life-saving immunisation. Having travelled so far it was particularly humbling and I can't emphasise enough how important it is that their work continues. They need all our help to make sure it does.

The mothers were young and proud, conscious of doing all they could for their babies just as any mother would. It struck me how calm they were: there was a lot of laughter yet there was also perfect order. The women waited patiently with the kids, no one was yelling or screaming, it was all very peaceful and it echoed the tranquillity of this idyllic jungle setting. As long as I live I'll remember the river, the people and their perfectly kept houses behind those picket fences.

A little later I stood on the jetty with Mungo, watching a group of older kids splashing around in the water.

'I cannot tell you how glad I am to be back,' Mungo said. 'This is the best job, Charley. It's absolutely brilliant.'

He was right, it was.

At last it was time to say goodbye, the villagers gathering to see us off. Back in the boats we were soon racing downriver and getting much wetter than on the way up. It was far less scary in the daytime and the pilot was really going for it. He threw the boat down the rapids without batting an eyelid and I got completely soaked on four separate occasions. Now and again we'd pass small boats with flat roofs carrying dirt bikes, their riders all kitted out for the jungle. I bet the riding up there is just fabulous. Another trip, perhaps – I had already vowed to myself that I would come back.

Retracing our steps to Ketapang, we spent the night there before jumping back on the *Hutan Express* and crossing the delta to the mouth of the Kapuas. It was 28 June and suddenly I could sniff the end of the trip ahead. I had mixed feelings – over the past few days I'd been missing Olly and the kids terribly, but at the same time this really was the journey of a lifetime. Better make the most of it, I told myself.

Then, starving hungry, I joined the others for frogs' legs and puff adder.

24

Two Hundred and One Horsepower

We arrived in Bali on the evening of 29 June, taking a flight from Pontianak. It was a shame to leave Borneo by plane but our UNICEF trip had been a detour, and we really had no choice.

Russ was waiting for us, and I hoped he had news on the route ahead. We'd put a deposit on a boat to take us from Kupang to Darwin but I had no idea how we were going to get to Kupang itself. Sitting down with a map and a beer, Russ, Mungo and I discussed the journey. But if I'd been hoping for enlightenment, I was out of luck. It turned out that even the Kupang–Darwin stretch was still a bit sketchy.

'Don't worry, we've got the boat,' Russ said. 'It's just that when I saw a picture of it my first reaction was "Oh my God!"'

'That sounds promising.'

'It looked better once they'd blown the picture up a bit.'

'How far is it to Darwin?' Mungo asked.

'Four hundred and fifty miles. The boat ought to do about twenty knots, but apparently the currents are against you so it can take up to four days.'

'Four days!' I didn't like the sound of that. After our experiences in Vietnam and Nikoi I'd decided I wasn't much into boats. But Indonesia is, of course, a series of islands. If we weren't going to fly, a boat was the only option. I turned to Mungo. 'What do you think?'

Mungo thought for a moment. 'Well,' he said carefully, 'if the skipper's an Aussie and he's done it before a few times . . . He must know what he's letting himself in for. If he's confident it's OK then yeah, I'd put my life in his hands.'

'I tell you something,' Russ said with a nervous grin. 'You wouldn't want to be on that boat in rough weather. Not from the picture I saw . . . Having said that,' he added quickly, seeing our expressions, 'I suppose you don't really know about a boat until you step on to it. Right now our priority is to get to Kupang. Lucy and I weren't able to get anything concrete sorted back in London, but Jo stayed up all night to find and organise a boat, and this morning I met up with an Australian guy called Steve to finalise the plans. He said he's got a speedboat that could take us part of the way.'

Now we'd had a chance to discuss things properly, Russ called Steve, who offered to take us as far as the Gili Islands tomorrow night, and then on to Bima. From there we could pick up a *phinisi*, a traditional sailing boat a bit like a dhow. If we sailed overnight on the *phinisi* we could get to Flores via Komodo, again on the speedboat, giving us just enough time to catch a ferry to Kupang. A little complicated, but still – sorted.

But it was the journey from Kupang to Darwin that still worried me, and I'd learned to listen more closely to my instinct. There is something to be said for not tempting fate and already we'd lost the engine on one boat then managed to hole another half an hour from shore. Between here and Darwin we had about nine days at sea and while I was up for the fun of it, I was still a little apprehensive. At least I had a new good luck charm with me. Back in Borneo I'd lost the St Christopher I'd been wearing the entire journey. I had phoned my wife and she bought a new one, had it blessed and sent it out with Russ. The next morning I fastened it carefully round my neck and thought of Olly and the kids back home.

On the way out of the hotel we bumped into four Bondi Beach life guards from Sydney called Harry, Chappo, Tom and Terry. They were making a documentary with their counterparts here –

they told us that a couple of hundred tourists drown in the waters around Bali each year. The lads were fans of the *Long Way* series and asked if I would deliver a card to their mate 'Box' when I got to Sydney. They also asked me to ride a moped with them down to the marina for their TV show. I had to get to the boat somehow and, never one to turn down the chance of two wheels, I happily accepted.

Down at the marina, Steve introduced us to Andy, the Indonesian guy who would skipper the boat. We were supposed to leave at three p.m. but it was already gone four. I was concerned because the boat had no lights and it would be dark by around half six. We were at the south-eastern tip of Bali and had to get to Trawangan on the north-western tip of the Gili Islands – a trip of at least two hours.

While we waited for the paperwork to be sorted, I asked Andy if he'd been that way before. He replied that he'd been there in this very boat – something I found reassuring, remembering how I'd felt when Ahong told me he'd never crossed from Nikoi to Borneo before. I asked Andy what the weather was going to be like. Right now it was blisteringly hot, the sky a perfect blue and the water sparklingly calm.

'There is high tide and neap tide,' Andy told me. 'At high tide the water is very big, but it's better at neap tide; only the wind is bad then.'

'What is it today?'

'High tide.'

By the time we were finally cleared to go it was quarter to five. Mungo was excited by the prospect of sailing on what he called a 'proper boat', all clean lines and very sleek. It could reach a speed of forty-nine knots, which was pretty bloody fast. I checked the pilot's console to make sure we had all the right stuff like GPS and radar. It did, but no matter how well equipped the boat was and how unfazed Andy seemed to be, I knew we were going to arrive at Trawangan in darkness and on a boat without lights.

'What do you reckon, Russ?' Mungo asked as we got settled.

'Great. Crossing shark-infested waters in pitch-darkness. Just what "by any means" is all about.'

'We've got petrol and horsepower,' I said. 'That works for me.'

Backing away from the marina we made our way out of the harbour. The sea was calm, but then of course it was sheltered here. As we picked up speed I went and stood to the side of the wheel, Russ squatting on the seat in front, the wind whipping at our hair and spray stinging our faces.

'I spoke to Lucy just before we left,' Russ called out over the whine of the engine. 'The boat from Kupang is definitely on its way.'

'Did they say any more about how long it would take to get to Darwin?'

'Four days minimum.'

Four days . . . Ah, well. We'd seen a boat in the harbour that Russ thought was roughly the kind of thing we'd be going on: thirty-seven feet, maybe. Up close it didn't look too bad. I decided not to worry any further – there was nothing more I could do now until we reached Kupang.

Gradually the land mass began to dwindle and we were soon in choppier sea, the bows smacking rapidly rising waves that formed a swell like mountains far to the left. Glancing back to Mungo I saw seat cushions disappearing over the stern.

'Hey, Andy,' I yelled. 'We lost the cushions.'

He slowed down, turned the boat and there they were. It bothered me that we'd lost something overboard, particularly so soon after we'd set off.

'Jesus,' I muttered. 'Somebody's telling us not to go today.'

'Hey, Charley,' Mungo called as if he'd heard me. 'Take a look.'

I stared at where he was pointing. The sun was already going down and at first I couldn't see anything except the rapidly greying waves. Then I spotted it. A shark's fin, slicing through the water. A little shiver worked through me.

'Are there a lot of sharks in these waters?' I asked Andy.

'Oh yeah,' he nodded. 'Lots and lots of sharks.'

Lots and lots of sharks. And we would be negotiating rocks and God knows what else in the dark with no lights. Perfect.

At ten past six I was scanning our position on the GPS. The sun was sinking fast and I reckoned in twenty minutes we would be in complete darkness. We still had at least forty minutes, maybe an hour to go. 'It's dark in less than half an hour,' I muttered to Andy.

Andy nodded. 'We have to be careful of rocks,' he said, 'and floating wood. There's a lot of floating wood off the island.'

I kept one eye on the horizon now as it got steadily darker.

'Oh, well,' Russ said. 'At least we did that night exercise in Southampton.'

'With lights and buoys and waypoints,' I reminded him. 'That was the River Hamble, mate, not the open sea.'

By six-thirty-five the ocean was black. I stood at the gunwales as we raced through the darkness.

'By the way,' Russ said. 'Bits of the boat are falling apart.' Leaning over the side, he flapped at a thick rubber band that went all the way round the hull. It was hanging off like a broken seal on a fan oven.

'I don't believe it,' I said. 'Why is it that every boat I step on, there's something not working?'

Suddenly the engine note changed, rising savagely in pitch. Moments later Andy cut the power and the bows dipped hard into the swell, sending the whole vessel into a sideways roll.

'What is it?' I said through the gloom. It was so dark I could only just make out his face by the lights on the console.

'There's something caught in the propeller.'

We'd clearly run into the kind of debris he'd warned us about. He put the boat into reverse and slowly wound on the power, the little alarm sounding on the dash. For a moment the gears wouldn't engage. That's it, I thought. We're fucked.

God, I hate boats.

But Andy worked the prop gently backwards and at last whatever had caught came loose and the familiar whine started up once again.

I fingered the St Christopher Olly had sent, and peered into the darkness with hot tongues of wind drying the sweat on my face. Let's just make it now, I thought. Please, please, let's just make it.

We got going again but now there seemed to be some confusion about which way to go. We had GPS and radar, but the mechanic was on one side of the console jabbering away and gesticulating while Andy was on the other doing the same. They were pointing in different directions and remonstrating with each other.

'That sounds comforting,' I said.

Russ didn't reply because at that moment we hit a big wave and he took most of it full in the face.

The argument seemed to die away quickly enough and Andy returned to his seat, the same relatively unflustered look on his face. We sped across the open sea again for a while but then the propeller snagged for a second time. Fucking hell, I thought – here we go again. It was the left-hand engine this time and the mechanic had to hang over the back with a torch while Andy put the thing into reverse. In open water, in the dark, on a boat with no lights, in shark-infested seas. By any means, Charley, I told myself; by any bloody means.

We got going again and kept the speed down this time. Andy picked out the glow of a lighthouse and knew immediately where we were. Keeping the lighthouse on our left we motored on until finally we saw more lights dotted along what must be the shore ahead. Andy brought the boat round in a circle, explaining that we had to come in from the north to make sure we avoided a line of rocks that would tear the bottom out.

There was no marina, no jetty; he just drove the big boat onto the beach and we jumped out. Land at last. It had been fun but with the engine dying it had played havoc with the old nerves and we still had another eight days at sea to come.

There are no cars on the Gili Islands. Walking up the beach with our gear we found a horse and cart taxi.

'It's like a *songthaew*, only without an engine,' Russ said.

'At least we got here,' I told him. 'From Bali to Gili by two hundred and one horsepower.'

The narrow, dusty street where our hotel was situated was heaving all night long, so we decided to have a night out on the tiles. There was music everywhere and tourists were flocking in from the other islands. I was still up with the dawn, mind you, taking a swim in the sea while many revellers were drunkenly making their way back to their hotels.

Considering the amount of Jack Daniel's and coke Russ put away he was in surprisingly good form, as was Mungo. We wandered the length of the narrow road looking for a horse and cart to take us to where we were supposed to meet the speedboat. Without cars, and with most of the tourists now in bed, there was a real peacefulness to the place. The bars looked very different in the daytime with their open-air tables and thatched shelters; the sea dotted with dive boats and the ragged outline of islands across the bay.

We'd arranged to meet Andy at eight, but having trawled up and down the road in the back of a horse cart, there was still no sign of him. He finally appeared at nine o'clock, by which time the three of us were flapping around like parrots. Andy was very apologetic; he'd had to go miles to get fuel and it wasn't just a case of pulling up at a petrol station. He had to fill jerricans and find someone on a moped to ferry them.

We sailed east for nine hours to reach Bima, and I loved every minute of it. The humidity that had made Vietnam, Laos and Cambodia so tough had dissipated, leaving a much drier heat, far easier to deal with. As we travelled further east the scenery began to change. The islands became more arid and barren, with fewer trees and hardly any jungle.

We crossed the water without incident, Andy and the mechanic doing a fantastic job. The sea finally settled into a breezy but gentle chop; the engines kept going and we didn't hit anything. We passed fishing boats and dive boats, and one old guy paddling a surfboard with a pair of oversized flip-flops. Skirting the southern lip of the Flores Sea, we skimmed across bay after bay, passing golden beaches, and others made of black volcanic rock or pure coral.

It was working out, I thought, smiling to myself. This was the most awkward part of the expedition in terms of locating transport, and it was actually working out. Nine hours after we'd set off we rolled into the harbour at Bima, knackered and hot and covered in dried salt from the constant spray. From here we hoped to catch the *phinisi*. There were one or two in the harbour – one particularly spectacular one with a white hull and dark wooden wheelhouse. It was the *Bidadari*, our boat, and it looked absolutely fabulous. Andy took us alongside where a tall, blond-haired American was leaning on the rail.

'Are you expecting us?' I yelled.

'I think so,' he grinned. 'I'm Nick, by the way.'

It was a superb-looking boat, completely refurbished, with twin masts, and a dining room, salon and cabins below. Nick showed us the 'speedies', as he called them: a couple of dive boats upturned in the bows. Above was a sun deck where one of the crew was facing Mecca in prayer. After an open speedboat all the way from Bali, this was pretty luxurious.

I spotted another *phinisi* across the bay: an old, skeletal wreck resting on a sandbar. You could really see the shape though, the castle-like quarters at the stern and the upturned prow. Even old and falling apart there was a kind of elegance about it. Boats in that condition are often taken to Bali and refurbished. For about £250,000 you can buy one pretty much to your own spec. Made completely of wood, they're ultra-seaworthy and fitted with diesel engines so you can take them wherever you want.

It was now Tuesday night, and we needed to reach Flores to catch the two p.m. ferry on Thursday. We were planning to steam out to Komodo this evening and see if we could see the dragons tomorrow. The idea was that Andy would stay on Bima tonight and bring the speedboat to Komodo or Rinca the next day to meet us. Then he'd take us on to Flores, though, given his trouble this morning, he was a little concerned about refuelling and he was looking less than sure about the whole situation – he didn't know Bima very well. Even if he refilled the jerricans tomorrow, he would use most of it reaching Komodo, and wasn't sure where he'd get any more.

'Hang on a minute,' Russ said. 'Is there any way this boat can tow the speedboat?'

'I don't see why not,' Nick said, slapping at a stray mosquito, 'but you'll have to ask the captain.'

Once we had the captain's agreement, the crew attached the speedboat to a tyre, then fastened two ropes from that to the stern. And with that we were under way; next stop the Komodo dragons.

25
Dragon's Breath

Komodo was stunning: golden white sands set in a turquoise sea, and 2 July was another glorious morning. We'd been steaming along at a gentle six knots and I'd slept very well. I doubted the same could be said for Andy and the poor mechanic, mind you, who must have been slapped around in the speedboat towed along behind. They were such good guys and they'd worked so hard. On deck at six-thirty I'd given them an encouraging wave but they just grinned impassively, smoking cigarettes. We had decided it would be easier on them if we went back to Bima to get the ferry instead of trying to get to Flores. At full chat we could do it in a couple of hours and when they dropped us off they'd be that bit closer to home.

We headed to Rinca, a little way south from Komodo. The island is part of a World Heritage Site and the local people have learned how to coexist with the huge lizards. The dragons mainly eat carrion, but can hunt if they need to. Their main prey is buffalo. Their bite causes an infection, so when they attack their prey they usually have to follow it around for a couple of days afterwards until the toxins take. The dragon's saliva contains up to sixty different types of bacteria. With swift medical care an adult human might survive, but not a child, so the locals have to be careful. Only last year a young boy had died from septicaemia.

Tying up to a wooden jetty we were greeted by signs forbidding camp fires and guns. As we climbed the path that circled the base of a rocky slope I realised this was another of those stop-and-pinch-yourself moments. Komodo dragons – incredible. I felt like David Attenborough.

'Actually, I think he might be coming out here,' Nick said. 'Someone from the BBC is coming anyway.' He pointed across the rocks to where half a dozen macaque monkeys were watching us. 'Those little guys use their tails to fish for crabs, apparently.'

'They do what?' I stared at them, amazed.

'They dangle their tails in the water to attract crabs. The crab grabs the tail with its pincers then the monkey whips it out of the water and eats it.'

'With melted butter and a glass of Sancerre, I hope?' I was laughing. 'How did they work out how to do that?'

'I have no idea, but it's the only place in the world where macaques do it and the BBC is going to try and catch it on film.'

Close to the village we saw a couple of baby dragons soaking up the sun. They were about two or three feet long and grey coloured with massive heads and long curling claws. When they're young they can climb trees, but as they get older they use their claws for fighting and tearing the flesh of their prey.

It was incredibly hot and the landscape had a stark beauty that felt somehow prehistoric. We walked along a dry river bed littered with fallen leaves and exposed roots curled like snakes at the bases of ancient trees. There was a silence here that smacked of predators.

We crossed short stretches of swamp, the jungle rank with rancid water and the smell of dragon shit. Gradually the trees thinned out and we climbed a hill to discover another world, a high, barren plateau, the only vegetation a handful of palm trees.

We saw plenty of macaques and the odd buffalo but no sign of any adult dragons. Apparently July and August was mating season and most of them were probably off in the bush somewhere trying to get it on. Probably best not to interrupt that, come to think of it. We came across some old nests, though; great holes scraped in the ground where the female would lay up to thirty eggs that took nine months to hatch.

Nothing hunts these creatures – they're top of the food chain. It's amazing to think no westerner knew they were here until 1910. It's easy to see how the beasts got their name, though: the adults are colossal. The largest wild one ever seen was over ten feet long and weighed a hundred and fifty pounds. Their tail is as long as their body and they use it to balance on their hind legs. They are also incredibly powerful, with over sixty serrated teeth. I tried to imagine coming across one in the wild, back when no one knew they existed. With their forked tongue, scaly skin and massive claws, it's no wonder they were referred to as dragons.

We walked for a couple of kilometres but still couldn't find any adults so we went back to the village. Lo and behold there was a big male lying between the cafe and the toilet block. Completely unconcerned by us, he got to his feet, flicked his tongue and took off with an ambling overarm gait. They are truly awesome creatures – they can live for fifty years and run at twenty miles an hour if they need to. They can also leap about fifteen feet, so getting close really isn't a good idea.

It was a strange sensation, being around them – almost like travelling back in time. I thought that if I lived here I'd feel perpetually hunted. The villagers build their homes on stilts and at night the ladders are pulled up.

After our walk round the island Russ and I set off for a dive in the RIB. Poor Mungo couldn't join us. He was capable enough, but ten years ago he'd suffered a spontaneous pneumothorax and couldn't take the risk. Pneumothorax was one technical term etched for ever into the 'Charley Book of Everything' – it means a collapsed lung. It had happened to Olly just as Ewan and I were about to leave on Long Way Down. I felt for Mungo, this was one of those places you just have to dive, and the last bit of R&R before the long haul to Darwin.

We'd just witnessed something of a prehistoric world and now we were in another world again. Descending about fifteen metres, I gazed the length of a reef that seemed to go on and on – a forest of weaving, waving colours like hundreds of heads of hair billowing in a breeze. I'd never dived anywhere like this: perfect visibility, perfect conditions. I glimpsed puffer fish, sea turtles and moray eels, and angel fish that at first glance seemed to be part of the coral. Great shoals swam up to investigate – fantastic.

Russ paused to check his air and somehow managed to let go of the camera. It was wrapped in a partially inflated airbag and instead of sinking it rose all the way to the surface. He didn't realise at first and spent some time looking for it among the coral, hoping that it hadn't gone to the bottom. It was only when he glanced up that he could see it floating close to the boat. All at once a hand reached out from above and grabbed it.

'There's a crack in it,' he told me as we climbed aboard once again. 'Moisture in the lens. It's a real shame, I doubt we'll get anything from it.'

'Regular Jacques Cousteau, aren't you, mate,' I said. 'Never mind.'

Back on the *phinisi* we grabbed something to eat and thanked Nick and the crew before returning to the speedboat for a mad dash back to Bima, where we hoped to catch the ferry and hook up with Anne, who was already on board.

We passed the ferry just as it was approaching the dock. Back on land we joined the massive crowd waiting behind a pair of iron gates. There were so many people; it was as if all of Bima had descended – not only passengers carrying cases and boxes, bags and bundles, but curious onlookers. There were kids selling cans of a cold drink called Pocari Sweat, women kneeling on rugs offering everything from red beans to marrows and cucumbers. It was chaos: the only thing I'd experienced that was even vaguely similar had been in Aswan with Ewan, waiting for the ferry to take us the length of Lake Nasser. Everyone was crowding around us asking what we were doing and where we were going; there were so many people that for the first time we were a little concerned about our gear. Finally the blue gates opened and we were pushed and

Preparing to sail from Nikoi to Pontianak on the Yeremia.

After half an hour, things started to go wrong.

The Yeremia's lifeboat. Not a reassuring sight.

Delivering vaccines for
UNICEF in Borneo.

On a speedboat from Bali – great fun.

The Oelin. Beautiful in calm waters in Timor, Indonesia. Not so pretty when the waves are four metres high.

Me, Mungo, Warwick and Tony. We survived!

The team together on the Wicked campervan – Darwin to Alice Springs.

The pub in Daly Waters. I didn't leave my bra behind but I did leave some pink fluffy handcuffs (don't ask).

Noel let me ride his favourite camel.

Dinky the Dingo and his owner James Cotterill.   Shearing time at the sheep station . . .

With Dave 'The Outback Man' just outside Marree.

Alan and the Road Train.

Kelly the solar-powered car. Probably wouldn't work in Britain.

The Nissan Ute – a classic vehicle for the Australian outback.

Riding through the mountains on a horse called Basil.

Riding into Sydney with my daughter Doone.

Made it!

With my beautiful family and the brilliant By Any Means team. I couldn't have done it without them.

jostled, people elbowing and shoving, almost bundling us over as the entire throng swarmed for the gangplank. It would have been easy to feel a bit panicked or threatened even, but I just told myself to roll with it. The arrival of the boat was clearly a big deal on Bima.

Eventually we got on board and it was just as busy there with people cramming the gangways and stairs, running up and down and shouting like mad things.

'What are they running for?' I asked no one in particular. 'We've got at least a couple of hours until we leave.'

'They're running to get a seat,' a voice said from behind me. 'It was the same in Bali.'

I turned to find Anne smiling at me.

'Hello,' I said. 'We missed you.'

'This place is mad, Charley. It's like this all the time.'

Two nights and almost two full days of madness. 'We booked a couple of cabins, didn't we?' I said hopefully.

She nodded. 'You're sharing with Mungo and it's very, very hot.'

The four of us enjoyed a dinner of rice and chicken with a spicy jalapeno sauce. Maybe the fieriness got into the conversation somehow, I don't know, but things got a little heated afterwards.

'The boat is in Kupang,' Russ said, biting into a slice of melon. 'The Australian guy who skippers it is called Warwick and he goes back and forth all the time to trade. I'm still not convinced, but we don't have any choice, there's nothing and no one else. I think we'll have to take it.'

'We already know that,' I said, a little irritated. 'I've been saying we've got to take it from the moment we booked it.'

'Yeah, but you haven't seen it.'

'But I *have* been told it's seaworthy. In fact I was told exactly what you just said weeks ago.'

'I know, but I've *seen* it.'

'What exactly is the matter, Russ?' We were staring at each other now.

'You don't know what you're talking about. You haven't seen it.'

'Well, you've only seen a photo of it.'

'Look.' He jerked a thumb at Anne and Mungo. 'It's my responsibility to ensure you all make it safe to Darwin. I'm just trying to make sure we have a seaworthy boat.'

'Fine. But why are you getting so narky?'

'I'm not. It's you.'

It was a ridiculous argument, I know. I think underneath it all we were feeling a bit apprehensive about that last sea leg. Anyway, I found Russ on deck later and apologised.

When we docked in Flores about a hundred people got off but another three hundred got on. The stated maximum was nine hundred and ninety-eight and I counted roughly at least two thousand on board. I had a long chat with the captain: the ship had been listing to port all the way from Bima and he admitted that we were massively overloaded. But he didn't sell tickets, he just skippered, and with a shrug of his shoulders he told me that it was holiday season and this was normal. He'd been doing the route for years now and never had an incident.

The ferry was so overcrowded it was actually hard to move around; people were crashed out in corridors, the stairwells, every inch of the deck, entire families camped out on rough sleeping mats with their luggage in cardboard boxes lying alongside them.

I didn't see Russ all day: he had left his cabin at five a.m. and was nowhere to be found. It was at this point I discovered that he had decided to fly from Timor to Darwin instead of taking the boat. Our Indonesian guide wanted him to confirm the flights and when he couldn't find him he asked me. It was a bit galling to find out that way, but I suppose it was Russ's decision. Finally, we located him sleeping in a 'crew only' section of the deck: his cabin window wouldn't open because sacks of potatoes had been piled up outside and the only air came from a vent surrounded by cockroaches.

I was adamant I was not going to fly no matter how bad the boat was. I wanted to stay true to the spirit of our original idea. Russ suggested the spirit had been broken anyway because I'd flown from Batam to Borneo then from Borneo to Bali, but I pointed out that I'd only done that because of our obligations to

UNICEF. If we hadn't had the vaccination programme I'd have found another way off Nikoi.

The ferry finally docked in Timor and I watched as the mania took over. Crowds of orange-clad workers waited impatiently for the gangplank to come down. As soon as it did a mass brawl ensued. People were clambering over each other, others were leaping from the sides, ducking under the ropes, falling off and trying again – it was like watching lemmings piling over a cliff. Sheer mayhem, and easily the most eye-popping boat trip I'd ever been on.

Once we made it ashore we met Warwick, the skipper of the boat that would take us to Darwin. He was about thirty-five with a shaven head and blue mirror-lens sunglasses. He was joined by an older guy called Tony who worked as first mate. Tony was talking as we approached and I picked up the words 'fifty-knot winds'.

'Fifty knots?' I said in horror.

'That's what it can get up to,' he said. 'But it won't be anything like that.'

'It'll be a rough crossing, though?'

'Not rough, mate. A bit bumpy, maybe.'

The ferry captain had told me that if the sea was calm then the crossing to Darwin would be fine, but if it was rough we should stay at home, go inside and shut the door. But bumpy or rough there was no way I was backing out, though I did want to see the boat first just to be sure.

'How long do you think it'll take?' I asked Warwick.

He made a face. 'It ought to take four days but with the kind of weather we've been having you need to prepare for six, or even seven maybe.'

Six or seven, God, I'd been thinking four at the most. With a quick glance at Mungo I asked Warwick to show us the boat.

'Mate,' he said as we headed for the bay, 'if it's only going to be you and Mungo that'll work, actually, because we've already got a couple of passengers on board. Cyclists. Andreas and Lena, a German and a Lithuanian. They sleep on deck most nights so it'll be OK.'

Cutting through an alley between two harbour buildings we came to the bay where a variety of boats were moored. 'There she is,' Warwick said, 'the wooden one, the *Oelin*.'

I looked where he was pointing. Without doubt she was the prettiest boat out there: a small *phinisi* with its high prow and the wheelhouse at the stern.

'You built her?'

Warwick nodded. 'Over in Kalimantan – me and my brother. We were told it ought to take three months but allowed a year. Anyway, five years later, there she was. People think she's teak but she's made from the local timber, Kalimantan ironwood.'

'What do you think, Charley?' Russ had come with us and was standing alongside me.

'I think she looks terrific. I'm going to have a closer look, but we'd better say goodbye now because if she's as sound as she looks I'll just stay on board.'

'OK. Take care then and I'll see you in Darwin.'

I gave him a hug and said goodbye to Anne, who was also going to fly. After a couple of bad experiences on small boats then having to take the ferry all the way from Bali, she'd had her fill of the sea. So, it would just be Mungo and me for this last stretch. With two other passengers on board perhaps that was just as well.

We stowed our gear on Warwick's little speedboat and got aboard. 'Six days then, Warwick,' I said.

'I reckon. If we go straight across we'll be smack into the wind all the way and it'll be really tedious. We're going to hug the coast for about half the time then scuttle across. It's another ninety miles, but it'll be more comfy.'

'Comfy is fine with me. I hope you've got lots of seasickness pills aboard.'

'We've got a few,' he said. 'Why, do you reckon you'll need lots?'

'No . . . I might lose a bit of weight along the way, but I can take it.'

The boat was fabulous, exactly the kind of thing we wanted. There was plenty of space, and I loved the fact it had been built using traditional techniques. Ironwood is really durable, it's heavy, but that's good in a wooden boat. Warwick said the *Oelin* could withstand pretty much anything.

The two passengers, Andreas a grey-haired German guy and his girlfriend Lena, showed us below. There was just one large cabin with six bunks so that ought to be cosy; the walls were panelled and there were plenty of books in the bookcase. The whole place had a warm, encouraging feeling. It might be a bit of a tight fit if the weather was bad, but Andreas and Lena reiterated that they liked to sleep on deck.

The boat was clearly well maintained and Warwick had all the necessary safety equipment. He had a full safety checklist, the dos and don'ts etc, and told me he'd been sailing one way or another since he was fourteen. He was skippering unofficially at fifteen and had his ticket by the time he was nineteen. He was very relaxed, a real easy-going Aussie, and he seemed to know exactly what he was doing. We'd heard word from Kupang that Warwick was the only guy around who would make the crossing at this time of year and I suppose you could take that one of two ways. I asked why it was so difficult and Tony explained that there was high pressure after high pressure in the south. That created the constant easterly winds that blew so violently up here.

Once aboard that was it: I'd made my decision and was sticking with it. Itching to get going, Mungo and I stood gazing at the grey stone buildings that dominated the shore. Warwick had taken our passports over to immigration and he was hoping we'd be away by four. So was I.

I could scent the end of the journey now, and like a horse I was bolting for home.

'This is the last leg, Mungo,' I said.

He nodded. 'You'll be the only one who made it all the way, do you realise that? Three set out but only one made it.'

'What do you mean?'

'I mean Russ went home and so did I.'

'You were injured.'

'I know, but whatever the reason, you're the only one who made it all that way.' He shook my hand. 'I don't want to tempt fate, buddy, but congratulations.'

*

The estimated time of departure came and went and still Warwick wasn't back. At last he returned and explained that while things were moving, this was Indonesia, and we were some way off yet. 'I reckon the paperwork will be done by about seven, but I think we should wait and leave first thing in the morning.'

'The morning?' First six or seven days and now the morning – I could feel my heart sinking all over again.

'You see those bamboo rigs?' He pointed up the bay to a whole string of sailing boats that were here and there. 'They're not lit at night and we don't want to hit any. It'd be safer to wait till first light.'

He was right, of course, but I was still gutted.

'Are you superstitious, Charley?' he asked.

I showed him the half-dozen or so charms hanging from my wrist. 'No, Warwick, I'm not superstitious at all.'

'They say you should never set sail on a Friday anyway. It's an unwritten rule of the fisherman. We'll leave at first light tomorrow. Now, I don't know about you, mate, but I'm ready for a cold beer.'

26
A Little Rough and Bumpy

It wasn't just the beer, of course. Being sailors we broke out the rum, and at 57 per cent proof, we got absolutely hammered.

First light seemed to come around far too quickly and when I woke up I had to think long and hard about where I was. Then I remembered I was in Kupang and had at least six days at sea ahead of me. My head was pounding, my stomach felt like a washtub and we'd not even left the mooring. It would have been a good time to go home. But I couldn't, so instead I crawled out of bed and stumbled on deck.

'It's your fault,' I told Warwick, who was grinning at my self-induced misfortune.

'I know, mate. That funnel in your mouth, that wasn't fair, was it?'

I helped winch the tender on board: the little metal dinghy we'd used to get ashore last night after we'd worked out that the alcohol we'd consumed needed to be soaked up by some solids. That done, Warwick passed me the handle for the anchor winch which proceeded to shear off at the first turn. I stood there with it dangling uselessly in my hand. Warwick took it from me and with a grim shake of his head told me to assume the position.

He explained that Andreas and Lena were working their

passage by doing the cooking and cleaning, which was great for us because it meant fewer chores and more leisure time. To begin with at least, I was all for that. Between them Warwick and Tony fixed the winch handle and we got the anchor up.

'We lose the odd one now and again,' Warwick told me. 'It's an occupational hazard and we carry spares in the hold. Cyclone anchors, Charley.' He winked at me. 'Just in case.'

Back in the wheelhouse he opened the flap in the windscreen to let some air through and showed me how to set up the autopilot on his laptop. With the waypoints already programmed, the course was logged. I stood back and watched as the old-fashioned ship's wheel steered itself. It looked very strange, the wheel spinning first left then right then left again all by itself. Mungo and I decided it wasn't the autopilot at all – there was a ghost on board. We named him Joe.

It was a crystal-clear morning and cruising along the northern coast of Timor we would be sheltered from the weather. After we hit the open sea we'd continue for about ninety miles then run south-east for Darwin.

'It's an easier ride,' Warwick assured me again. 'This way the wind is with us and we ride the waves a bit like a camel rides the sand dunes, you know what I mean?'

'Sand dunes, sure,' I said. 'Did I ever tell you that I did the Dakar?'

'You did, mate, yeah, last night. About three times.'

I was all for an easier crossing and this morning I couldn't think of a better place to be than on this boat. It was lovely; the wooden hull painted a bright orange, the wheelhouse pink. Warwick said the colour scheme was his wife's idea. It was extremely pretty and the Kalimantan ironwood gave it real character.

Mungo and I agreed that for all our arguments and flapping around, Warwick had turned out to be exactly the kind of skipper we needed. He knew these waters like the back of his hand and had spent twenty years fishing, first with his father then on his own boat. He had that uniquely Aussie wit and the first day and night were just wonderful. The company was great, the sea calm and with the grey hills of Timor on our right we were skipping along with barely a judder.

I loved the boat. Compact and atmospheric, it was the kind of vessel I'd like to have taken from Nikoi to Borneo. The wheelhouse was panelled in wood and every time we went inside, Joe would be steering. The other end was devoted to the galley – a bench fastened against one wall and a table and couple of stools. Outside on the poop was the fridge, and a hatch that opened on to a ladder leading down to the propeller. At night we'd sit and watch the most amazing flashes churned up in the wake – a kind of phosphorous green.

Tony reckoned the hatch was where Indonesian sailors traditionally took a poo. We, of course, had a small toilet (though you had to be careful with the flush) and a shower cubicle. Whenever the hatch was open someone had to be there to make sure no one else fell through. Not falling overboard was the only really hard and fast rule on the boat.

'It's boring,' Tony said. 'We have to turn around and come back to look for you. Interrupts the journey, mate, and that's a real bummer.'

They made the journey regularly and carried various cargoes. On the trip over they'd brought a whole load of building materials for an Australian who was constructing a house, as well as giving passage to an Irish kid and an English girl.

It was great fun and very relaxing. We took our time, stopping now and then for a swim and rolling out a 400 lb line in the hope that passing tuna would bite. I'd check it occasionally for debris – plastic bags mostly. But no matter how many times I rebaited it we didn't get so much as a sniff.

It took a little while to slow down to the pace of the boat – we were trundling along at about six or seven knots and things just happened when they happened. The sun was shining, the sky was blue and I spent a lot of time up front resting against the upturned tender, with my gaze fixed on a flat and brilliantly blue horizon. There was nothing ahead save a pod of dolphins surfing the bow wave. I'd never been up close with dolphins before and I leant over the rail to watch them darting ahead and leaping out of the water. Warwick told me it was quite unusual, dolphins were pretty shy of boats up here.

After dinner Mungo and I went forward again to watch the

same flakes of phosphorescence we'd witnessed at the propeller. Every now and then the shaft of brilliant green would be criss-crossed by jagged lines created by dorsal fins that told us the dolphins were there although we couldn't see them. It was a strange phenomenon and in complete darkness with the stars above and the wind in my hair, it was really quite magical. Warwick showed us the Southern Cross, a crucifix of stars that southern hemisphere sailors use to find south at night, using the twin pointers that accompany the constellation.

Sunday dawned a little cloudier, but with calm seas and no hint of any real weather we carried on with land on the starboard side. I was feeling pretty happy, looking forward to crossing Australia and finally seeing my family. I'd slept well last night, we stuck to a beer at sundown and I was in my bunk by nine and awake by six. The day slipped by and as we went to bed on the second night the sea was still calm.

At one a.m. I was jerked upright by the most incredible bang. I was out of my bunk and staggering to stay upright as the whole boat seemed to roll to one side. Mungo was on his feet and the pair of us crabbed our way to the steps then out on deck where we stood gripping the rail and staring into absolute blackness.

For a moment it was terrifying: I couldn't see anything and all I could hear was the straining diesel engine and the thundering of the sea. This was as black a night as I'd seen; no trace of light, not even a hint of grey. The wind was like a banshee and waves were crashing against the hull. I realised it was a wave that had woken us.

'Jesus, Mungo,' I yelled. 'This is incredible.'

He threw up, 'blew the chunks' as he put it. The movement of the boat had taken all sense of balance and he just ducked his head and chundered into the wind – bad move: it all flew back into his face.

Turning back to the wheelhouse door I could just make out Warwick in the glow of the GPS screen, a cigarette burning between his fingers.

'You all right, Charley?'

'Yeah, Mungo fed the fish but we're fine. That wave just now woke us up.'

'Better get used to it, mate, we're coming into some weather.'

'It feels big.'

'It's big enough. I reckon we've got about three metres. She might swell to four or five before we're done. We just have to roll with it.'

He was different. For the first time I could see a serious side to him; the set of his face, the expression in his eyes and the calm, quiet way he was speaking. 'Best go below, mate. Don't want you going overboard, do we?'

Back in my bunk I felt easier, the light-headedness I'd experienced on deck was gone. I looked over at Mungo.

'Are you all right, dude?'

'Yeah, I'll be fine.'

Everything seemed accentuated by the darkness: the sound of the waves, the engine . . . it really did seem to be straining but that might have just been my imagination. There was only one engine on this boat, no back-up other than an outboard which wouldn't get us anywhere. Shifting onto my side I peered at Mungo where he lay prostrate with one foot on the floor.

'Are you sure you're all right?'

'Charles. Since when did you care so much about me?'

'I don't know, since we shared that room together in Borneo, I think.'

He squinted at me. 'Look, I know the trip's almost over and your wife is on her way, but stay on your side of the cabin, all right?'

'Good to see you didn't lose your sense of humour along with your dinner, eh?'

'Ha-bloody-ha.'

Warwick had warned us that when we came out from the shelter of Timor all the currents converge and that probably accounted for the savagery of the wave that woke us. I hadn't really had any idea what he meant, but I did now and I was just a little nervous. I had images of that old boat where water flooded the hold. This was a much smaller boat and like the other boat it was made of wood and if the same happened here . . .

It didn't bear thinking about.

I couldn't sleep, so I went back up top. Warwick was sitting with his arms folded, Joe ghosting the wheel.

'That is so weird,' I said, watching it shifting sharply from side to side. With the swell it was harder to stay on course and the wheel was spinning quite violently. 'Pity about the weather,' I added. 'I was really enjoying myself.'

Warwick made a face. 'The weather report says it's getting worse.'

'Worse?'

'It can always get worse, Charley.'

I did sleep again, though I had to get used to the see-saw motion, the shudder as we climbed massive waves then dipped into the troughs. The noise was incredible: the engine, the wind, the sound of a boiling sea.

As dawn broke on Monday 7 July I was on deck holding the rail and feeling more than a little seasick. I hadn't vomited but the thought of food wasn't good and the way this boat was yawing there was every chance that I'd throw up. What had been a great little boat trip was now something else altogether. The seas were mountainous, the swell beyond four metres, and we were struggling to make progress. Up and down, side to side, torrents of water rushing over the bows and slapping the sides before pitching us into cavernous grey troughs that I was sure would swallow us up.

The day wore on slowly. Yesterday and the day before had flown by with the sunshine and the sails up. There had been lots of laughs and banter. Now the world was different and I had a feeling of trepidation that I knew would be with me until we hit dry land. Already we'd had a couple of bad experiences on boats and I had a nagging concern that I was tempting fate. But this was the penultimate leg of the journey and by far the most treacherous: we had to do it and if we made it safely the sense of achievement would be monumental.

Mungo came up to catch some fresh air and we stood together at the rail. 'This is still only the Timor Sea,' I said. 'We've got at least eighteen hours before we get to Australian waters.'

He nodded.

'Stunning, isn't it?' A little rush of adrenalin caught up with me and looking out from that tiny, wooden deck I was overtaken by the sheer power of the sea.

'Are you worried?' Mungo asked. 'I mean, this is serious weather, and we were told that Warwick's the only guy who'd risk crossing at this time of year.'

For a moment neither of us said anything.

'We'll get there,' he added, as if to affirm his own convictions.

'Your life in his hands,' I reminded him. 'That's what you said when we talked about it in Bali: if he's a confident skipper, you'd be happy to place your life in his hands.' I held on tightly now to the rail, my whole body at forty degrees as another wave hit and the boat shuddered into yet another massive trough. 'Well, here we are, dude. Your life in his hands, and mine too.'

'We'll be fine,' he said.

'Of course we will.'

Still we stood there, the wind tearing my hair and peeling the skin on my face. 'Did you ever see *The Perfect Storm* – George Clooney and Mark Wahlberg? Everyone in that bar praying they'd just make it home. It's a true story, you know.'

He looked sideways at me. 'Let's go below,' he said.

The weather closed in. For hour after hour it was nothing but crashing waves and the guttural rattle of the engine, the moan of the wind and the tearing sound of wood as if the hull was going to give way any minute. Lying on my bunk I could feel spots of water leaking in from above. Everything seemed stifled; we couldn't stand up or move around, we couldn't go outside. We were confined both physically and mentally and that stopped conversation. The mood on board was serious – we were alone with our thoughts, either lying prone or holding on to something in the galley or wheelhouse. As the hours ticked by my mood got darker and darker.

'God, I'm pissed off,' I said, sitting upright. 'Right now I'd rather be anywhere in the world than out here.'

Mungo smiled. 'Me, too. Fickle fuckers, aren't we? When the sun's out and the sea is flat we're happy as pigs in shit.'

'And when the shit hits the fan all we do is run for cover.'

'Human nature, I guess.'

'My wife is flying out on the nineteenth, Mungo. I can't believe

I'm actually going to see her. I haven't seen her or my kids for three months and now it's only just a few days. It's been really hard for her this time – this idea came up so soon after Long Way Down and that wasn't in the plan.' I stared at the floor, the confines of the cabin closing in so hard it was as if I couldn't breathe. 'Jesus,' I muttered. 'What the fuck am I doing on this boat?'

Mungo didn't say anything further and I slipped into silence. I was feeling queasy and alone. The world had stopped: there was only the vulnerability of this little boat and the vastness of the ocean. I was as far away from my family as I think I ever could be and for a moment or two I was tearful. Then I thought about how my sister Telsche is always with me. I'd felt her presence when we rode through the rain in Cambodia, and if I thought about it I could feel her now. I was aware of the St Christopher around my neck and I was so glad Olly had had it blessed before she sent it out to me. Lying back I gripped it hard, staring at the wooden panelled ceiling, water dripping on my face.

As it got dark I was in the wheelhouse once more with Warwick. Mungo was below talking to Lena, and Tony was having a kip.

All of a sudden we heard a thud, a real bang on the roof directly above our heads. Eyes wide, Warwick rushed out on deck. I could see him through the windshield peering up at the roof of the wheelhouse. He stood there for a moment then crabbed his way to one side of the boat and then the other. He went aft to the poop deck and came in through the galley door, his eyes hunted and his brow furrowed. For the first time since I'd met him he looked a little freaked out.

In the wheelhouse he slid down the stairs. 'Where's Andreas?' he said.

Mungo looked up. 'I don't know.'

'Lena, where is Andreas?'

She was on her feet, her face white. Stepping past her Warwick took a quick glance into his cabin then came back up the steps. He went outside again, the boat rolling so viciously he was staggering the length of the deck. The wind was horrific, flapping his shirt so hard I could almost hear it. We tipped into another trough and surf boiled over the side. Losing his footing Warwick had to grab the mast to avoid being washed overboard. And beside me, as if to accentuate the madness, the ship's wheel was spinning left and right.

He was facing the wheelhouse now. Glancing up, a smile of relief suddenly creased his face. Moments later, and soaking wet, he was back inside.

'He's in the bloody Zodiac. He must have slipped over – that was the thud we heard – and when I went out the first time he was flat on his back and I couldn't see him. Jesus Christ, Charley, that was a fucking moment. Man overboard in this weather. No chance, mate, no bloody chance at all.' With a shake of his head he grabbed a cigarette from a crumpled pack stuffed into the netting above the dash.

I spent the rest of that night and the next day lying in a clammy heat on my bunk. The weather was so bad we hardly ate – certainly not a proper meal anyway. If we tried to move around we felt sick or kept bashing into things, and it was too dangerous to go out on deck.

Tedium and fear, that would be my abiding memory I decided, as I lay there watching Mungo with an arm across his eyes.

'We'll be glad we did it when we've done it.' I was trying to sound encouraging.

'Pretty hairy with Andreas last night, though. God only knows what would've happened if he had gone overboard.'

'He'd have drowned, Mungo. There's no way we could've turned the boat and found him in time.'

Mungo tried to sit up but then thought better of it. 'Bit bloody stupid being up on the roof in the first place.'

I was looking at my GPS. 'Do you know how fast we're going?'

'Enlighten me.'

'Four miles an hour.' It was suddenly very depressing. 'Do you know how far we've got to go still?'

'Nope.'

'Two hundred miles. Two hundred miles at four miles an hour. Jesus, Mungo, how long is that going to take?'

Now he did sit up. 'How long was the flight from Timor?'

'About two and a half hours.'

He lay down again.

It just went on and on, hour after hour with waves at four metres: we'd climb one side and roll down the other and all we could do was stay in the cabin and withdraw emotionally. All conversation stopped and like a pair of zombies we just lay there trying to ride it out.

The longer it went on the more I could feel that this was not only testing physically, it was testing on the mind. I found myself beginning to think we'd never see land again. Finally, though, some semblance of humour broke out.

'When we hit the beach I'm going to have a meal of earth,' I said aloud. 'I'm never going to buy a boat; I'm never going in a boat. In fact I doubt I'll ever go swimming again.'

At three a.m. I was awake and went up to the wheelhouse where as usual Warwick was on watch. It didn't feel so bad now. Perhaps I was just getting used to it, but the waves didn't feel as big and everything seemed a tiny bit quieter.

'How are you, fella?' I said.

'Good. The weather came good. Did you notice?'

'Yeah, it doesn't feel so smashy.'

'There are no guarantees for the morning, though.'

'No?'

He shook his head. 'We'll be crossing what they call the hundred metre bank, shallower water. It could get rough again but it won't last too long.' He pointed to the computer screen. 'That lumpy bit there is Bathurst Island.' He tapped a mass of land north of the Australian mainland. 'If we go in and hug the coast we'll be in calm water.'

'Let's do that then, shall we?'

'Why not. We'll cut the engine, put the sails up and do a few checks. See how much water we've taken on, see what needs repairing and check the engine. Can't do it in this weather, turn the engine off in this – it's too dangerous.' He nodded to the galley. 'We'll shut her down, have a good feed, then it's sixty miles to Darwin.'

'Only sixty?'

'About that: I reckon we should be in around four, maybe four-thirty on Thursday morning.'

'Fantastic.'

'The last stretch, mind, when we come out from the point, that'll be rough as hell.'

My heart sank. 'Worse than this?'

'Maybe not quite as bad.'

'Is this really bad, Warwick? I mean do you think it is or are we just a couple of Poms being a bit pants?'

He laughed. 'I tell you what, Charley, it's bad enough that we'll need to repair what's broken; fix a few leaks.' He paused and scratched his shaven scalp. 'How bad it is from Bathurst Island will depend on how we hit the current. If it's going in, we'll go faster but it will be rougher – we'll be pushed nose deep in the waves every inch of the way.'

I cannot tell you how good it was to switch off the engine and get the sails up. When dawn broke we could see Bathurst Island, our first glimpse of Australia – the final continent on this marathon journey. Mungo and I were on deck, the sun was out and we were in calm seas for the first time in days.

The whole atmosphere changed. In calm weather the boat oozed relaxation, the laughter returned, the conversation and the jokes. With the sails up we were still moving but there was no sound other than the breeze and the cry of gulls. The sea was flatter and in the distance tuna were jumping as if in mockery at our line.

I could feel the tension slip away, the tightness in my shoulders and the ache in the pit of my stomach. I felt as though we'd almost made it and I realised what we'd achieved.

'Can you believe this?' I said to Mungo. 'That's Australia over there. Think back to when we got on the bikes at my dad's house. I can't believe we've actually made it. In less than twenty-four hours we'll be in Darwin.'

27

Recovery of Friendships

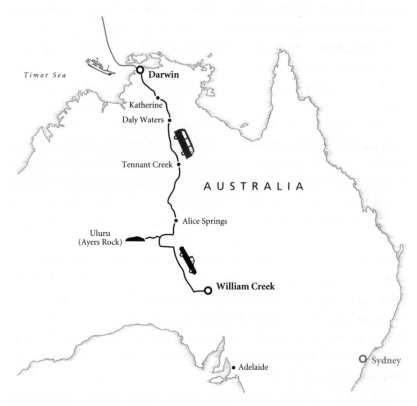

At quarter to seven on the morning of Thursday 10 July I stood on the deck of the *Oelin* as we motored into Darwin Harbour.

'Mungo!' I called out. 'Mate, we've done it. We're in Australia.' I punched the air and danced a jig on the deck. 'Yes,' I said. 'Yes! Yes!'

I could hardly believe it. After all that planning, the weeks and weeks of travelling, we'd finally made it all the way to Darwin. It was almost three months to the day since we had left London, but my God had it been worth it.

The harbour was sheltered by a stone wall, the sea as flat as it had been all the way from Bathurst Island. We had expected those last sixty miles to be really rough, but when we came around the point the ocean had been like a millpond. No longer confined to our berths, Mungo and I had sat on deck, chatting away as the sun went down.

I looked out to sea for one last time. It had taken six days to cross, three of which had been unbelievably difficult. On that last section before Bathurst Island the swell had risen to well over four and half metres and we'd been in troughs so deep there was nothing but a wall of water surrounding the boat.

'I'm so glad we did this,' I said. 'I'm so glad we didn't chicken out.'

'Congratulations, Charley,' Mungo said. He shook my hand and slapped me on the back. 'It's been a pleasure travelling with you.'

Russ and Anne were waiting for us on the wharf.

'How are you?' Russ called out.

'Not bad at all, thanks.'

'I won't ask what it was like.'

As soon as we reached the wharf I jumped down and sprawled flat on my stomach, hugging and kissing the concrete. I could have quite happily eaten it. Dry land at last. For a time back there I'd wondered if I'd ever see it again.

It was only after we'd cleared customs and I had a moment to myself that it really hit me: I'd actually made it. Sitting on the bed, looking out of the window, it was as if no time had passed. I was back in Dad's drive, throwing a leg over that cherry-red bobber, friends and neighbours waving us off, the rain, the lump in my throat and the wobble in my chin. Now here I was in Darwin having been through all those countries by any means possible. A wave of emotion washed over me and the tears welled up – I couldn't help it. After three long months on the road, it was a bittersweet moment. I thought of my family, all my friends, and all the support they gave me, and amid it all my heart went out to Françoise, my great friend in London. As we'd pulled into Venice on the *Orient Express* I'd found out she was terminally ill, and from what Olly had said on the phone, she didn't have much time.

The journey wasn't over yet, of course – we still had to get to Sydney. But the Timor–Darwin crossing had been the hardest leg. During the really bad thirty-six hours or so, there had been moments when I'd almost gone mad I was so miserable. Halfway across I would have given anything just to get off the boat and never set foot on one again. But looking back now, having weathered the storm, I wouldn't change places with anyone.

We spent the night in Darwin, and the following morning had to figure out a way to get the nine hundred miles south to Alice Springs. After considering various options we decided to rent a Wicked Bus – second-hand camper vans that you see all over the place. Each one is individually painted by a bunch of bikers, and people use them as an inexpensive way of getting around. It seemed like the perfect vehicle to take us into the outback. Someone had painted a sign on the dashboard – 'Don't fucking swerve for kangaroos or you will roll bad'.

I think being at sea for so long must have affected my sense of direction because driving out of Darwin I got lost. There didn't seem to be any road signs and we ended up at a dead end and then a shopping centre car park. Eventually Mungo wound the window down and asked someone.

Finally we found the right road and left Darwin. This was thirsty-looking country with dust in the air, the tarmac bordered by skinny trees and banks of yellow grass. Glancing at the map, I was struck once again with how vast Australia is – almost as big as the US.

Once I'd re-established my sensory GPS I realised how good it was to be on the road again. One way or another we'd been at sea pretty much since Borneo. I drove with one hand on the wheel, lost in my thoughts as the road became a limitless line of tarmac disappearing into the distance. Alice was a two-day drive away and we planned to get there tomorrow evening. We took our time – the van wasn't fast and the roads were pretty clear. We hit some dirt for a while and had to wait at an outback crossing as a humungous train rattled by. Back on the black stuff we got out of the van and with music blaring be-bopped away in the middle of the deserted road. Demob happy, the lot of us.

Ironically the fact that the team had been split for the few days it took to cross from Darwin turned out to be a good thing. Up until that point we'd been on the road for three solid months and it was the first real disagreement. Russ told me he'd opted to fly largely because he felt that given the tension, three of us in such close confines might end up with someone going overboard or something (at least metaphorically). The reality was that a little time apart had allowed things not only to cool down, but be placed in their proper perspective. Often once a situation has come to the fore friendships can be all the deeper for it. That was certainly the case with Ewan and me in Africa; and now the three of us were together again we were getting on like a house on fire. The bus journey was an absolute scream; we chased trains, played music, made up the craziest songs. We'd accomplished something special here and the spirit was fantastic.

That night we stopped in a town called Daly Waters, which was close to an aerodrome the Americans used as a staging post in World War Two. Pulling in, I saw a red traffic light and auto-matically stopped. We sat there and a couple of people came out and gave us a funny look. Then we noticed a sign that said the light was the most remote in Australia and we realised it was always on red. That about typified the place, a clutch of mad buildings half-hidden in trees with the heat of the sun beating down on the dusty road. We wandered into a crazy-looking pub crammed with all sorts of memorabilia, bank notes from across the world, road signs, even bras and knickers hanging from the ceiling. Across the road there was a ramshackle shop with a wrecked helicopter half buried in its roof, while next door there was a couple of petrol pumps with a sign that said: 'Fill your car up and come over to the pub to pay'.

The rumble of a V-twin grabbed my attention. As I turned I saw a guy roll up on a big old cruiser.

'Hello, mate,' I said. 'Nice bike.'

He peered at me. 'Charley – what are you doing here? Loved the series, mate; very inspirational. Is Ewan with you?'

'Not this time. I've come from Ireland, heading for Sydney.'

'Right, right. So what bike are you on?'

I explained about 'By Any Means', all the forms of transport I'd been on, and how I'd just crossed from Timor on a boat built from Kalimantan ironwood.

'All the way from your dad's place, eh? Sounds great,' he said, nodding. 'Name's Steve McGrath by the way.' Steve explained that he was doing a lap of the country with some old friends. They'd been talking about it for forty years, and now they were all retired they'd finally got around to it. They were staying the night in town and a little later we met up for a few beers and a chat. We settled down at the back of the pub in what they called the 'outback servo'. A local guy was playing guitar on a small stage, singing everything from Johnny Cash to 'Waltzing Matilda' with a stream of filthy jokes thrown in.

There were four of them on the trip – Steve and his childhood friends Jack, Terry and Chris. There was a fifth member of the gang but unfortunately he'd been diagnosed with leukaemia and was due to have a bone marrow transplant. They had been on the road a month already and were having a whale of a time. Tonight was no exception – we talked bikes and travel, we talked life, and if they overheard another conversation at another table they'd jump right in. It was a great evening.

That night the temperature plummeted and I was cold for the first time since I could remember. In the morning we hooked up with the boys again and rode pillion out to the old aerodrome, where they showed us a display of photos of the place and let me ride the length of the runway on a couple of their bikes. Chris told me that having gone their separate ways since school, the trip was 'a recovery of friendships', which I thought was a really nice way of putting it.

Leaving town I forgot to fill the tank and had to go back. Of course there was nobody at the pumps so I trotted over to the bar.

'Just fill her up then tell us how much it was,' the girl serving told me.

Wonderful – her perfectly laid-back response reflected our mood exactly, and I knew this was the ideal way to end the expedition.

We spent an easy day cruising down to Alice, the stark, rocky outback shimmering into the distance. We were just chilling – good music on the radio, Mungo mooning the oncoming traffic, the normal kind of thing boys get up to on a road trip. Late in the afternoon with the tank half empty I rolled past a petrol station thinking we'd have plenty to get us to the next one. But an hour or so later the gauge was on red and then the light came on. The next town was still seventy kilometres ahead and the last thing we needed was to run out. If you do that in a diesel you get air-locks in the injectors and it's a bastard to try and bleed them.

Spotting a picnic area with a couple of campers parked up, I pulled in and wound down my window. There were some people sitting at a table and I called out to them, asking if they had any spare diesel. They shook their heads. My heart sank. To have come all this way just to run out of fuel in the Australian outback; how typical is that? Just then another van pulled in driven by an elderly guy, his wife sitting alongside him with their dog. Walking over, I asked them if they had any diesel, explaining that we were about to run out.

'That'll be a bugger,' he said. 'I've got a jerrican in the back, you can have that.'

I couldn't have been more relieved – he'd really saved our bacon. I emptied the ten-litre jerrican into the tank while we introduced ourselves. His name was Kevin Mitchell.

'Thanks, Kevin,' I said as we paid him. 'Have a drink on us.'

He looked at the money and gave me a wry smile. 'I'll pick up a slab.'

Twenty-four cans of beer straight from the cold room; come Friday you see plenty of guys with a slab or two slung over each shoulder.

'Do that,' I said. 'And thanks again.'

We finally made it to Alice Springs and the next morning hooked up with Dave 'The Outback Man', his brother Ken and their mate Gary. Dave – a stocky guy with a thick, grey beard and Akubra hat – had been dubbed 'The Outback Man' by Australian TV and was pretty well known in the area. Along with Ken and Gary, he would be guiding us to the South Australia border in utes and had brought along some food and swag bags so we could have at least one night under the stars. They won't mind me saying that they were all knocking on a bit – Dave said they had four hundred and fifty years of outback experience between them. He was great company, full of jokes and quips, and between him and his brother they had us in stitches.

We were making for Uluru, known to many as Ayers Rock, but before we left town Dave took us to meet Noel Fullerton. Originally we had hoped to make Alice in time for the annual camel race, but because of the long haul from Timor to Darwin, we'd just missed it. Noel had been organising the race for almost forty years. At seventy-four with a white beard and long white hair, he made the Outback Man look like a city slicker. Wearing a pair of battered jeans and a leather waistcoat with a bandanna tied round his head, he explained that he had been working with camels almost all his life, taking people on safaris into the desert where some half a million camels roam wild.

'I always tell 'em,' he said, 'riding a camel, you've got a one in ten chance of breaking a leg. So bear that in mind.'

He told me that when he first came to Alice it had a population of just five thousand. This really was the heart of the old country – even in 1926 there had been just twenty-eight white men and eight white women. The first camel race was run in 1970 and started out as a bet between Noel and his mate Keith Mooney-Smith, who raced a pair of camels along the dried Todd River bed. Now the Camel Cup is an annual event and Noel still supplies a lot of the mounts. It takes place at the Lions Club track in the middle of a dusty park, which is where I met him.

Noel introduced me to 'Number 26' – a tall, grey, regal-looking camel who had raced the day before. He kneeled down so I could climb into the saddle. Noel suggested I walk him round the track a few times while he saddled another. And then he casually mentioned that he had entered me in a belated two-man race against one of the locals.

Russ, who was looking on from the fence, asked if I needed a crash helmet.

'Only if he comes off,' Noel told him.

Sitting there on a kneeling camel with a lap of the track ahead of me, I felt like a 500 GP racer from the seventies – back in the days when you had to bump-start your machine and jump on. The guy I was racing was experienced and he had that 'I'm going to kick your Pommie arse' look in his eye.

Noel cracked his whip like a starting pistol and we were off. I stood in the stirrups, with my opponent heading for the first bend. Meanwhile Number 26 wheeled sharply to the right and dived for a gap in the fence, his massive tongue hanging out the side of his mouth. I tried to haul him round, but he was having none of it. The gap was too small, but that wasn't going to stop him trying. We came clattering into the fence and I only just got my right leg out of the way before it was crushed. He still managed to crunch my left leg, though, bruising my shin and tearing a slice of leather from the toe of my brand-new R. M. Williams Outback boots.

Undeterred I went back to the start and the bugger tried to do the same thing again. But I was ready for him this time, and with a tighter rein I brought him round and took off after the guy who was going to kick my arse: which he did. We raced once more and still he beat me, but for a greenhorn Noel said I'd done all right. The others had gone ahead in the trucks and with Noel's permission I rode the camel out to meet them.

En route to Ayers Rock we stopped for something to eat at the Stuart's Well Roadhouse; where Dinky the Dingo plays piano. He's world-famous apparently, having played duets with all sorts of well-known people.

'Don't touch him and don't make eye contact,' his owner James Cotterill told me. 'He can be a bit of a boy and after all, he's not a dog.'

A little nervously I sat down on the piano stool in a cafe full of people. I played with two fingers while Dinky, who looked like a cross between a tawny Alsatian and a Eurasian wolf, climbed onto the keys and proceeded to howl.

After I was done Russ sat at the piano and Ken looked over with an 'Oh no, not again' sort of look on his face. 'Can he actually play?' he asked me.

'Yes,' I said, 'he can.'

They played a pretty good duet, Russ blasting out some rock 'n' roll while Dinky paced the keys and yowled as if he'd been shot.

Back in the truck we left town on a single-lane highway, a few sparse trees the only landmarks in an otherwise empty landscape. An hour or so later the rock just lifted from the desert – a magnificent great flat-topped hill that dominated the surrounding area.

'No, mate,' Dave said, before I could speak. 'That's Mount Conner. Everyone makes the same mistake; no worries.'

Shortly after, the road curved to the right and there was the rock, smoother and rounder than Mount Conner and a bright, vivid red. Made of coarse-grain sandstone, arkose, it sounds almost hollow when you tap it – the last remaining piece of a once vast mountain range that has gradually been eroded away. Dave told me that only about a fifth is above ground – the rest is under the sand. The aboriginal people call it Uluru and for countless years they've been coming here because it's a place of life when the rest of the desert is parched. The desert was parched now: the region we were heading into hadn't seen rain in four years and even when it does rain it's still just about the driest region in one of the driest places on earth.

There was nothing Dave didn't know about Uluru, the desert, the wildlife. The outback had been his backyard all his life and he loved it. Leaving the main road for dirt we were very quickly into deep red dust that hugged the wheels and kicked up great clouds behind us. Dave said we were on the largest cattle ranch in the world, and when there was water in the ground some twenty-thousand head wandered this area alone.

It was the perfect place to camp. Dave suggested a couple of trees in a dip about fifty yards off the road and I bumped across the scrub with no problem. Russ got stuck. He always gets stuck – I'm beginning to think he does it on purpose. He rolled a truck on Long Way Round, when we did the Dakar he got stuck in the sand and he got stuck again on Long Way Down. We were thinking about a fire and he was still calf-deep in red dust with the wheels spinning.

'You've got to lock the front hubs,' I yelled.

'What?'

'The front hubs, you've got to lock them.' Heading over, I made the adjustment and he was able to drive out.

Dave got a fire going with plenty of air underneath, while I dug a pit so that when it was burning properly we could move it. I watched the sun go down over the desert – a vast emptiness with straggly trees and boulders and acres of red dust. Before I rode a bike round the world I hated camping. Now I can't get enough of it and I counted myself very lucky to be spending the night sleeping under the Southern Cross in the Australian outback.

While I dug the hole Ken was standing over me, sipping from a water bottle half-filled with Johnnie Walker.

'Looks like a urine sample,' his brother told him.

'Whisky, mate. Don't worry, Charley, there's plenty of beer and a cheeky little red for you blokes.'

The next thing I knew he was blasting the Australian National Anthem from the cab of his truck.

They cooked a fantastic dinner of steak and fried potatoes and they really did have a few bottles of the cheeky red in the back of the truck. After dinner we shot the breeze, telling jokes and laughing. When it got late I picked up my swag bag and headed for the patch of ground in front of my truck that I'd painstakingly cleared and graded. Swag bags are all-in-one waterproof sleeping bags, with pillow, mattress and duvet built in. Crawling into mine, I was reminded that Australia is the most toxic country in the world, with something like seven of the world's ten most venomous snakes. Luckily, just as I settled in, Mungo broke wind as only Mungo can, and I knew then that the smell would keep them at bay.

On Monday morning I woke to sausages, bacon, tomatoes and fried eggs – these outback boys really know how to live. Fully fed we were on the dirt again and I was driving, the road pretty gnarly, hoping to catch a road train. Road trains are monstrous bull-nosed trucks that haul three massive trailers, creating a single vehicle with more than forty wheels. We were pretty sure we could find one that would take us as far as the South Australian border.

Suddenly, out in the middle of nowhere, we came across a John Deere 670D, a huge vehicle used to flatten the washboard corrugations cars cause on dirt roads. The back end was all engine, while the cab sat in the middle. The front was a long proboscis with a huge blade underneath. Standing beside one of the massive wheels was an old boy in a baseball cap and a pair of those really short shorts that Aussies like to wear. He had a bushy grey beard and a skinny little pipe clamped between his teeth.

'That's Popeye,' Dave said. 'Let's say hello.'

Popeye was pleased to see us; out on the road he didn't get many visitors.

I introduced myself, and asked him about his truck.

He grinned. 'It's a big toy to play with, that's for sure.' He said he had been grading the road with this particular company for ten years.

'And you're out here by yourself?'

'Yep. I see the odd person now and again. Cars go by, blokes like you. Every once in a while I have to nurse a cyclist back to health, someone who has no idea how big this country is and isn't carrying enough water. But yeah, I'm by myself. No other bloke wants to come out here.'

I took a moment to gaze at the nothingness all around us. 'But where do you live? How do you get home?'

'I've got my house and that with me,' he said. 'I'm a gypsy. I live on the side of the road.'

He told me he had a daughter in Alice Springs and went back now and again to get supplies, but he was sixty-three years old and there was no way he could get a job in town. No one wanted to be stuck out here on their own, but the road still had to be graded. He did a few weeks at a time then went back for a day or so, but it wasn't uncommon for him to be here for fourteen weeks or more. He carried 14,000 litres of diesel and now and then a tanker would come out to replenish his stock. He maintained the grader himself, fixing punctures and doing whatever else was needed. He even let me have a go at grading a piece of Australian dirt road myself.

He was a great guy to talk to and so chirpy; the pipe stuck in his mouth clearly a fixture. No wonder they called him Popeye. I asked him if Olive Oyl was at home, but he shook his head.

'Nope, not any more.'

Bidding goodbye to Popeye we headed for the road train in Coober Pedy; a tiny dot in a vast, rocky desert where they mine opal. Dave said there were at least a million shafts out in the field, some of them twenty metres deep. There was a sign suggesting that you didn't run, or walk backwards in that area.

'Photographers,' Dave explained. 'You'd be amazed how many people have been taking piccies and stepped backwards into a hole.' He shook his head. 'Twenty-metre hard rock-fall, that's not good. Best to stay on the road here; don't go out in the field.'

It was the road train, however, that dominated my thoughts: ever since we talked about crossing Australia I'd wanted to drive one. You don't find them anywhere else in the world; they have big rigs in the States but nothing like these. The ones we'd seen had those massive American bull-nosed tractor units, rather than the flat-fronted ones we're used to in Europe. There is something about the old Mack trucks, the Kenworths, that just reeks of raw power. Over here it was so much more accentuated, because when you're pulling three massive trailers, the word 'train' is the only way you could begin to describe them. When we'd overtaken one or been overtaken by one, they thundered across the ground as if they were alive. The clatter of the diesel, the coughing exhaust, the air horn . . . they were a real icon of the outback.

Dave had been in touch with his daughter Danielle, who knew a guy called Alan who drove a road train. Today Alan was carting sand, but he'd carried everything from pigs and sheep to cars and railway sleepers and he was happy to give us a lift. His rig had two trailers, and the tractor unit was an International S Line from the States. He told me that driving anything as big as this you had to keep your wits about you. It was incredibly long, and looking in the door mirror all I could see was trailer. It was four hundred and twenty horsepower, and with a twenty-speed splicer gearbox it was easy to forget what gear you were in.

Sitting behind the wheel with the window rolled down, driving a road train, an Australian icon ... now I really was in my element. I was only a few days away from my family and we were eating up the miles now, tarmac and desert slipping by as we rumbled down the road. You're up so high you feel invincible. I'd ridden motorbikes and lots of different cars, I'd raced a few bikes and cars at Goodwood but nothing compared to this. I imagined what it would be like to haul one right across Australia and it was easy to see how this kind of life could get deep into your blood. There was something about the vastness of this landscape, about the way the road just went on and on ... There was a real purpose to the journey, and it took the road and that landscape to a completely different level.

Alan dropped us off further south and we stopped for the night in William Creek, a stockman's town. The local blokes wore felt cowboy hats and body warmers with nothing underneath. We headed into a busy pub, with guys sitting at metal stools at the bar drinking from cans – the classic Aussie outback bar. I was introduced to a bush pilot, another mate of Dave's. I asked him what kind of planes he flew.

'None when I'm drinking,' he said with a laugh. 'Planes and beer don't mix, Charley.'

'And when you're not drinking?'

'Whichever one we haven't crashed at the time.'

28

Look Out for Motorcycles

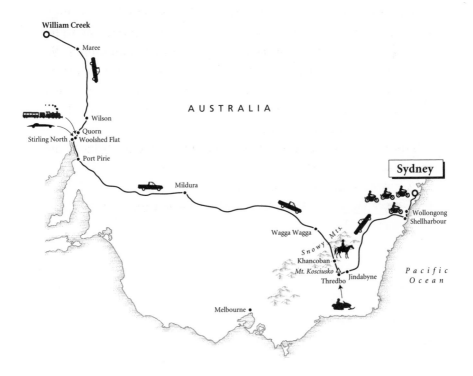

I woke up the next morning thinking about Valencia, where we'd scribbled our plans for the expedition on the back of a boarding pass. The last three and a half months had gone by in a heartbeat, and now we had just seven days to go before we reached Sydney. We headed back into William Creek where we bumped into

Neville, the pub landlord. He explained that the people we'd met last night weren't local stockmen as we'd first thought; they were just passing through. Because of the drought the cattle ranch, which was the only local employer, had as few as three hands working. If not for the pub, William Creek wouldn't exist at all. According to Neville it was the smallest, driest and most remote town in all Australia, with a population of about six.

Once south of town we found ourselves in a desert of sage brush and red sand – the most arid place I'd ever been. Dave showed us the way to Coward Springs. This tiny oasis, dotted with palm trees, is the only water in the area – camel trains used to stop here on the way to Alice. It has a naturally hot pool, which bubbles up from the ground, and is home to a colony of birds. The waterhole has been reinforced with railway sleepers and a fence, and as we walked over we met a family coming out.

'Have you been in the water?' I asked the little boy. 'Was it warm?'

He nodded.

'Was it worth it?'

'Ah yeah, maybe.'

Pushing open the gate I stripped to my shorts and stepped into the warmish water, natural jets bubbling up beneath me.

'This water's very wet,' Dave stated. 'It takes much longer to dry.' Then he jumped in, fully clothed, hat and all. 'That'll get the washing done.'

Further down the road we stopped at the ruins of an old house – just a couple of walls and a fireplace, really. Collecting some wood and brush we got a fire going and cooked hotdogs for lunch. From there we drove into absolute nothingness. We were on the lip of a salt lake that stretched as far as the eye could see. At fourteen metres below sea level this was the lowest point on the entire continent and the mud beneath was tidal.

Further south we came across the Dingo Fence – a wire mesh construction that cuts across the horizon. Like a fox in a henhouse, dingoes are indiscriminate killers, and if they get among the sheep they can cause carnage. The fence starts on the east coast at Surfer's Paradise and runs inland for five thousand kilometres. It's not that high but dingoes don't jump, and the bars on the cattle grid truck crossings are wide enough to discourage them.

Making it to Marree before the sun went down, we set up camp just out of town and I dragged over a fallen tree for firewood. Dave bent a length of corrugated iron into a three-sided windshield, and taking the axe I threw a couple of swings but the blade just kept bouncing off the branches. Ken brought out a chainsaw which ought to have made life easier but the bloody thing wouldn't start and it was dark before we managed to get the fire going.

The town of Marree is at the junction of the Oodnadatta Track (the aboriginal trading route across the Tirari Desert) and the infamous Birdsville Track that runs all the way to Queensland. It's here that the standard-gauge railway line from Adelaide joins the narrow-gauge line that goes on to Alice Springs. When Dave first left school he worked on this stretch of railway, and he told us that the trains would leave Adelaide on Tuesday morning and get here about midnight. Then everyone and everything would be transferred across the platform to another train on the narrower line for the remainder of the journey.

After dinner we had a few beers and some wine. Ken decided we didn't have enough alcohol so he went into town to pick up some more. When he came back he told us there was a hooley going on at the pub. We could hear the raucous singing from across the road – a bunch of Caterpillar drivers were celebrating the end of a refresher course and the grog was flowing, the sing-song gathering pace. What could we do? We joined in. Ollie, who had joined us in Darwin, Mungo and I bailed out a little earlier than the others but we were still completely out of it. For some reason, right in the middle of the street, I decided to take Mungo's legs from under him and he went down like a tree. Demob happy, I suppose. Ollie piled into me and for the next ten minutes we wrestled in the dust like schoolboys, almost breaking our Nikon camera.

At first light with pounding heads and dodgy stomachs we regretted it bitterly. Ollie was convinced he'd broken his little finger so I had to strap it to his ring finger. I knew then it would be a delicate day.

Driving very gently, we headed towards a town called Quorn, stopping for a cup of tea at Gordon Litchfield's sheep station. Gordon was a mate of Dave's, a thoughtful soul with a cowboy hat and bushy moustache, who had a team of shearers working on his flock. Never mind four years of drought – in this part of the country it had barely rained in ten.

'It must be a hard life,' I observed.

'Hard, yeah right.' He rolled his eyes at Dave. 'Try whatever they call two steps down from hard, mate, and you might be getting close.'

Further south we came across a clutch of old buildings and a broken-down Land Rover half buried in sand. This was home to Talc Alf, a stone carver and philosopher who had interesting ideas on the alphabet and particularly Barack Obama. From the letters in Obama's surname Alf had worked out that he might just be the saviour of Western civilisation. I suppose if Obama gets elected we'll find out if he's right. Alf had converted an old washing machine with belts and pulleys so he could power it by riding a stationary bicycle. Jumping on, I pedalled for a while, giving the old man's clothes a bit of a stir. If nothing else, the bike would set me up nicely for the solar-powered car.

We'd heard about the car back in England and had contacted the people involved to see if it was possible for me to drive it. We were due to meet up with them the next morning, but by chance we were staying at the same campsite, so we got our first glimpse of 'Kelly' that same night. Shaped like a bullet, it arrived in a black-and-yellow trailer, towed by a coach with a V8 engine that ran on LPG. The team – known as the RAA Kelly Gang – were electronics specialists from the University of South Australia. The 'Kelly' car was the Mk II version – an improvement on the original, which had, naturally, been called 'Ned'. Kelly had taken part in the three-thousand-kilometre race from Darwin to Adelaide, specifically designed for these kinds of concept vehicles. The Kelly Gang used the tow-coach as a mobile classroom, travelling around the schools in South Australia trying to get students interested in learning about electronic engineering.

Looking like a cross between a road-going stealth bomber and a cockroach, Kelly was inched out of the trailer on hydraulics. Almost black, she sat very low and streamlined, with four wheels on struts like the undercarriage of the aforementioned bomber. The bodywork was made from hundreds of individual panels that reminded me of scales on a reptile. I know, I'm mixing metaphors, but this was one weird-looking motor car, believe me. The team were going to give Kelly a run out and had promised to let me drive a few miles. First, though, we were leaving town on a steam train and would hook up with them further down the road.

The next morning Dave's nephew Duane showed up in a 1954 Holden to take us to the station. The Holden is the archetypal Australian motor car. Duane had restored the car himself – an FJ six-cylinder with a column gear change. He told me that most people in Oz had a story to tell about this little beauty, and it often involved the back seat. Ours had seen back-seat action of the handcuff variety and I don't mean the pink and fluffy kind. Formerly a police car, it had a rail where the cops cuffed crooks before taking them down to the station. I had a little trouble with the gears – so much so that Duane had to lift the bonnet and do something to the gearbox. After that I drove across town with no further trouble to some old siding sheds.

We were travelling on a steam locomotive on part of the old Ghan Railway that ran from Port Augusta to Alice Springs. Originally it only went as far as Marree and from there the passengers transferred to a camel train. The camels came from Afghanistan and the train was originally called the 'Afghan Express' – later shortened to The Ghan. This was only a small section and, a bit like the Watercress Line in England, it is a self-funding operation where the drivers and firemen give their time voluntarily.

For a laugh I lay down on the tracks, my impression of a Buster Keaton movie. It was just a bit of fun but seeing my antics the driver slammed on the brakes and the locomotive came to a sudden, screeching stop, belching smoke as if they'd missed me by just a few inches.

'Please don't do that again.' He was pretty terse. 'Mate, you have no idea how long it takes to stop one of these.'

It wasn't the best of starts.

Russ was in seventh heaven. He'd wanted to find a steam train ever since we decided on the route. The engine had been built in England back in 1951; a W-class 4-8-2: the numbers denoting the number of wheels, four, eight and two. I'd driven the sister engine to the *Mallard* which had been built much earlier and this was a different layout. But on the footplate, shunting backwards towards the platform it was just the same: the feel of the thing, the heat, the hiss, the incredible clanking noise. I remembered Bob (the driver at the Watercress Line) telling us that there was nothing as dead as a cold steam engine and nothing more alive than one with a fire in the box. He was right; even if you're not particularly into them, steam trains have a way of attaching themselves to your soul. It was very atmospheric – the smell of sulphur, the rushing sound from the boiler like a massive pair of bellows.

As with all steam locomotives, the water level in the boiler was critical. Fired by burning coal, the boiler fuels the steam chest that in turn fuels the pistons. It is fed by injectors and regulated by a pair of safety gauges – too much water creates its own problems but if there is too little the engine becomes a time bomb. The most important job for the fireman is to keep a check on the water levels and that was my responsibility. As we rolled through the Australian countryside I kept one eye on the gauges, especially going up and down hill. Every now and then I would open the injectors to suck water from the tender into the steam chest and when the levels were back to what they should be I'd shut them off again. The pressure was measured by two gauges: one for the steam we had available and one for the steam we'd actually use. The massive pistons that kept the wheels rolling operated on a bed of steam and the more pressure they were under the faster they pumped.

It was a great way of chewing up some miles but it was a complete contrast to the solar car, which we joined a little further up the road. Kelly really did look like a cockroach, especially from the back. In order to drive you had to lie in the cockpit, and when the roof was on you were completely enclosed, which was quite claustrophobic. There were dials and gauges telling you the wattage available, and a screen to use for reversing because you couldn't look behind.

It wasn't difficult to drive, though it did have a tendency to drift into the middle of the road. You started the engine by pressing a green button and the throttle was a dial fixed in the middle of the go-kart-style steering wheel. It was actually capable of 120 kph, which wasn't half bad, and had a power output of 1.1 kilowatts. At full chat it sounded a bit like a motorbike.

I was a bit nervous to be driving it – this was the team's pride and joy, after all, and a really important invention. Their inventions had implications for all kinds of solar power, and there I was beetling along the open road in the middle of South Australia. But once I was over the nerves I really enjoyed it, and began to wonder if – with the price of oil being so high – the solar car might not be the way forward, at least in some countries.

The days were skipping by now and the next morning, 18 July, we were back in the Nissan pickups we'd rented in Alice. These were as much a part of Australia today as the Holden had been in the 1950s – the 4x4 ute being the vehicle of choice for a hell of a lot of Australians. Ours had carried us from the Northern Territories, across the deserts of central Australia and into colder and muddier country down south.

It was five hundred kilometres to Khancoban, where we would pick up some horses to carry us into the Snowy Mountains. I was looking forward to that – we'd yet to ride horses on this trip and, of course, more people have used horses to get around than any other mode of transport in history.

Along the way we stopped on the outskirts of a blink-and-miss-it town – I think it was called Griffith. There were no signs, just a couple of houses, a petrol station and what looked like some kind of ironworks.

Wandering over, Russ realised it wasn't an ironworks but a

steel artworks gallery. The closer we looked the more we could see and some of the work was amazing. Famous faces, movie stars and rock singers, political heroes – all shaped from steel plate. There were full-size sculptures too that looked 3D but were actually flat, and Russ spotted an amazing piece.

'Charley, you've got to look at this,' he said. 'It's incredible.'

It was a motorbike racer from bygone days. Cut from a piece of steel, maybe six feet by four, it was standing upright, rusting in the breeze.

'We have to see if we can find the bloke that runs this place,' Russ said. 'See if that bike racer is for sale.'

The sign above the gate indicated the owner was called Ron Clarke, but there didn't seem to be anyone around. Russ tried calling a number he found on the fence while I took a wander round the back. The place was all locked up but as I was standing there a little old guy in a battered Akubra hat came shuffling across the yard. I asked if he was Ron and he said that he was. Then I asked if the motorbike racer was for sale.

'That old piece? Fuck, I made that back in the fuckin' day.' Ron swore a lot. About every other word. We went round the front where I introduced him to Russ and Mungo and he squinted at each of us in turn.

'Must be fifteen fuckin' years, now I think about it. This fella wandered in one day and asked me to make something to honour his brother. He'd been a motorbike racer, one of the best in Australia the fella reckoned, eight times Aussie champion or something. Anyway he got himself killed somewhere round here in a semi.'

'His brother asked you to make it?' I said.

'Yeah, showed up here asking what the fuck I charged and I told him about thirty-five dollars a yard. Is that all? he said. Fuck, I could have something for under two fuckin' grand then. Course you fuckin' could, I told him. But I can't make it for you, mate, because I've got the mafia swarming all over me and they'd want a fuckin' piece.' He looked puzzled suddenly, as if something was bothering him. 'Don't I know you?' he said to me. 'I've seen you some fuckin' place before. You look like that joker on the TV – *Top Gear* or something.'

'*Long Way Round*,' I suggested. 'I made a show called *Long Way Round* which was shown here.'

'*Long Way Round*, that's it. But you didn't come round this way, did you – not to this fuckin' penal colony?'

'Is it still like that?' Russ asked him.

'Fuck, yeah. The way the coppers treat you. This is the crime capital of Australia.' He pointed to the empty road. 'I had some joker in just the other day wanting to take the fuckin' place over. I told him. You're trying to press-gang me into your fuckin' workshop. You can't do that – take over a little fuckin' Pommie. It's just not on, you fuckin' idiot. We invented it.'

'You're from England?'

'Of course, I'm a cockney. Came over here when my dad lost his job. We were heading for the opal mines but ran out of fuckin' money.'

'You don't sound like a cockney,' Russ said.

Ron looked sideways at him. 'That's because I've been here for fuckin' *ever*.'

'Do you want to sell the motorbike racer?'

He thought about that.

'Why is it still here?' I asked him.

'Because the fella never found anywhere for it. No bastard would let him put it up.'

Russ told him we could display it in our warehouse, but we didn't have enough Australian dollars in cash. We did have US dollars though, and offered five hundred.

'US?' he snorted. 'What the fuck do I want with US? They're not worth fuck all.'

'They're worth about the same as an Aussie dollar,' Russ said quietly.

I wasn't sure about this. The piece, brilliant though it was, had been specially commissioned by the man's brother and there was something about us buying it that didn't seem right. Having said that, it had been here fifteen years already and it was pretty rusty. If we didn't buy it then who would?

We kicked the idea around for a while, taking a look at Ron's workshop. He was an incredible artist, drawing the pattern on steel plate and then cutting it with the acetylene torches. As well as the portraits, he'd created a life-size coach with a team of four horses and a massive Caterpillar truck like the ones those guys had been driving in Marree. Nothing was too big or too complicated. He told us he'd been in newspapers all over the world and had a full page in *Live to Ride* but he was paranoid – absolutely convinced everyone was out to get him. Even with Mungo filming and talking about the TV and *Long Way Round*, he still didn't seem to get who we were. Every now and then he'd peek out from under the brim of his sweat-streaked hat and ask if we were Catholics or Mormons. The Catholics were gathering in Sydney, apparently, and the Mormons had been trying to take him over for years.

Finally, disappearing into his workshop, he came out with a framed photograph of a guy called Johnny Shields riding a BSA 350. This was the guy he'd used as a template – in 1956 he'd been both senior and junior Australian road racing champion. Ron said there was no way the brother would be coming back for him, not after all this time, so we upped our offer to $1000 and loaded Johnny into the back of the Nissan.

That night I spoke to Olly, who told me that Doone had had an accident. She'd been sailing, and moving from the dinghy to the motor boat she got her hand trapped. The doctors thought that she'd either damaged the scaphoid (which is what I'd done on the Dakar) or torn a tendon, but they wouldn't be able to tell for sure without doing a CAT scan. The earliest they could do that was on Monday but by then Doone would be in Australia, so they put a split cast on her hand and suggested we get it looked at over here. Apart from that mishap everything at home was fine. Olly was yet to do any packing but she told me the girls were beside themselves with excitement.

All I had to do now was get to Wollongong. On Saturday 19 July I woke up feeling pretty chirpy. We were heading for the Snowy – one of the major rivers in Australia. It's fed by snow melt from the Snowy Mountains in New South Wales and the main trunk runs from Mt Kosciuszko, the highest mountain in the country. Three rivers converge here: the Thredbo (which used to be called the Crackenback), the Snowy and the Eucumbene. The confluence is at a place called Jindabyne and from there they travel as one, three hundred and fifty kilometres to the sea in Victoria.

This is the place where Banjo Paterson wrote his famous poem, 'The Man from Snowy River'. His real name was Andrew-Barton Paterson, but he had a favourite horse called Banjo, and he took its name as a pseudonym. The poem is about a group of stockmen who try to recapture the colt of a famous race horse that escaped its paddock and is living wild with a herd of Australian brumbies.

I'd ridden quite a bit as a kid back in Ireland: my dad's house had stables and we kept a few horses. I rode in *Excalibur*, of course, but my passion had dimmed when I heard Tommy Rochford tearing through the woods on his Enduro. Before long I worked out that you didn't need to groom or muck out a motorbike, so horses were suddenly relegated to second place in my affections.

We'd arranged to meet a sixty-year-old trail guide named Peter Cochran and a stockman called Barry Paton, a tall, rangy guy who'd been mustering in this area for almost as long as he'd been walking. With his thick moustache and his hat worn low, he looked every inch the Australian cowboy. He was the genuine article, complete with a stock whip which he let me have a go at cracking. It's nowhere near as easy as you'd think and every time I flicked it out it recoiled to sting me. Barry had been using one forever, of course, and after a couple of demonstrations from him I got the hang of it.

Being a stockman isn't a job, it's a way of life and some of the stations the guys work on are enormous. Like cowboys in the US, stockmen use working dogs – kelpies – to help with the cattle. They have rodeos and outback polo matches and their gear, particularly the saddle, is very specific. Originally they used 'park' saddles, which were pretty much the same as English ones, but over the years various types of 'stockman' saddles evolved. Some have pommel horns like Western saddles, but they're distinctive mostly because of high knee rolls and a cantle that shapes to the small of your back.

So far we'd been travelling south-south-east from Darwin, but from Khancoban it was east all the way. I was so glad we would be riding a few miles on horseback. This was beautiful country and perfect for riding; serene-looking valleys where cattle grazed and kangaroos fed their young, the hillsides mottled with trees.

We met up with Peter Cochran, a sixty-year-old trail guide, and a stockman called Barry Paton, a tall, rangy guy who'd been mustering in this area for almost as long as he'd been walking. Peter led a palomino Arab down from the truck.

'This one's called Hellfire,' he said, 'and there's good news. He's not bucked anyone off for a week.'

'That's because he's not been ridden for a week,' I called back.

Actually his name was Basil and he was a very nice horse. As I swung up into the saddle, I was conscious that I'd not done much riding lately. I'd practised a bit in London before we left, but prior to that I hadn't been on a horse since Ewan and I rode in Kazakhstan during Long Way Round. The saddle Peter had given me was more comfortable than the one I'd had then, thankfully – a really well-sprung rig called a 'half breed' that had been designed specifically for hill country. I walked Basil up and down the trail, backing him up and trotting him in a circle so we could get used to each other before we set out. A horse wants you to be in charge, and it's really important that they have confidence in you. They can feel whether or not you can ride properly, and years ago I learned that the first thing you do with a new horse is let him know that you know what you're doing.

At this time of year the horses weren't shod – the ground was soft so there was really no need. Peter explained that you can tell a brumby from a domestic horse at a distance because of the way it walks. The nerve endings in a horse's hoof are all in the middle pad and over the years unshod wild horses have developed a way of walking where their foot is slightly crimped.

With Barry as trail boss, we followed a grassy track into the woods, heading for a place called Keeble's Hut, which had been built in 1942 as a fishing lodge. It was a bright, chilly morning – the first really cold day we'd experienced in a couple of months and a reminder that it was winter in Australia. The weather had started warming up when we got to Turkey and it had been hot ever since until we reached the Australian winter.

Riding side by side, Barry and I chatted away like old friends. I realised that cowboys and dirt-bike riders share similar injuries. We tend to ride in the same kind of country and take the same kind of falls, and the two of us spent much of the morning swapping pain stories.

He told me that with the ongoing drought, the amount of guys like him still working had fallen rapidly. Also, the larger stations, such as the one we'd crossed further north, tended to use small planes and choppers to muster the stock. Back in the days of Banjo Paterson (who also wrote 'Waltzing Matilda'), this whole area was thick with sheep and cattle – real stockmen country. The interior of the country had been opened up in 1813, when a group of men on horseback first crossed the Blue Mountains from Sydney. In World War Two, stockmen from New South Wales took their horses to Palestine to fight with 'The Australian Light Horse'. Unfortunately the British wouldn't ship the horses back again, and they ended up in the UK, nicknamed 'Walers'.

I was learning so much more about Australia than I'd imagined I would. As you get closer to the end of these expeditions things tend to get a little rushed, but we were covering three thousand miles on this continent – one sixth of the entire journey. Originally, reaching Darwin safely had been my main goal. But since then we'd crossed right through the outback, and now here we were in the heart of the mountains.

Around mid morning we stopped for a breather at a small hut in a clearing where the horses could eat. We were close to a place called Scammell's Lookout, the place where a soldier named Clews began surveying the area after World War Two. Since then, fourteen dams and seven hydro-electric power stations have been constructed. The hut was known as Geehi, and it was used by bush walkers and stockmen. Barry said there were a few here and there along the trail. After stretching our legs for a while we were back in the saddle. We crossed and recrossed the river, fording shallow streams and using small bridges designed for hoofs not wheels. It was wonderful to be trotting along in the open air, travelling on horseback just as the settlers had done in the days of Banjo Paterson.

We met Peter again at lunch time; he'd brought the horse truck to Keeble's Hut and had prepared a meal for us. After lunch we rode alongside the highway for a mile or so before beginning our climb into the mountains. I was loving every minute. Earlier I'd taken Basil for a bit of a gallop and it was just like being on my dad's film set again, racing a horse I didn't know through deep woods – only this time I wasn't wearing armour.

It was a shame to leave them, but later that afternoon we had to say goodbye and carry on in the Nissans. Unsaddling the horses, we thanked Barry and Peter and jumped back in the utes, driving into snow with black rocks bulging on either side. Visibility was way down – the sun had gone and the sky was closing in.

We spent the night in an eco lodge called Bimblegumbie, close to the Thredbo Ski Resort, a Bohemian kind of place with a roaring fire and great views across the valley. Tomorrow would be 20 July, our one hundredth day on the road. In less than two days I would see my family again.

The plan had been to cross the mountains on skidoos. That night we met Huw, a local guide, who told us we could try but it wasn't likely we'd make it. He was staying in the lodge, so we sat down together with a map and he pointed out the problems. High winds had been forecast, which would make the one possible route impassable. We'd been hoping to rent a couple of skidoos but Huw told us that given the area was a national park, there were only certain places you could ride one and you had to be licensed. We might have made it as pillions with the ski-patrol perhaps, but he doubted we'd have been able to go under our own steam.

As it turned out, we were not able to go at all. When we woke on Sunday morning we quickly realised there was no chance: a gale was blowing at a hundred and thirty kilometres an hour and the road on the other side of Perisher Valley was closed. It was a shame; we'd come this far and skidoos were the last different form of transport we'd planned for the expedition. It was a reminder of how vast Australia truly is. The temperatures in

Darwin had been up in the thirties, but down here the road was blocked by snow.

I couldn't help reflecting that the journey was nearly over – the chequered flag in sight. There was no point in wasting the chance to see some snow however, so we decided to take the skitube through the tunnel into the National Park. It is three kilometres from Bullock's Flat right through the Ramshead Range to Perisher. Skidoos can only be ridden in certain areas; you have to have a licence and primarily they're used by the ski patrol. The tunnel had been built as a kind of dry run for Sydney harbour, and they used it to test the design and equipment before starting on one that went under water.

At the other end were the ski-runs where it was blowing so hard the lying snow was creating a bit of a blizzard. This was a high plateau with the runs dipping between the summits and low cloud blanketing any kind of view. Hugh introduced us to a couple of guys from the ski patrol and they took us part of the way along Charlotte's Pass.

It was bloody freezing, two up on a Polaris two-stroke. We took a road marked by poles in the snow, riding between thick fir trees and black rocks. The snow was banked up around us, some of it deep and flat and slippery as sheet ice. We went as far as we could before the blocked road thwarted us. Turning back again we stopped at what must be the most bizarre and remote petrol station in the world: just a couple of pumps – one diesel and one unleaded – in the heart of the mountains, with snow and rocks all around. They were used by the ski patrol when they needed to access areas too remote to be reached on one tank of fuel alone.

There are more than a hundred and seventy guys patrolling this area and most of them are volunteers. They buy their own uniform, their own food and organise their own accommodation. They're effectively paying to be up there and they make sure that if anyone gets injured, they're carried off the mountain as quickly as possible. The training is incredibly rigorous and they have to know the landscape like the back of their hand. Every slope is named, every gulch and valley, every orientation point; though none of the names appear on any map. Every member of the ski patrol has to be able to get to any point in Perisher Valley in the quickest possible time.

On Sunday night I could hardly sleep, and on Monday morning I was awake at five-thirty, like a child at Christmas. Our last day on the road. We were heading for Wollongong by ute, or rather a place just down the road called Shellharbour, where Lucy had organised some chalets for us all to stay and celebrate. As well as Olly, Doone and Kinvara we would be joined by Sarah, Russ's girlfriend, as well as his daughter Emily and his parents Jill and Tony. We'd have a party tonight, that's for sure.

The journey was almost over. The night before, over dinner, Russ and I had spent an hour or so recalling some of the people we'd met. Like Natalia, the Croatian girl who had to hide in her basement for three months, Cenk, who'd been such a laugh in Turkey, and Fahti, the poor kid who couldn't wait to get out of the *dolmus*. We talked about Mahmood, who'd guided us through Iran, Fariba the taxi driver, the guys on the container ship, the potters in the slums of Mumbai. We'd never forget the old priest at Varanasi or the family on the barge in China.

To cap it all we'd finished up in Australia, where I reckon we'd met as many archetypal Aussies as was possible. It's a beautiful country – a huge continent filled with incredible mountains and deserts, snow-capped mountains, rivers and beaches, not to mention the fifty-thousand-year-old aboriginal culture. There is pretty much everything you could wish to see on this continent, but as with any Western civilisation, it has its share of bureaucracy. The customs guys at Darwin had given us the usual hard time with our paperwork, and now – on the very last day – we had a run-in with the New South Wales Police.

On the way across country a cop passed my truck in a Holden. For some reason he flashed his lights. The next thing I knew he'd made a U-turn and pulled Russ over.

'He's not happy with Johnny,' Russ told me when I went back. 'That and the fact I was doing a hundred and thirty in a one hundred kilometre zone. And apparently my wheels were across the white line.'

'He flashed me as he went by just now.'

'Why didn't you tell me? I'm looking at a two hundred and forty-three dollar fine and three points that'll go on my licence in England. Jesus, you come eighteen thousand miles only to get pulled by the Old Bill in Australia.'

It was a minor setback but the cop, in his baseball hat and shades, was definitely not happy about the fact we were driving with the tailgate down on Russ's truck. It had been that way since we'd loaded the sculpture, and it was true it did block the view of the number plate. The copper said it was illegal but we'd passed loads of police cars since Griffith and none of them had pulled us over till now.

Russ fixed the tailgate with bungees so the number plate was visible and with Johnny suitably sorted, we took off again.

It was cold and wet and we'd come down from the green of the mountains into flatter, scrubbier country. One by one the miles slipped by and, a couple of hours later, we were in Shellharbour.

Now I was really excited, my heart hammering in my chest. Searching for the chalets close to the beach, I was physically twitching with the anticipation. I made a turn and another turn and then another, but could I find the place? No chance. I was getting quite frustrated when I nosed the truck round a final corner and saw Doone and Kinvara jumping up and down on the pavement.

My heart almost leapt out of my chest. There was my wife looking so beautiful with her long blonde hair and her wonderful smile. I couldn't believe just how much I'd missed her. I hit the horn, Russ hit the horn and we pulled up and piled out with Doone and Kinvara screeching with excitement. They were in my arms finally: the Boorman pod together again, the self-contained unit that we are. It hit me then perhaps for the first time, or maybe I just allowed myself to really admit it for the first time, but these last few months had been the hardest parting yet. We were together now, though, and all I wanted to do was hold them.

Russ was cuddling Emily, hugging his mum and dad and kissing Sarah, all at the same time. I was still clinging to Olly and the kids and for a few moments the emotions were almost too much. It was at this point that our friend David Kent, who had flown out to help with arrangements on the last leg, pointed out that we'd left the two Nissans in the middle of the road with the engines running.

Lucy stepped forward, and we both gave her a hug. 'You have to pass that on,' Russ told her.

'To everyone back in London,' I added. 'Without you guys we'd never have left Ireland.'

A couple of hours later I wandered outside into gardens that sloped to the beach. Next door had a massive Newfoundland dog with them. He bounded up, the whole of his back end wagging along with his tail.

'Hello, mate,' I said. I stroked his head and he licked my hand as if I were a long-lost friend who had just come back to him. 'You know what,' I told him, 'on the twelfth of April I left my dad's house in a place called Annamoe and since then I've been on my way here. Me, Russ and Mungo: we crossed the world on boats and buses and motorbikes, we've ridden on trains and elephants and horses. I drove a tuk-tuk and a speedboat.' The dog was listening intently. 'We almost sank off Nikoi Island. We saw dragons on Rinca and dived off Komodo. We survived a ferry that had far too many people on board then crossed the sea on a boat made from Kalimantan ironwood.'

'Finally found someone who'll listen to you, have you, Charley?'

Russ's voice came from behind me. I looked up with a smile. 'I was just telling him how we got here,' I said. 'In a dinghy and a Citroën, a couple of bicycles across Paris and the *Orient Express*.'

'Not to mention a Yugo and a Ural, a concrete truck . . .'

'And a pair of Royal Enfields,' I added. 'Dirt bikes through a monsoon in the jungles of Cambodia.'

'And tomorrow we'll cross the Sydney Harbour Bridge on a couple of BMWs.' Russ looked out to sea. 'It just shows what can be accomplished when two mates scribble an idea on an old boarding pass. Kind of romantic, isn't it?' For a moment he was a little thoughtful. 'I've learned such a lot on this trip. The people, the cultures, the land. We've crossed half the world with no back-up and no one's given us a hard time, no one's threatened us. I don't remember being really bothered once. I think I've realised that no matter where you go, people care about the same thing. All they really want is a little respect, some compassion maybe if it's needed, some understanding.'

'Russ,' I said. 'Mate, you're getting all philosophical on me.'

He grinned. 'Am I? Yes, I suppose I am.'

'It's all right, I understand. I feel the same way. One of the things I always find is that no matter what anyone tells you about a place, you need to find out for yourself: your preconceptions never turn out to be right.'

He went back inside. I could hear my daughters talking about tomorrow, heatedly discussing who would ride pillion with whom. Russ was right. Nothing is how you imagine it's going to be, but as long as you've got the right attitude, you'll be OK. I remembered again what Lewis Gordon Pugh had said about people travelling by their faces. It was true; if you had a smile for someone, more often than not they had one for you. If you were respectful, so were they. We'd got by just by being who we were.

Inside, I grabbed Olly and the kids and the four of us took a wander along the beach, Doone with a split cast on her arm and Kinvara showing me where the doctors had operated on her lip. It was wonderful to have Olly beside me, talking to her about what I'd done and what we were about to do. I was taking my family back to some of the places I'd been. I wanted to show them some of the sights so they could experience a little of my journey themselves. I'd done something similar after Long Way Down and by the time we got back to London everything would be back as it should be. If I'm honest it was as it should be already. After being on the road and on my own for so long, I felt whole again.

A little later that afternoon we went down to the local BMW dealer to pick up the bikes we would ride into Sydney. We were hoping to hook up with a bunch of local bikers, just as we'd done in England, and create a little convoy for the final leg. Russ's dad Tony would be riding along with David Kent, who promised me he'd ride shotgun for Olly. She had only recently passed her test and would have either Doone or Kinvara on the back, so David said he'd make sure she was given plenty of room. Russ would alternate between taking Sarah and Emily on the back of his bike. En masse we would roll into Sydney.

And that's exactly what we did. About three hundred bikers joined us along the coast from Wollongong – skirting Sydney so we could come in from the north. I rode up front, first with Kinvara and then Doone on the back. We followed the road to a fantastic sweeping bridge, where the cliff climbed on our left and massive rollers crashed on rocks below. I looked across and there we all were – me and Olly, Doone and Kinvara, all together, all on motorbikes. With Kinvara hanging on tight I popped the front wheel and suddenly it was April again – I was back at my dad's place in Annamoe for a visit. My old childhood friend Tommy Rochford had got that old Yamaha of mine running and while he and I chatted, Doone and Kinvara took turns riding the bike on the lawn I'd churned up as a kid.

As we came into Sydney we rode under a massive sign that said: 'LOOK OUT FOR MOTORCYCLES'. It felt like an iconic moment, and suddenly I was very emotional. We'd started on bikes and we'd finished on bikes and as we entered the tunnel to pass beneath the harbour, heading for the Shangri-La Hotel, the thunder of motorcycles echoed off the walls like the beat of a thousand drums.

Moments later we were back in bright sunshine, the ironwork of the bridge above our heads. Glancing across at Russ, I punched the air. 'Yeah, baby. We made the bridge!'

Doone and I fell in alongside Olly and Kinvara and we rode two abreast now, with the glistening blue harbour below us. Down there on the headland, like a ship's sails billowing in the breeze, was the most recognisable opera house in the world.

'Fantastic,' I murmured. 'Absolutely marvellous.'

Appendix

Country	Day Number	Day	Date	From
Ireland	1	Saturday	12 April	Wicklow
UK	2	Sunday	13 April	Kilkeel
	3	Monday	14 April	Douglas
				Liverpool dock
				Liverpool
	4	Tuesday	15 April	Coventry
				Ace Cafe, London
				Shoreham-by-Sea
				Brighton
	5	Wednesday	16 April	Dover
France	6	Thursday	17 April	Calais
				Paris
				Paris
Italy	7	Friday	18 April	On train
				Venice station
				Venice
Croatia	8	Saturday	19 April	Venice
				Porec
	9	Sunday	20 April	Motovun
				Zagreb
	10	Monday	21 April	Vukovar
Serbia				Ilok
				Backa Palanka
	11	Tuesday	22 April	Roma community, Novi Sad
Via Bulgaria				Novi Sad
	12	Wednesday	23 April	Belgrade
Turkey	13	Thursday	24 April	On train
	14	Friday	25 April	Istanbul
	15	Saturday	26 April	Istanbul – Europe
				Istanbul
	16	Sunday	27 April	Safranbolu
Georgia	17	Monday	28 April	Samsun
	18	Tuesday	29 April	Border
	19	Wednesday	30 April	Kutaisi
				Tbilisi
Azerbaijan	20	Thursday	1 May	Arrive Baku
Iran	21	Friday	2 May	Baku
				Iran border – Astara
				Astara
				Astara town

To	Transport	No of Forms of Transport	Notes	Section Mileage	Total Mileage
Kilkeel	Classic motorcycles	1		128	128
Douglas	Scallop trawler	2		63	191
Liverpool dock	Passenger ferry	3		80	271
Liverpool station	Black taxi	4		10	281
Coventry	Train	5		116	397
Ace Cafe, London	Motorcycle convoy			97	494
Shoreham-by-Sea	Routemaster bus	6		81	575
Brighton	RNLI lifeboat	7		7	582
Dover	Mark I Land Rover	8		89	671
Calais	Laser sailing dinghy	9		25	696
Paris	Vintage Citröen DS car	10		184	880
Paris Gare de l'Est	Bicycle	11		2	882
On train	*Orient Express*	12		320	1,202
Venice	*Orient Express*		via Switzerland	476	1,678
Venice hotel	Water taxi		and Austria		
Venice	DAY IN CITY			0	1,678
Porec	Hydrofoil	13		63	1,741
Motovun	Yugo car	14		20	1,761
Zagreb	Yugo car			121	1,882
Vukovar	Croatian local bus	15		173	2,055
Ilok	Working barge	16		23	2,078
Backa Palanka	Taxi			3	2,081
Roma community, Novi Sad	Carpet lorry	17		21	2,102
Road to Novi Sad	Scrap cart			1	2,103
Belgrade	Serbian bus	18		54	2,157
On train	*Balkan Express* train	19		244	2,401
Istanbul	*Balkan Express* train			350	2,751
Istanbul	REST DAY			0	2,751
Istanbul – Asia	Turkish ferry	20		3	2,754
Safranbolu	*Dolmus*	21		255	3,009
Samsun	*Dolmus*			229	3,238
Hopa, Georgia border	*Dolmus*			344	3,582
Kutaisi	Ural motorbike	22		96	3,678
Tbilisi	Ural motorbike			40	3,718
On train	Train (*Baku Express*)	23		299	4,017
Baku	DAY IN CITY in UAZ truck	24		0	4,017
Astara, Iran border	UAZ truck and GAZ 21 Volga			145	4,162
Astara	Lajvar	25		1	4,163
Atara town	Tractor			1	
Bandar-e Anzali	Taxi			83	4,246

Country	Day Number	Day	Date	From
	22	Saturday	3 May	Bandar-e Anzali
	23	Sunday	4 May	Tehran
				Tehran
				Tehran
	24	Monday	5 May	Shahr-e-Kord
				Esfahan
	25	Tuesday	6 May	On train
	26	Wednesday	7 May	Bandar-e Abbas
Dubai	27	Thursday	8 May	Bandar-e Abbas
	28	Friday	9 May	Dubai, UAE
	29	Saturday	10 May	Dubai, UAE
	30	Sunday	11 May	Dubai, UAE
	31	Monday	12 May	Dubai, UAE
	32	Tuesday	13 May	On container ship to India
	33	Wednesday	14 May	On container ship to India
India	34	Thursday	15 May	On container ship to India
	35	Friday	16 May	Mumbai
	36	Saturday	17 May	Mumbai hotel
				Mumbai station
	37	Sunday	18 May	Train to Delhi
				Delhi station
	38	Monday	19 May	Delhi
	39	Tuesday	20 May	Agra
	40	Wednesday	21 May	Kanpur
				Outskirts of Mirzapur
				Mirzapur bus station
				Ramnagar
				Varanasi Ghats
	41	Thursday	22 May	Varanasi
	42	Friday	23 May	Varanasi hotel
				Varanasi
Nepal	43	Saturday	24 May	Gorakhpur
				Sunauli
				Butwal
				Narayani River
	44	Sunday	25 May	Tharu Lodge, Chitwan
				Tharu villages
				Hetauda
	45	Monday	26 May	Kathmandu
				Kathmandu suburb
	46	Tuesday	27 May	Chaubas
	47	Wednesday	28 May	Kathmandu
	48	Thursday	29 May	Kathmandu
				Sagarmatha National Park

To	Transport	No of Forms of Transport	Notes	Section Mileage	Total Mileage
Tehran	Mercedes cement truck	26		217	4,463
Tehran	Iranian taxi (female driver)	27		3	4,466
Tehran	Metro	28		5	4,471
Shahr-e-Kord	Bus (Express Coach)	29		253	4,724
Esfahan	Express Coach			56	4,780
On train	Train (Iranian sleeper train)	30		470	5,250
Bandar-e Abbas	Train and taxi			25	5,275
Bandar-e Abbas	DAY VISITING ISLAND			0	5,275
Dubai, UAE	Ferry	31		140	5,415
Dubai, UAE	DAY IN CITY			0	5,415
Dubai, UAE	DAY IN CITY			0	5,415
Dubai, UAE	Overnight on container ship	32		0	5,415
On container ship to India	Container ship				5,415
On container ship to India	Container ship				5,415
On container ship to India	Container ship			1,135	6,550
Mumbai	Container ship				6,550
Mumbai	DAY IN CITY			0	6,550
Mumbai station	Black & yellow taxi	33		2	6,552
Train to Delhi	Local train	34		852	7,404
Delhi station	Rajdhani Express	35		3	7,407
The Imperial hotel	Bajaj tuk-tuk	36		5	7,412
Agra	Royal Enfields Bullet	37		124	7,536
Kanpur	Agra local taxi	38		176	7,712
Outskirts of Mirzapur	Tata truck	39		227	7,939
Mirzapur bus station	Piaggeo tuk-tuk	40		2	7,941
Ramnagar	Jeep	41		37	7,978
Varanasi Ghats	Rowing boat	42		5	7,983
Varanasi	Ricksahw	43		1	7,984
Varanasi	DAY IN TOWN			0	7,984
Varanasi station	Tuk-tuk	44		1	7,985
Gorakhpur	Train	45		128	8,112
Sunauli	Ambassador taxi	46		59	8,171
Butwal	Tractor	47		15	8,186
Narayani river	Local bus	48		50	8,236
Tharu Lodge, Chitwan	Dugout canoe	49		3	8,239
Through Tharu villages	Elephant	50		2	8,241
Hetauda	Jeep	51	via Narayanghat	10	8,251
Kathmandu	Taxi	52		85	8,336
Kathmandu suburb	UNICEF van	53		5	8,341
Chaubas	Bus	54		29	8,370
Kathmandu	UNICEF van			34	8,404
Kathmandu	DAY IN CITY			0	8,404
Sagarmatha National Park	Helicopter		Lukla & Tengboche – at 3800m	0	8,404
Kathmandu	Helicopter			0	8,404

Country	Day Number	Day	Date	From
	49	Friday	30 May	Kathmandu
China	50	Saturday	31 May	Guangzhou, China
	51	Sunday	1 June	Guangzhou
	52	Monday	2 June	Fengkai
				Wuzhou
	53	Tuesday	3 June	Yangshuo
	54	Wednesday	4 June	Yangshou
				Guilin
				Nanning
Vietnam	55	Thursday	5 June	Pingxiang
				Dong Dang
	56	Friday	6 June	Hanoi
				B52 lake
				Hanoi
	57	Saturday	7 June	Halong City
				Halong Bay
				Floating village
				Floating village
	58	Sunday	8 June	Cat Ba Island
				Cat Ba Island
				Hai Phong City
				Nam Dinh
	59	Monday	9 June	Dong Ha
				Vinh Moc
Laos				Khe Sanh
				Dansavanh, border
	60	Tuesday	10 June	Mueng Phine
				Savannakhet
	61	Wednesday	11 June	Pakse
				Tha Muong, Champasak
Cambodia				Khon Phapheng falls
				Voen Kham
	62	Thursday	12 June	Stung Treng
				Across river
				Kratie
				Stung Trang
				Chamcar Leu

To	Transport	No of Forms of Transport	Notes	Section Mileage	Total Mileage
Flight to China	Plane	55		1,763	10,167
Guangzhou	Arrived by plane then DAY IN CITY			0	10,167
Towards Fengkai	Cement barge	56		40	10,207
Wuzhou	Taxi			88	10,295
Yangshuo	Local bus	57		146	10,441
Liugong village	Bamboo raft		made from plastic	0	10,441
Guilin	Van	58		29	10,470
Nanning	Train	59		239	10,709
Pingxiang, border	Taxi			127	10,836
Dong Dang, border	Taxi			2	10,838
Hanoi	Minsk motorcycles	60		222	11,060
B52 Lake	*Xe Om* (motorbike taxi)			0	11,060
Hanoi bus station	Tri-wheel motorbike for disabled			0	11,060
Halong City	Public bus	61		76	11,136
Halong Bay	Minibus			3	11,139
Floating village	Junk	62		3	11,142
Floating village	Rowing boat			3	11,145
Gia Luam, Cat Ba Island	Junk			5	11,150
Hai Phong City	Speedboat	63	got cancelled as dangerous	16	11,166
Hai Phong City	Public fast boat	64		14	11,180
Nam Dinh	Minibus	65		52	11,232
Towards Dong Ha	*Reunification Express*	66		289	11,521
Vinh Moc	Military jeep	67		19	11,540
Khe Sanh	Military jeep			68	11,608
Lao Bao, border	Military jeep			5	11,613
Keng Tueb village Mueng Phine district	*Songthaew*	68		44	11,657
Savannakhet	*Songthaew*			92	11,749
Pakse	*Lod Mei* (bus)	69		117	11,866
Tha Muong, Champasak	Slow boat	70		34	11,900
Khon Phapheng falls	*Songthaew*			52	11,952
Voen Kham, border	*Songthaew*			9	11,961
Stung Treng	Rocket boat	71		7	11,968
Kratie	Honda 250 dirt bikes	72		92	12,060
Across river	Local ferry	73		1	12,061
Stung Trang	Dirt bikes			9	12,070
Chamcar Leu rubber plantations	Dirt bikes			59	12,129
Beng Mealea	Dirt bikes		via Kompong Thmor and Kompong Thom and Dam Dek	53	12,182

Country	Day Number	Day	Date	From
	63	Friday	13 June	Beng Mealea
				Phnom Kulen
	64	Saturday	14 June	Siem Reap
	65	Sunday	15 June	Siem Reap
Thailand	66	Monday	16 June	Siem Reap
				Sisophon
				Road to Poipet
				Poipet & Thai border
				Aranyaprathet
	67	Tuesday	17 June	Bangkok
	68	Wednesday	18 June	Bangkok
Malaysia	69	Thursday	19 June	Butterworth
	70	Friday	20 June	Kuala Lumpur
Singapore				Danga Bay
	71	Saturday	21 June	Singapore
	72	Sunday	22 June	Singapore
Indonesia	73	Monday	23 June	Singapore
				Bandar Bentan Telani, Bintan
				Kawal, Bintan
	74	Tuesday	24 June	Nikoi Island
	75	Wednesday	25 June	Nikoi Island
				Kawal, Bintan
				Tanjung Pinang, Bintan
				Batam
	76	Thursday	26 June	Pontianak
				Teluk Melano
				Ketapang
				Sandai
				Rando Jungkal
	77	Friday	27 June	Riam Dadap
				Rando Jungkal
				Sandai
	78	Saturday	28 June	Ketapang
	79	Sunday	29 June	Pontianak
	80	Monday	30 June	Bali
	81	Tuesday	1 July	Gili, Trawangan
				Bima
	82	Wednesday	2 July	Boat towards Komodo
				Rinca

To	Transport	No of Forms of Transport	Notes	Section Mileage	Total Mileage
Phnom Kulen	Dirt bikes			27	12,209
Siem Reap	Dirt bikes			82	12,291
Siem Reap	REST DAY			5	12,296
Siem Reap	*Coyonne* (elephant truck) and wooden boat	74	via Angkor Wat	10	12,306
Sisophon	Taxi			79	12,385
Road to Poipet	Bamboo train	75		1	12,386
Poipet & Thai border	Taxi				
Aranyaprathet	*Songthaew*	76		5	12,391
Bangkok	Mercedes bus	77		164	12,555
Bangkok	REST DAY			0	12,555
Train to Butterworth	Train	78		688	13,243
Kuala Lumpur	Bus	79		236	13,479
Danga Bay	Hire car	80		197	13,676
Singapore, Raffles marina	Wakeboard	81		12	13,688
Singapore	REST DAY			0	13,688
Singapore	REST DAY			0	13,688
Bandar Bentan Telani, Bintan	Ferry	82		26	13,714
Kawal, Bintan	Holden Kingswood	83		35	13,749
Nikoi Island	Water taxi	84		6	13,755
Nikoi Island	Cargo boat	85	Went 10 miles out and had to return due to hole in boat	20	13,775
Kawal, Bintan	Water taxi			6	13,781
Tanjung Pinang, Bintan	Car	86		15	13,796
Batam	Ferry	87		24	13,820
Pontianak	Batavia plane	88		369	14,189
Teluk Melano	*Hutan Express* speedboat	89		152	14,341
Ketapang	Pickup truck	90		62	14,403
UNICEF project – Sandai	Speedboat	91		98	14,501
Rando Jungkal	Moped	92		14	14,515
Riam Dadap	Motorised canoe	93		25	14,540
Rando Jungkal	Speedboat			25	14,565
Sandai	Motorcycle & pickup truck			14	14,579
Ketapang	Speedboat			98	14,677
Pontianak	*Hutan Express* speedboat			214	14,891
Bali	Plane	94		709	15,600
Gili, Trawangan	Bemo, X2K speedboat	95/96		68	15,668
Bima	X2K speedboat	97		212	15,880
Boat towards Komodo	*Phinisi*	98		60	15,940
Rinca	*Phinisi*			15	15,955
Bima	X2K speedboat			75	16,030

Country	Day Number	Day	Date	From
				Bima
	83	Thursday	3 July	Onboard ferry
	84	Friday	4 July	Maumere – ferry
	85	Saturday	5 July	Kupang
	86	Sunday	6 July	At sea
	87	Monday	7 July	At sea
	88	Tuesday	8 July	At sea
	89	Wednesday	9 July	At sea
Australia	90	Thursday	10 July	At sea
	91	Friday	11 July	Darwin
	92	Saturday	12 July	Daly Waters
				Alice Springs
	93	Sunday	13 July	Outskirts of Alice Springs
				Along road
				Uluru
	94	Monday	14 July	Campsite in outback
				(near Mount Conner)
				Coober Pedy
				Road to William Creek
	95	Tuesday	15 July	William Creek
	96	Wednesday	16 July	Marree
	97	Thursday	17 July	Quorn
				Pitchie Ritchie Engine
				Shed
				Woolshed Flat
				Stirling North
	98	Friday	18 July	Mildura
	99	Saturday	19 July	Khancoban
				Geehi
	100	Sunday	20 July	Thredbo
	101	Monday	21 July	Thredbo
	102	Tuesday	22 July	Shellharbour
				Wollongong

The modes of transport that are included in this chart are only those which moved Charley forward on his journey across the world.

As taxis were sometimes used to get from one unique form of transport to the next, these have not all been included in the final count of vehicles.

To	Transport	No of Forms of Transport	Notes	Section Mileage	Total Mileage
Onboard ferry	Ferry	99		50	16,080
Ferry – Maumere	Ferry			358	16,438
Kupang, Timor	Ferry			70	16,508
At sea	*Phinisi* boat	100		145	16,653
At sea	*Phinisi* boat			142	16,795
At sea	*Phinisi* boat			117	16,912
At sea	*Phinisi* boat			104	17,016
At sea	*Phinisi* boat			105	17,121
Darwin	*Phinisi* boat			30	17,151
Daly Waters	Wicked camper van	101		349	17,500
Alice Springs	Wicked camper van			557	18,057
Outskirts of Alice Springs	Nissan ute	102		2	18,059
Along road	Camels	103		2	18,061
Uluru	Nissan ute			312	18,373
Campsite nr. Mount Conner	Nissan ute			20	18,393
Along road	Road grader	104		1	18,394
Road to William Creek	Road train	105		20	18,414
William Creek	Nissan ute			471	18,885
Marree	Nissan ute			170	19,055
Quorn	Nissan ute			210	19,265
Pitchie Ritchie Engine Shed	Classic Holden	106		1	19,266
Woolshed Flat	Steam train	107		9	19,275
Stirling North	Solar car	108		10	19,285
Mildura	Nissan ute			332	19,617
Khancoban	Nissan ute			467	20,084
Geehi	Horses	109		10	20,094
Thredbo	Nissan ute			28	20,122
Back to Thredbo	Skitune and snowmobile	110/111		15	20,137
Shellharbour	Nissan ute			255	20,392
Wollongong	BMW motorcycle	112		5	20,397
Sydney	BMW motorcycle – convoy			81	20,473

Total number of forms of transport: 112
Total number of miles: 20,473

The other journey

By Any Means was about all the wonderful people and places between Ireland and Sydney that you miss if you fly there by plane. It's been an amazing journey that was only possible by sharing different modes of transport with local people. But there's an even more important journey going on, which we witnessed in Nepal and Borneo. That's the journey that UNICEF makes every day, doing whatever it takes to deliver life-saving vaccines to children in remote and isolated rural areas.

Immunisation has achieved real successes. Today, vaccines protect nearly three-quarters of the world's children against major childhood illnesses. However, more than 1.4 million children still die each year from diseases that could have been prevented by cheap vaccines.

With UNICEF, we followed the trail of a vaccine from where it's picked up in Borneo to its final destination and saw all the logistical problems that are involved. We travelled on bikes, in minivans and on speedboats, shooting rapids, all the time having to make sure the vaccines stayed cold. It took us sixteen hours to get the vaccine to a small village where children needed inoculating and it was sometimes pretty hairy stuff. But these guys do this all the time, all over the world.

When you go to the places that I've been, and see the work that UNICEF does with children in often desperate situations, it touches your heart and it often makes you feel very sad. But at the same time, it makes you feel hopeful that people like UNICEF are out there, helping to look after the kids.

UNICEF relies entirely on voluntary donations to get these vaccines out there, as well as to provide the trained doctors and nurses to give the vaccines. Without the donations made by the UK public, many more children would die around the world from preventable diseases. So please dig deep and give whatever you can. Your donation really does save children's lives.

To find out more, visit www.unicef.org.uk/byanymeans

UNICEF, the United Nations Children's Fund, is the world's leading children's organisation, reaching children in more than 190 countries around the world. We work with families, local communities, partner organisations and governments to help every child realise their full potential. We support children by providing them with health care, nutrition and education. We protect children affected by crisis including war, natural disasters and HIV.

UNICEF is not funded by the UN. Instead we rely on voluntary donations to fund our work for children worldwide. UNICEF needs help from people like you in order to continue supporting and protecting children from the effects of poverty, conflict and disasters. Even the smallest donations can make a huge difference to a child who has nothing.

If you live in the UK you can help UNICEF by donating, by taking part in a fundraising event or by lending your voice to our campaigns. Please do something to help the world's children online at:
www.unicef.org.uk/byanymeans

Alternatively, you can donate by calling **0800 037 9797** or by sending a cheque to:

UNICEF
By Any Means
Freepost CL885
Billericay
CM12 OBR
United Kingdom

If you are outside the UK there are still many ways to support UNICEF. Please visit www.supportunicef.org to find out more.

Acknowledgements

Olivia, Doone, Kinvara and the whole Boorman clan

Russ Malkin

Lisa Benton, Sarah Blackett, Ollie Blackwell, Mike Clark-Hall, Rob Drake, Joanna Ford, Jeff Gulvin, Corin Holmes, Anne Holst, Amber Latif, Sarah Lawrance, Jo Melling, Liz Mercer, Mungo, Stephanie Newman, Hannah Palmer, Alex Pipkin, Catriona Scott, Robin Shek, Tom Swingler, Lucy Trujillo

Special Thanks To:
Ace Cafe, Munir Akdogan, Robert Ashworth, AST, Deepak Bajracharya, Bali Film Centre, Baron Speed Shop, Cenk Baysan, BBC, Haci Bekir, Bimblegumbie, BMW, Breitling, Bremont, Boatbookings.com, John Boorman, Cristel Boorman, Robert Bu, Dave Burge, Shiyi Cao, Caucasus Travel, Channel Swimming and Piloting Federation, Citroën, Classic Car Club of Thailand, Peter Cochran, Coventry Transport Museum, Simon Crellin, Danubium Tours, Richard Darwood, Mahmood Darya, Davenport Lyons, Davida, Geoff Duke, Durbar Associates, Matt Elmes, Enia Carpets, Exmed, Yangshou Expat, Explore, Explore Georgia, Explore Indochina Ltd, Richard Gauntlett, Rina Gandhi, Garmin, Trevor Gibbs, Global Events and Expeditions, Gritti Palace, Hachette, The Hatton Family, Warwick Hill, Hotel Danuv, Pete Huckle, Infocus Asia, Steve Jameson, Stanka Jankovic, Jebel Ali Golf Resort & Spa, JK, Olja Jovovic, Kentec Mail and Courier Service, Robert Kirby, Land Rover, Laser, Edwin Lerrick, Darren Loveday, Steve Loveday, Maersk Company, Magic Carpet Travel, Manx Fishing Producers Organisation, Martin Mayhew, Maxout Hydrosports, John McGuinness, Media Insurance, Wencenlaus Mendes, Mid Hants Railway, Chiara & Alessandro Mingardi, Minsk Club Vietnam, Richard Moxon, Nikoi Island, National Geographic Channel, Nikon, Catherine & Rem Niessen, Nissan, Old Burma, Omnibuzz, Micheal Oram, Orient Express Trains and Cruises, Taotao Peng, Pop Films Asia, Rick Pope, Richard Quayle 'Milky', Raa Kelly Solar Car Team, Nick Ray, RNLI, Royal Enfield, Sea and Sky Travel, Zuar Shafiev, Shangri-La Hotel Sydney, Snowy Mountain Ski Patrol, Songline Cruises, Sonic Communications Ltd, John South, Steampacket Ferry Company, Steve Jameson, Stormforce Sailing, Kevin Sullivan, Swissotel, Singapore, Taj Hotel Group, The Pitchie Ritchie Railway, Tourism New South Wales, Tourism Australia, Trango Disaster and Response Services, UNICEF, Universal, Ural Motorcycles, V-Media Works, Visa World, Rob Warner, Wicked Campervans, Wild Horizons

Images in this book were taken on Nikon digital cameras.